ARTHURIAN LITERATURE
XXXIII

ARTHURIAN LITERATURE

Incorporating *Arthurian Yearbook*

ISSN 0261–9946

Editors
Elizabeth Archibald, *Durham University*
David F. Johnson, *Florida State University, Tallahassee*

Assistant Editor
Anna Dow

Editorial Board
James Carley, *York University*
Helen Cooper, *University of Cambridge*
Julia Crick, *King's College London*
Tony Hunt, *University of Oxford*
Marianne Kalinke, *Illinois University*
Norris Lacy, *Pennsylvania State University*
Ceridwen Lloyd-Morgan, *Cardiff University*
Andrew Lynch, *University of Western Australia*
Ad Putter, *University of Bristol*
Felicity Riddy, *University of York*
Alison Stones, *University of Pittsburgh*
Toshiyuki Takamiya, *University of Keio*
Jane H. M. Taylor, *Durham University*
Raymond H. Thompson, *Acadia University*
Michael Twomey, *Ithaca College*

Arthurian Literature is an interdisciplinary publication devoted to the scholarly and critical study of all aspects of Arthurian legend in Europe in the medieval and early modern periods. Articles on writings from later periods are included if they relate very directly to medieval and early modern sources, although the editors welcome bibliographical studies of all periods. Articles may be up to 20,000 words in length; short items, of under 5,000 words, are published as Notes. Updates on earlier articles are also welcomed.

Material for consideration should be sent to Boydell & Brewer: contributors should follow the style sheet printed at the end of XII of the series. The contents of previous volumes are listed at the back of this book.

Arthurian Literature XXXIII

Edited by
ELIZABETH ARCHIBALD AND DAVID F. JOHNSON

D. S. BREWER

© Contributors 2016

All rights reserved. Except as permitted under current legislation
no part of this work may be photocopied, stored in a retrieval system,
published, performed in public, adapted, broadcast,
transmitted, recorded or reproduced in any form or by any means,
without the prior permission of the copyright owner

First published 2016
D. S. Brewer, Cambridge

ISBN 978-1-84384-450-1

D. S. Brewer is an imprint of Boydell & Brewer Ltd
PO Box 9, Woodbridge, Suffolk IP12 3DF, UK
and of Boydell & Brewer Inc,
668 Mt Hope Avenue, Rochester, NY 14620–2731, USA
website: www.boydellandbrewer.com

A catalogue record for this book is available
from the British Library

The publisher has no responsibility for the continued existence or accuracy
of URLs for external or third-party internet websites referred to in this
book, and does not guarantee that any content on such websites is,
or will remain, accurate or appropriate.

This publication is printed on acid-free paper

Typeset by
www.thewordservice.com

CONTENTS

General Editors' Foreword   vii

Contributors   ix

I   From 'The Matter of Britain' to 'The Matter of Rome': Latin Literary Culture and the Reception of Geoffrey of Monmouth in Wales   1
Georgia Henley

II   Chrétien's British Yvain in England and Wales   29
Erich Poppe

III   Edward III's Abandoned Order of the Round Table Revisited: Political Arthurianism after Poitiers   70
Christopher Berard

IV   'Thanked Be God There Hath Been But A Few Of Myne Auncytours That Hathe Dyed In Their Beddes': Border Stories and Northern Arthurian Romances   110
Ralph Hanna

V   T. H. White's Representation of Malory's Camelot   140
Louis J. Boyle

VI   ἹππόΤησ ὉΠρεσβύΤησ: *The Old Knight* An Edition of the Greek Arthurian Poem of Vat. Gr. 1822   158
Thomas H. Crofts
with a translation by *Thomas H. Crofts* and *Dimitra Fimi*

GENERAL EDITORS' FOREWORD

This volume of *Arthurian Literature* ranges from the reception of Geoffrey of Monmouth in Wales to the Camelot of T. H. White. Georgia Henley discusses Latin literary culture in medieval Wales, evaluating the intellectual and literary context in which Geoffrey of Monmouth's seminal *Historia regum Britanniae* was received. She makes the case for discarding the binary distinction of 'Welsh vs Latin' in favour of a view of medieval Wales as a multilingual culture in which Latin and Welsh existed side-by-side and the classical tradition had a significant influence on Welsh literature.

We are pleased to be able to publish a revised version of Prof. Erich Poppe's 2016 O'Donnell Lecture in Celtic Studies, in which he shines a bright comparative light (in terms of both plot and lexis) on Chrétien's *Ivain*, the Middle English *Ywain and Gawain* and the Middle Welsh *Owein*, otherwise known as *Chwedyl Iarlles y Ffynnawn* (*The Tale of the Lady of the Well / Countess of the Spring*). In his reading of these poems, Poppe effectively demonstrates Peter Clemoes' axiom that to read 'Medieval Welsh literature alongside that of Middle English' is to recognize how great a debt English literature owes to the Celtic tradition for its Arthurian inspirations.

Christopher Berard returns to the subject of Edward III's abandoned Order of the Round Table to argue that, while Edward's 'un-Arthurian' tactics at Crécy made his association with the legendary king problematic, his victory at Poitiers and the capture of the flower of French knighthood – and of Jean II of France himself – rendered that association apt once more. Portraying himself as an Arthurian 'King of Kings' enabled Edward to negotiate a treaty with, and seek ransom for, the French king without undermining his own claim to that throne.

Ralph Hanna considers *Ywain and Gawain* and the Alliterative *Morte Arthure* in the cultural and political context of the turbulent history of the borders and of two great northern families, the Percys and the Nevilles. In spite of the popular image of the 'uncouth / violent North', he argues that northern romances diverge from the popular insular pattern of usurpation, exile and return, focusing instead on more domestic themes and on 'the failure of mere martial prowess to offer meaningful achievement'. He sees *Ywain and Gawain* as a response to criticism of romance in texts such as *Cursor mundi*, stressing the importance of both time and 'trowth'.

GENERAL EDITORS' FOREWORD

Louis Boyle explores T. H. White's treatment of Malory's Camelot, demonstrating ways in which, rather than contradicting Malory's portrayal of the iconic locale, White explores gaps left by Malory in the fabric of his tale. In White's version of the story, Camelot is an unstable signifier. In Malory, Boyle argues, the use of the name 'Camelot' fades as its importance diminishes, to the point where this most famous of locales is referred to exclusively as 'Winchester'. In White, however, notions of 'home' have greater importance, and the use of the name 'Camelot' in this version 'lays bare disruptive forces that are nuanced in Malory', particularly in relation to gossip and hearsay. It may be unclear where Camelot actually is, but for White it becomes Arthur's centre, his ground zero.

Finally, continuing our recent tradition of publishing lesser-known, shorter Arthurian texts, this volume includes an edition and facing page translation of the fragmentary medieval Greek poem Ἱππότης ὁ Πρεσβύτης / *Hippotēs ho Presbutēs*: *The Old Knight*. Thomas Crofts (ed. and trans.) and Dimitra Fimi (trans.) present the text and English translation of this fascinating poem together for the first time, rendering it accessible to a much wider audience. It offers a surprisingly cynical view of the Arthurian court, with the anonymous Old Knight defeating all his famous opponents.

We are grateful to all our contributors and also to our Editorial Board for their careful reading and recommendations; to Caroline Palmer, Boydell & Brewer's Editorial Director, for her patience and support; to our Editorial Assistant Anna Dow for her invaluable contribution to the preparation of this volume for publication; and to the Department of English Studies at Durham University for their financial support.

Elizabeth Archibald
Durham UK

David F. Johnson
Tallahassee, Florida

CONTRIBUTORS

Christopher Berard holds a doctorate in Medieval Studies from the University of Toronto. He has taught British Literature at the University of Toronto and Trent University. He is currently preparing a book on the history and politics of Arthurian imitation in Plantagenet England.

Louis J. Boyle is Professor of English and Chair of the English Department at Carlow University in Pittsburgh, Pennsylvania. His research interests centre on Malory and T. H. White, but he has also written on the field and practice of technical writing. He is the author of *T. H. White's Reinterpretation of Malory's* Le Morte Darthur (2008). His current project focuses on gossip, hearsay, slander and idle talk in Malory.

Thomas H. Crofts is the author of *Malory's Contemporary Audience* (2006), as well as several book chapters and articles on Arthurian and other Middle English literature. He teaches medieval literature at East Tennessee State University, where he is also Director of the Minor in Classical Studies.

Ralph Hanna is Professor of Palaeography, Emeritus, and Emeritus Fellow of Keble College, Oxford. He researches materials in medieval manuscripts, mainly Anglo-Latin, and maintains a lively relationship with libraries. His many publications include editions of *Golagros and Gawane* and *The Awntyrs of Arthur*.

Georgia Henley is a Ph.D. candidate in the Department of Celtic Languages and Literatures at Harvard University. Her dissertation, 'Monastic Manuscript Networks of the Anglo-Welsh March: A Study in Literary Transmission', examines transmission networks of historical writing and hagiography in the Anglo-Welsh March and their impact on thirteenth- and fourteenth-century literary culture in England and Wales. She co-founded the Welsh Chronicles Research Group and website and is editing forthcoming volumes on Gerald of Wales and Geoffrey of Monmouth.

Erich Poppe is Professor of Celtic Languages and Literatures at the University of Marburg, Germany. His main research interests are processes of textual transfer and adaptation in medieval Wales and Ireland, Middle

Welsh syntax and the history of Celtic Studies. Together with Ceridwen Lloyd-Morgan he is co-editing *Arthur in the Celtic Literatures* for the University of Wales Press, forthcoming in 2017.

1

FROM 'THE MATTER OF BRITAIN' TO 'THE MATTER OF ROME': LATIN LITERARY CULTURE AND THE RECEPTION OF GEOFFREY OF MONMOUTH IN WALES

Georgia Henley

The Welsh reception of Geoffrey of Monmouth's *Historia regum Britanniae*, an important facet of Geoffrey's reception into the vernacular literary cultures of medieval Britain, is a topic that has fascinated and at times stymied scholars of Arthurian literature over the years.[1] The *Historia* was first translated into Middle Welsh in the mid-thirteenth century, and by the mid-fourteenth century at least six distinct Welsh versions circulated, the result of several acts of translation and redaction.[2] This proliferation of translations and manuscript copies suggests a considerable popularity in Wales.[3] Scholarly attention to this important group of texts, known collec-

---

[1] Note that the title of Geoffrey's history is *De gestis Britonum* in an early group of manuscripts; he also uses this title to refer to the work in *Vita Merlini* (ll. 1525–9); for discussion see *Geoffrey of Monmouth, the History of the Kings of Britain: An Edition and Translation of* De Gestis Britonum (Historia regum Britanniae), ed. M. Reeve, trans. N. Wright, Arthurian Studies 69 (Woodbridge, 2007), p. lix. I owe sincere thanks to the anonymous reviewer of this article for very useful and gracious comments, to Paul Russell for valuable discussion of an earlier draft of this paper, to Joshua Byron Smith and Ben Guy for discussion of various points and to the audience of a session at the 50th International Congress on Medieval Studies, Western Michigan University, Kalamazoo, 15 May 2015, for their responses and suggestions.

[2] They survive in approximately sixty medieval and early modern manuscripts. These versions are the Llanstephan 1, Peniarth 44, Dingestow Court, Peniarth 21, Cotton Cleopatra B v and Red Book of Hergest versions. They take the names of their principal or best-known manuscript witnesses, Aberystwyth, National Library of Wales, Llanstephan 1 (s. xiii[med]); Aberystwyth, National Library of Wales, Peniarth 44 (s. xiii[med]); Aberystwyth, National Library of Wales, 5266B (s. xiii[2]); Aberystwyth, National Library of Wales, Peniarth 21 (s. xiii/xiv); London, British Library, Cotton Cleopatra B. v (s. xiv[med]); and Oxford, Jesus College 111 (1382×1405). An early modern version is known as the *Brut Tysilio*.

[3] The Latin text also circulated in Wales: for example, four of the extant copies of the First

tively as *Brut y Brenhinedd* (*History of the Kings*), has been hampered by a lack of published editions and of translations into English. With several digital transcriptions now available, supplementing the earlier partial efforts at publishing and translating the texts in the twentieth century, the field is at last able to go forward.[4] Scholarship to date has focused on analyzing the differences between the various versions of *Brut y Brenhinedd*, their complex relationships to the Latin texts, and what the translators' modifications of their Latin exempla reveal about Welsh attitudes towards history, conquest and their English neighbours.[5]

Variant version of Geoffrey's *Historia* are of Welsh provenance and / or have Welsh glosses in them, nos. 55, 67, 70 and 163 in J. C. Crick, *The* Historia Regum Britannie *of Geoffrey of Monmouth, III: A Summary Catalogue of the Manuscripts* (Cambridge, 1989). For discussion see *The* Historia Regum Britannie *of Geoffrey of Monmouth, II: The First Variant Version: A Critical Edition*, ed. N. Wright (Cambridge, 1988), pp. lxxviii–xci. One Vulgate manuscript of known Welsh provenance is no. 112, London, British Library, Royal 13 D. ii (s. xii, provenance Margam Abbey), and possibly also nos. 48, 69 and 120. Margam Abbey is a candidate for the entry point of the Latin *Historia* into Wales.

[4] These texts are only partially edited and translated: for a partial edition of the Llanstephan 1 version, see *Brut y Brenhinedd: Llanstephan MS. 1 Version*, ed. B. F. Roberts, Mediaeval and Modern Welsh Series 5 (Dublin, 1971); for a transcription of the Peniarth 44 version see G. R. Isaac, S. Rodway, S. Nurmio, K. Kapphahn and P. Sims-Williams, 'Rhyddiaith Gymraeg o Lawysgrifau'r 13eg Ganrif Fersiwn 2.0' (Aberystwyth, 2013), http://cadair.aber.ac.uk/dspace/handle/2160/5811, accessed 22 October 2015; for an edition of the Dingestow Court version see *Brut Dingestow*, ed. H. Lewis (Cardiff, 1942); for transcriptions of the texts in Peniarth 21, the Red Book of Hergest and several other manuscript witnesses dated from 1300–1425, see D. Luft, P. Wynn Thomas and D. M. Smith, *Rhyddiaeth Gymraeg 1300–1425* (Aberystwyth, 2013), http://www.rhyddiaithganoloesol.caerdydd.ac.uk/en/texts.php?genre=history, accessed 15 March 2016; for an edition and translation of the Cotton Cleopatra version see *Brut y Brenhinedd, Cotton Cleopatra Version*, ed. J. J. Parry (Cambridge, MA, 1937). For a list of manuscripts see P. Sims-Williams, *Rhai Addasiadau Cymraeg Canol o Sieffre o Fynwy* (Aberystwyth, 2013), p. 13; B. F. Roberts, 'Astudiaeth Destunol o'r Tri Chyfieithiad Cymraeg Cynharaf o *Historia regum Britanniae* Sieffre o Fynwy, Ynghyd ag "Argraffiad" Beirniadol o Destun Peniarth 44' (unpublished PhD dissertation, University of Wales, 1969), pp. xliii–xlvii; and *The* Historia regum Britanniae *of Geoffrey of Monmouth, with Contributions to the Study of its Place in Early British History*, ed. A. Griscom (London and New York, 1929), Appendix II.

[5] See, for example, Sims-Williams, *Rhai Addasiadau*, an important article soon to be published in English (in a shortened and revised form) as 'The Welsh Versions of Geoffrey of Monmouth's History of the Kings of Britain', in *Adapting Texts and Styles in a Celtic Context. Interdisciplinary Perspectives on Processes of Literary Transfer: Studies in Honor of Erich Poppe*, ed. A. Harlos and N. Harlos (Münster, forthcoming 2016); B. F. Roberts, '*Brut y Brenhinedd*, ms. National Library of Wales, Llanstephan 1 Version', in *L'Historia regum Britannie et les 'Bruts' en Europe, Tome 1: Traductions, adaptations, réappropriations (xiie–xvie siècle)*, ed. H. Tétrel and G. Veysseyre (Paris, 2015), pp. 71–80; P. Y. Lambert, 'À propos de la traduction galloise du ms. London,

The circumstances of the origins of these Welsh translations, however, remain murky – they were likely monastic, though even this is not certain – and the initial motivations and intentions of the translators are very much open to interpretation. When exactly Geoffrey's Latin text reached Wales, and why it first appeared in Welsh c. 1250, is also unclear. Furthermore, the status of Latin-language literature and historical writing in Wales has not been adequately understood or appreciated to date, with Latin literary culture often passed over in favour of studies of Welsh-language literature and historical writing.[6]

The present study addresses this last desideratum, demonstrating that Latin was in fact a very important part of Welsh literary culture. It argues that Welsh-language literature and historical writing arose out of, and alongside, Latin writing and should not be considered as separate from it. This interpretation has the potential to alter scholarly perceptions of the intellectual and literary context into which Geoffrey's history was received in Wales, shedding light on this important group of Welsh texts, their ideologies and the circumstances of their translation into Welsh. The centrepiece of this discussion is not *Brut y Brenhinedd* itself, but the background and context into which Geoffrey's history was received in Wales – necessary groundwork before the Welsh texts can be fully understood.

The following pages demonstrate that Geoffrey's *Historia* was met in Wales by a vibrant literary culture of Latin writing, extant in a number of genres and original compositions which reveal a high degree of Latin learning, and that this literary culture exhibited an awareness of and interest in its own classical heritage and connection to the Romano-British past. This second point is accomplished through a discussion of the twelfth-century prose text *Breudwyt Maxen Wledic* (*The Dream of Maxen Wledic*) and the

---

British Library, Cotton Cleopatra B. V', in *L'Historia regum Britannie*, ed. Tétrel and Veysseyre, pp. 81–104; M. Faletra, *Wales and the Medieval Colonial Imagination: The Matters of Britain in the Twelfth Century* (New York, 2014), pp. 25–6; J. B. Smith, 'Literary Encounters in the Anglo-Welsh Borderlands: 1138–1400' (unpublished PhD dissertation, Northwestern University, 2011); C. Chance, 'Ethnicity, Geography, and the Passage of Dominion in the *Mabinogi* and *Brut y Brenhinedd*', *Proceedings of the Harvard Celtic Colloquium* 29 (2009), 45–56; M. Warren, *History on the Edge: Excalibur and the Borders of Britain, 1100–1300* (Minneapolis, MN, 2000), pp. 60–80; Roberts, 'Astudiaeth', pp. xxviii–xxxix.

[6] By 'Latin literary culture' I mean historical, literary, scientific and religious writing in Latin, as well as the methods of Latin education, that formed a large part of the intellectual heritage of literate societies in medieval Western Europe. An exception to this trend is C. Davies, *Welsh Literature and the Classical Tradition* (Cardiff, 1995). For a recent study of the multilingual environment of South Wales and the March, and the Welsh translated texts it produced, see H. Fulton, 'Translating Europe in Medieval Wales', in *Writing Europe, 500–1450: Texts and Contexts*, ed. A. Conti, O. Da Rold and P. Shaw, Essays and Studies 68 (Cambridge, 2015), 159–74.

extent to which it recognized a Romano-British past in Wales. Perceived ancestral links between Wales and the classical world, specifically Rome and Troy, would have reinforced the strength of their connection to the Roman past and to the Latin language amongst Welsh literati – the writers and receivers of Geoffrey's history.[7] The present study has the additional goal of advocating a dissolution of the binary opposition of 'Welsh vs Latin', instead presenting evidence for a multilingual culture in medieval Wales which accepted both languages, fluidly, as its own. The quality, extent and cultural centrality of this multilingualism is perhaps exceptional in Wales, by virtue of its historical origins as a Roman province, as 'in one form or another Latin and Welsh (or the earlier Brittonic language antecedent to Welsh) have co-existed and interacted in Wales from the Roman period onwards'.[8] Without entering into the debate about the linguistic transition from Latin to Brittonic in the sub-Roman period, this study argues that Latin enjoyed a special status in Wales because of how Welsh literati, who were responsible for producing translations of Geoffrey of Monmouth, perceived the classical inheritance of both their history and their literature.[9]

---

[7] By 'Welsh literati' I refer to those who were part of learned Welsh culture, i.e. oral and book learning which existed in either Latin or the vernacular, generated for the benefit of secular and non-secular audiences alike. This includes both monastic / ecclesiastical learning and the secular *cyfarwyddiaid* (storytellers), *beirdd* (poets) and *ystorïwyr* (historians) who would have operated in the vernacular, though generic categories employed by secular and non-secular writers overlapped, particularly in the cases of history and poetry. By using the terms 'learned Welsh culture' and 'Welsh literati', I aim to sidestep the problems of the phrase 'Welsh tradition', which can be a catch-all that does not adequately account for source material nor articulate the exact relationship between written and oral sources. For the standard view of the oral transmission of Welsh sources see C. B. Davies, *Professional Interpreters and the Matter of Britain* (Cardiff, 1966); S. Echard, *Arthurian Narrative in the Latin Tradition* (Cambridge, 1998), pp. 194–5; B. F. Roberts, 'Geoffrey of Monmouth, *Historia Regum Britanniae*, and *Brut y Brenhinedd*', in *The Arthur of the Welsh*, ed. R. Bromwich, A. O. H. Jarman and B. F. Roberts (Cardiff, 1991), pp. 97–116 (pp. 109–13). For a new view, see J. Byron Smith, *Walter Map and the Matter of Britain* (forthcoming).

[8] Quoting P. Russell, '"Go and look in the Latin books": Latin and the Vernacular in Medieval Wales', in *Latin in Medieval Britain*, ed. R. Ashdowne and C. White, Proceedings of the British Academy (London, forthcoming 2016); I am very grateful to Paul Russell for allowing me to consult this article in advance of its publication. I do not mean to suggest that Wales is unique in its perceived connections to Rome; in fact, this relationship plays out in interesting ways in different periods in Britain. For comparable studies of a perceived Roman intellectual heritage in Anglo-Saxon England, see *England and Rome in the Early Middle Ages: Pilgrimage, Art, and Politics*, ed. F. Tinti (Turnhout, 2014).

[9] This is not to say that the Welsh literati were one organized bloc, behaving in the same way across vast temporal and geographical areas; however, it is safe to say they received what was very likely a standardized Latin education, comparable to what was available elsewhere in Britain and on the Continent.

By demonstrating the high degree of Latin learning in Wales evident in extant Welsh Latin texts, and the special status afforded the language by contemporary perceptions of a classical heritage, this study necessitates a revision of some previous critical interpretations of *Brut y Brenhinedd*. As is well known, Geoffrey's political ambiguities mean that the *Historia* has been subjected to a multiplicity of interpretations, with most modern critics to date falling into one of two camps: those who think Geoffrey was a pro-Anglo-Norman tool of conquest propaganda, justifying and legitimizing the project of conquest by explaining how the Britons, and by analogy the Welsh, deserved to lose their sovereignty over the island of Britain;[10] and those who think he purposefully displayed just enough ambiguity and ambivalence to play both sides of the conflict, making him a product of the hybrid interface between Welsh, Anglo-Norman and Marcher culture and politics in the twelfth century.[11] Geoffrey's pro-Breton leanings have also been discussed at length, as has his playful subversion of Anglo-Norman historiographical forms.[12] Recent studies have revitalized a third option, that Geoffrey's immediate reception, provenance and projected aims point most obviously and simply to a pro-Welsh stance.[13] The benefit of this third argument is that it incorporates the Welsh perspective into considerations of Geoffrey of Monmouth's life, works and reception. This perspective requires an understanding of the underlying context

---

[10] See, for example, M. A. Faletra, 'Narrating the Matter of Britain: Geoffrey of Monmouth and the Norman Colonization of Wales', *Chaucer Review* 35.1 (2000), 60–85; F. Ingledew, 'The Book of Troy and the Genealogical Construction of History: The Case of Geoffrey of Monmouth's *Historia regum* Britanniae', *Speculum* 69 (1994), 665–704.

[11] M. R. Warren, 'Making Contact: Postcolonial Perspectives through Geoffrey of Monmouth's *Historia regum Britannie*', *Arthuriana* 8 (1998), 115–34; P. C. Ingham, *Sovereign Fantasies: Arthurian Romance and the Making of Britain* (Philadelphia, PA, 2001), pp. 15 and 21–50.

[12] The main proponent of this argument remains J. P. S. Tatlock, *The Legendary History of Britain: Geoffrey of Monmouth's* Historia Regum Britanniae *and its Early Vernacular Versions* (Berkeley and Los Angeles, 1950), pp. 396–402; see also E. M. R. Ditmas, 'Geoffrey of Monmouth and the Breton Families in Cornwall', *Welsh History Review* 6.4 (1973), 451–61; Roberts, 'Geoffrey', pp. 97–116. For Geoffrey's playfulness see, for example, V. Flint, 'The *Historia Regum Britanniae* of Geoffrey of Monmouth: Parody and Its Purpose. A Suggestion', *Speculum* 54 (1979), 447–68; and C. N. L. Brooke, 'Geoffrey of Monmouth as a Historian', in *Church and Government in the Middle Ages: Essays Presented to C. R. Cheney on His 70th Birthday*, ed. C. N. L. Brooke and G. Martin (Cambridge, 1976), pp. 77–91.

[13] O. W. Jones, 'Historical Writing in Medieval Wales' (unpublished PhD dissertation, Bangor University, 2014), and J. B. Smith, 'Literary Encounters in the Anglo-Welsh Borderlands', following, ultimately, J. Gillingham, 'The Context and Purposes of Geoffrey of Monmouth's *History of the Kings of Britain*', *Anglo-Norman Studies* XIII (1991), 99–118.

of Welsh literary culture: its languages, its manuscript production and its oral and written forms in the world of Welsh *cyfarwyddyd* (learning, lore), the common body of knowledge upon which learned Welsh poets, historians and genealogists drew.[14] An increased understanding of the *Historia*'s position in Wales is of benefit to any of the interpretations of Geoffrey's intentions outlined above.

Before I embark on a survey of the Welsh Latin literature that flourished before and after the impact of Geoffrey's history, I illustrate the necessity of understanding the role of Latin in Welsh literary culture through the following example. A critical view of *Brut y Brenhinedd* to have emerged in recent years is that the translations represent acts of reclamation of Welsh history after its appropriation by the Anglo-Norman colonizing elite.[15] In this reading, Geoffrey's translation into Latin of his *Britannici sermonis librum vetustissimum* (very ancient book in the British language) is 'an aggressive discourse of linguistic possession'.[16] By translating the *liber vetustissimus* from British into Latin, Geoffrey supplants the British-language source 'with the language of the dominant power'.[17] In order for this interpretation to work, Latin must be a language foreign to Wales and imposed upon it by the Anglo-Norman conquerors: Geoffrey takes possession of a purported history of the British people and renders it into a language foreign to that country, imposed upon it by a foreign and dominant power, epitomizing the colonial experience.[18] The British history is expropriated to an external audience: 'Geoffrey's translation [of the British history into Latin] thus makes the Britons more like his Latin-

---

[14] For discussion see P. K. Ford, 'The Poet as *Cyfarwydd* in Early Welsh Tradition', *Studia Celtica* 10/11 (1975–6), 152–62; B. F. Roberts, '*Ystoria*', *Bulletin of the Board of Celtic Studies* 26 (1974), 13–20.

[15] See, for example, Warren, 'Making Contact' and *History on the Edge*.

[16] Warren, 'Making Contact', p. 121; quotation of Geoffrey from *Geoffrey of Monmouth*, ed. Reeve, trans. Wright, pp. 4–5. *Britannicus* could mean either Welsh or Breton in this period. Interestingly, and perhaps tellingly, Geoffrey of Monmouth's contemporary Geffrei Gaimar takes it to mean Welsh: see *Estoire des Engleis*, ll. 6449–52 and 6459–61, ed. and trans. I. Short (Oxford, 2009), pp. 348–51: 'Robert li quens de Gloücestre / fist translater icele geste / solum les livres as Waleis / k'il aveient des Bretons reis. ... Geffrai Gaimar cel livre escri[s]t / [e] les transsa[n]dances i mist / ke li Waleis ourent leissé' (Robert earl of Gloucester had this historical narrative translated in accordance with the books belonging to the Welsh that they had in their possession on the subject of the kings of Britain. ... Geoffrey Gaimar made a written copy of [Walter Espec's] book and added to it the supplementary material that the Welsh had omitted).

[17] Warren, 'Making Contact', p. 122.

[18] Warren's reading in 'Making Contact' suggests that the Norman conquest of Wales had, as part of its agenda, the goal of discouraging or wiping out the Welsh language, something that was true in later periods of the colonization process, but not in the twelfth century.

literate readers – that is, more like everybody *with an official interest in written history*. ... While the *HRB* as a whole embodies the Britons' loss of history as well as their loss of language, it also resists their colonization by remembering their past.'[19] This interpretation, which views the Latin-literate audience and the British audience as separate groups, implies that Latin ('the language of the dominant power') and written history were not used by the Welsh prior to colonization. It implies that the native Welsh literati was essentially oral and did not have access to Latin texts. Consequently, the translation of Geoffrey's history back into Welsh as *Brut y Brenhinedd* is characterized as an act of reclamation, after Welsh narrative history had been appropriated, overwritten and disseminated in the language of the conquerors: 'The *Historia*'s receptions across the Severn (*ultra Sabrinam*) reclaim the past for the Welsh. ... These Welsh *Brutieu* repossess Briton history by returning it to the language of Geoffrey's ostensible source.'[20] The language of ownership is telling. Latin is not within the purview of the Welsh, nor is written language itself.

While the Welsh did indeed 'appropriate' elements of Geoffrey's history into their own vernacular literature – evidenced by, for example, the profound effect of the *Historia* on medieval Welsh genealogical tracts – and the English certainly, in turn, appropriated elements of the British history for their own political gain, viewing *Brut y Brenhinedd* as an act of re-appropriation does not take into account the important role that Latin played in the literary culture of medieval Wales.[21] As is demonstrated in the following pages, Geoffrey's history was not received into a culture devoid of Latin learning, but into a literate culture with a long-standing and robust relationship with Latin-language writing as well as a sensitive understanding of its own classical inheritance in that language. If the translations of Geoffrey's history into Welsh cannot be acts of re-appropriation, they must be something else, and this study offers some alternative possibilities at its conclusion.

---

[19] Warren, 'Making Contact', p. 122 (my emphasis). Though Geoffrey's history had indeed become the set-piece of Welsh written history by the mid-thirteenth century, the existence of the Welsh Latin annals indicates that written history was practised in Wales prior to the circulation of Geoffrey's text.

[20] Warren, *History on the Edge*, pp. 60 and 77.

[21] On the former point, see Ben Guy, 'Gerald and Welsh Genealogical Learning', in *Gerald of Wales: Texts and Contexts*, ed. G. Henley and A. J. McMullen (Cardiff, forthcoming), discussing Galfridian rulers in Welsh genealogies in relation to the Latin life of Gruffudd ap Cynan (*Vita Griffini filii Conani*). On the latter point a great deal has been written: see, for example, M. Fisher, 'Genealogy Rewritten: Inheriting the Legendary in Insular Historiography', in *Broken Lines: Genealogical Literature in Medieval Britain and France*, ed. R. L. Radulescu and E. D. Kennedy, Medieval Texts and Cultures of Northern Europe 16 (Turnhout, 2008), pp. 123–41.

The status of Latin in Wales: evidence for a vibrant Latin literary culture

From the point of view of Welsh literary audiences, writers and readers of history, Latin was an living language, available for writing poetry, hagiography, history, legal documents, hymns, penitentials and sermons, and was applied vigorously to these genres throughout the Middle Ages. As was the case elsewhere in the medieval West, 'Latin was unquestionably the language of the church in Wales. ... In Latin we expect prayers, hymns, sermons, elements of the service in Mass, penitentials, the books of the Bible, saints' lives, confessions, and even those texts further connected with church writings: commentaries on the Bible, records of church holdings. ... We have many of these texts surviving in a Welsh context.'[22] Not only did Latinate culture thrive within Wales, but its existence seems to have been recognized outside of it as well. In fact, some evidence suggests that Wales enjoyed a good reputation for book-learning, although that is not reflected in the manuscript record due to poor rates of survival. One example is Geoffrey's citation of the *liber vetustissimus* as his historical source, another Geffrei Gaimar's tacit acceptance of Welsh books as authoritative sources of learning.[23] There is no reason for Geoffrey's audiences to have assumed that Latin learning did not exist in Wales as well. Furthermore, Welsh Latin manuscript culture was so comparable to its English counterpart that the palaeographer Neil Ker on at least one occasion declined to distinguish between Welsh and English provenance, an indication that Welsh manuscript production, at least in some monasteries, was of a standard equivalent to that of their English neighbours.[24]

---

[22] S. Zeiser, 'Latinity, Manuscripts, and the Rhetoric of Conquest in Late-Eleventh-Century Wales' (unpublished Ph.D. dissertation, Harvard University, 2012), p. 10.

[23] See *Estoire des Engleis*, ll. 6449–61, ed. Short, pp. 348–51; I am grateful to Nicholas Watson for raising this point.

[24] Exeter, Cathedral Library, 3514 (s. xiii) is not localized to either England or Wales by N. Ker, *Medieval Manuscripts in British Libraries*, 5 vols. (Oxford, 1969–2002), II, 2 and 824. While identifying Welsh features, Ker classifies the manuscript as a hybrid with a 'core written ... in an unidentified British scriptorium' which was then expanded 'when the book had reached Wales'. J. Crick makes a definitive case for this manuscript's Welsh provenance, arguing in 'The Power and the Glory: Conquest and Cosmology in Edwardian Wales', in *Textual Cultures: Cultural Texts*, ed. O. Da Rold and E. Treharne, Essays and Studies 63 (Cambridge, 2010), 21–42 (p. 35), that it 'represents an assertion of intellectual and aesthetic standards' comparable to those in England and the Continent, 'staking out the place of Welsh history ... using the universal language, in texts copied in contemporary European script which a leading modern expert [Ker] was unable to localise to England or Wales'. This manuscript, with a core virtually indistinguishable from English productions, suggests that palaeographical standards in Welsh

Today, evidence for a longstanding tradition of Latin writing in Wales survives in a number of forms, including annalistic record-keeping, legal documents and poetry (see list below).[25] This can be divided into two categories: original compositions and evidence for the circulation of Latin authors in Wales gleaned from allusions to them in extant works. Though patchy in their survival, the extant Latin texts of medieval Wales attest to the richness of a now-neglected tradition.[26] The following list, though not exhaustive, constitutes a synopsis of extant or known Latin texts composed in Wales from the fifth to the fifteenth century:[27]

1. *Confessio* and *Epistola* by St Patrick, fifth century; possibly composed in Ireland, not Wales, but penned by a British author [28]
2. *De excidio et conquestu Britanniae* by Gildas, sixth century (London, British Library, Cotton Vitellius A. vi, s. x/xi); written in south-west England[29]

---

scriptoria were comparable to their equivalents in England. It also raises the problem of how the Welsh provenance of manuscripts now located in English libraries might be established without the presence of definitive Welsh symptoms such as genealogies or glosses; for further discussion, see P. Sims-Williams, 'The Uses of Writing in Early Medieval Wales', in *Literacy in Medieval Celtic Societies*, ed. H. Pryce (Cambridge, 1998), pp. 15–38 (p. 23). Exceptional cases such as the Black Book of Carmarthen (Aberystwyth, National Library of Wales, Peniarth 1) would not fit this description.

[25] I will not discuss at length the ecclesiastical texts in Latin which emerged from Welsh churches, such as sermons, masses and penitentials, as these have been studied elsewhere; see T. M. Charles-Edwards, *Wales and the Britons, 350–1064* (Oxford, 2012), pp. 625–50; *The Early Church in Wales and the West*, ed. N. Edwards and A. Lane (Oxford, 1992).

[26] Advocating that Latin was studied in Wales, Zeiser writes: 'That the Latin poetry of Wales needs renewed study is unarguable. ... Many twentieth-century surveys of medieval Welsh literature gloss over the survival of Welsh-Latin verse. Common compilation volumes of "medieval Welsh poetry" only include poems written in the Welsh language, adhering to the literal interpretation of "Welsh" as referencing language only rather than literary culture as a whole'; see 'Latinity, Manuscripts, and the Rhetoric of Conquest', pp. 2–3. Additional studies with this desideratum are Russell, '"Go and look in the Latin books"' (forthcoming); D. R. Howlett, *Cambro-Latin Compositions: Their Competence and Craftsmanship* (Dublin, 1998) and *The Celtic Latin Tradition of Biblical Style* (Dublin, 1995); G. Henley, 'Rhetoric, Translation and Historiography: The Literary Qualities of *Brut y Tywysogyon*', *Quaestio Insularis: Selected Proceedings of the Cambridge Colloquium in Anglo-Saxon, Norse and Celtic* 13 (2012), 78–103.

[27] The list is in approximate chronological order (as not all the texts are dated precisely), and a few exceptions to my classification of 'composition in Wales' are noted.

[28] *Libri epistolarum Sancti Patricii episcopi*, ed. L. Bieler, 2 vols. (Dublin, 1951–2); see also the *St Patrick's Confessio Hypertext Stack Project*, A. Harvey et al., Royal Irish Academy, 2011, http://www.confessio.ie, accessed 4 September 2016.

[29] *Gildas. The Ruin of Britain and other Works*, ed. and trans. M. Winterbottom, History from the Sources: Arthurian Period Sources 7 (London, 1978).

3. *Orationes Moucani*, s. vii²–viii¹ (London, British Library, Royal 2 A. xx, s.viii², fols. 42r–45r)[30]
4. *Historia Brittonum* by Nennius or pseudo-Nennius, AD 829/30, extant in at least five recensions[31]
5. *De raris fabulis*, ninth century (Oxford, Bodleian Library, Bodley 572, s. x); a text originally from Wales, though the form we have it in is from Cornwall[32]
6. the Harleian Chronicle, tenth century (A-text of *Annales Cambriae*, in London, British Library, Harley 3859, s. xi/xii, fols. 190r–193r)[33]
7. material from late eleventh-century Llanbadarn Fawr, including:
   - three poems by Rhygyfarch ap Sulien[34]
   - two poems by Ieuan ap Sulien[35]
   - eighteen distichs (Cambridge, Corpus Christi College, 199, *c.* 1085×1091, fols. 2r, 4v, 5r, 5v, 9v, 10v, 12v, 21v, 24r, 27r, 31v, 35r, 41v, 47v, 54r, 62v, 68v, 76r)[36]

---

[30] *The Prayer Book of Aedelulad the Bishop, Commonly called the Book of Cerne*, ed. A. B. Kuypers (Cambridge, 1902), pp. 219–20, dated by D. R. Howlett, '*Orationes Moucani*: Early Cambro-Latin Prayers', *Cambridge Medieval Celtic Studies* 24 (Winter 1992), 55–74 (p. 56).

[31] These are commonly known as the Harleian, Chartres, Vatican, Nennian and Gildasian recensions. The Harleian recension is edited and translated in D. N. Dumville, 'The Textual History of the Welsh-Latin Historia Brittonum', 3 vols. (unpublished Ph.D. thesis, Edinburgh University, 1976), I, 166–271, and translated in *Nennius. British history and the Welsh annals*, ed. and trans. J. Morris, History from the Sources: Arthurian Period Sources 8 (London, 1980), 18–43; the Chartres recension is edited in *The Historia Brittonum, vol. 2*, ed. D. N. Dumville (Cambridge, 1988); the Vatican recension in *The Historia Brittonum, vol. 3*, ed. D. N. Dumville (Cambridge, 1985).

[32] *De raris fabulis, 'On uncommon tales': a glossed Latin colloquy-text from a tenth-century Cornish manuscript*, ed. and trans. S. Gwara, Basic Texts in Brittonic History (Cambridge, 2004).

[33] Transcription by H. W. Gough-Cooper, 'Annales Cambriae: The A text, From British Library, Harley MS 3859, ff. 190r–193r', *Welsh Chronicles Research Group* (Bangor, 2015), http://croniclau.bangor.ac.uk/documents/AC_A_first_edition.pdf, accessed 27 August 2016.

[34] 'Carmen Ricemarch de psalterio' (Dublin, Trinity College, 50, *c.* 1079, fol. 158v), 'Planctus Ricemarch' (London, British Library, Cotton Faustina, C. i, part ii, *c.* 1115×1135), 'Carmen Ricemarch de messe infelici' (BL Cotton Faustina, C. i); ed. and trans. M. Lapidge, 'The Welsh-Latin Poetry of Sulien's Family', *Studia Celtica* 8/9 (1973–4), 68–106 (pp. 88–93), and Zeiser, 'Latinity, Manuscripts, and the Rhetoric of Conquest', pp. 314–15 and 332–7.

[35] 'Inuocatio Iohannis' (Cambridge, Corpus Christi College, 199, *c.* 1085×1091, fol. 1v); 'Carmen Iohannis de Uita et Familia Sulgeni' (Corpus 199, fols. 76r–78r); ed. and trans. Lapidge, 'The Welsh Latin Poetry of Sulien's Family', pp. 78–89, and Zeiser, 'Latinity, Manuscripts, and the Rhetoric of Conquest', pp. 316 and 322–31.

[36] Ed. and trans. Lapidge, 'The Welsh Latin Poetry of Sulien's Family', pp. 78–81, and Zeiser, 'Latinity, Manuscripts, and the Rhetoric of Conquest', pp. 317–21.

8. Life of St David (London, British Library, Cotton Vespasian A. xiv, c. 1200, fol. 61)[37]
9. Life of St Padarn (BL, Cotton Vespasian A. xiv, c. 1200, fol. 80)[38]
10. *De primo statu Landauensis ęcclesię*, a tract in the Book of Llandaf, early twelfth century (Aberystwyth, National Library of Wales, 17110E)[39]
11. the (lost) Latin exempla for *Brut y Tywysogion* (History of the Princes)
12. the (lost) Latin exempla for *Brenhinedd y Saesson* (History of the English)
13. lament and epitaph for the Lord Rhys ap Gruffudd (Aberystwyth, National Library of Wales, Peniarth 20, s. xiv^1, pp. 201–5)[40]
14. the Breviate Chronicle, late thirteenth century, though with earlier sources (B-text of *Annales Cambriae*, in London, The National Archives, E. 164/1, s. xiii^2, fols. 1r–13r)[41]
15. the Cottonian Chronicle, late thirteenth century, though with earlier sources (C-text of *Annales Cambriae*, in London, British Library, Cotton Domitian A. i, s. xiii^{ex}, fols. 138r–155r)[42]
16. *Cronica de Wallia*, late thirteenth century (Exeter Cathedral Library, 3514, s. xiii^{ex}, pp. 507–19)[43]

---

[37] R. Sharpe and J. R. Davies, ed. and trans., 'Rhygyfarch's *Life* of St David', in *St David of Wales: Cult, Church and Nation*, ed. J. W. Evans and J. M. Wooding (Woodbridge, 2007), pp. 107–55; *Vitae sanctorum Britanniae et genealogiae*, ed. A. W. Wade-Evans, History and Law Series 9 (Cardiff, 1944), 150–70.

[38] C. Thomas and D. Howlett, ed. and trans., '"Vita Sancti Paterni": the Life of Saint Padarn and the Original "*Miniu*"', *Trivium* 33 (2003), 1–129; *Vitae*, ed. Wade-Evans, pp. 252–69.

[39] *The Text of the Book of Llan Dâv reproduced from the Gwynsaney Manuscript*, ed. J. G. Evans and J. Rhys (Oxford, 1893), pp. 68–71; discussion in J. R. Davies, *The Book of Llandaf and the Norman Church in Wales*, Studies in Celtic History 21 (Woodbridge, 2003), 63–75.

[40] Printed in *Brut y Tywysogyon, Peniarth MS. 20*, ed. T. Jones (Cardiff, 1941), pp. 140–1, and discussed further below.

[41] Transcription by H. W. Gough-Cooper, 'Annales Cambriae: The B text, From London, National Archives, E. 164/1, pp. 2–26', *Welsh Chronicles Research Group* (Bangor, 2015), http://croniclau.bangor.ac.uk/documents/AC%20B%20first%20edition.pdf, accessed 27 August 2016.

[42] Transcription by H. W. Gough-Cooper, 'Annales Cambriae: The C text, From London, British Library, Cotton MS Domitian A. i, ff. 138r–155r', *Welsh Chronicles Research Group* (Bangor, 2015), http://croniclau.bangor.ac.uk/documents/AC%20C%20first%20edition.pdf, accessed 27 August 2016.

[43] Transcription by H. W. Gough-Cooper, 'Annales Cambriae: The E text, From Exeter Cathedral Library MS 3514, pp. 507–19', *Welsh Chronicles Research Group* (Bangor, 2015), http://croniclau.bangor.ac.uk/documents/AC_E_First_Edition%20%20.pdf, accessed 16 March 2016.

17. *Cronica ante aduentum domini*, late thirteenth century (Exeter 3514, s. xiii^ex, pp. 523–8)[44]
18. *Trucidare Saxones soliti Cambrenses*, c. 1200 (Leiden, Universiteitsbibliothek, Vossius Lat. F. 77, s. xiii^ex, fol. 144r–v; Cambridge, Corpus Christi College 181, s. xiv¹, p. 277)[45]
19. *Vita Griffini filii Conani*, twelfth century[46]
20. collection of Welsh saints' lives, twelfth century (BL Cotton Vespasian A. xiv, s. xii)[47]
21. *De situ Brecheiniauc* (Concerning the Establishment of Brycheiniog), twelfth century (BL Cotton Vespasian A. xiv, s. xii; London, British Library, Cotton Domitian A. i, s. xvi)[48]
22. praise poem to Geoffrey of Monmouth by Madog of Edeirnion, thirteenth century (Cardiff, Central Library, 2.611, s. xiii^ex, fols. 9v–10r)[49]
23. *De vera historia de morte Arthuri*, pre-1203[50]
24. five law texts, called 'Latin A, B, C, D, E', redacted, mid-thirteenth century to fifteenth century[51]
25. miscellaneous charters and *acta* issued by Welsh rulers, early twelfth century to late thirteenth century.[52]

Welsh manuscript survival is very poor, and most extant literature in Wales post-dates Geoffrey.[53] One very important exception is, however,

---

[44] Transcription by H. W. Gough-Cooper, 'Annales Cambriae: The D text, From Exeter Cathedral Library MS 3514, pp. 523–8', ed. H. Gough-Cooper, *Welsh Chronicles Research Group* (Bangor, 2015), http://croniclau.bangor.ac.uk/documents/AC%20D%20first%20edition.pdf, accessed 16 March 2016.

[45] Edited and translated by D. Howlett, 'A Triad of Texts about Saint David', in *St David of Wales: Cult, Church and Nation*, ed. J. Wyn-Evans and J. M. Wooding, pp. 253–73 (pp. 268–71).

[46] *Vita Griffini Filii Conani: The Medieval Latin Life of Gruffudd ap Cynan*, ed. and trans. P. Russell (Cardiff, 2005).

[47] *Vita Sanctorum Britanniae et Genealogiae*, ed. A. W. Wade-Evans, Board of Celtic Studies, History and Law Series 9 (Cardiff, 1944).

[48] A. W. Wade-Evans, ed. and trans., 'The Brychan Documents', *Y Cymmrodor* 19 (1906), 18–48.

[49] Printed in *Historia regum Britanniae: A Variant Version Edited from Manuscripts*, ed. J. Hammer (Cambridge, MA, 1951), p. 18. For discussion of this poem see J. Byron Smith, 'Literary Encounters in the Anglo-Welsh Borderlands', pp. 48–51.

[50] Edited by M. Lapidge, 'An edition of the *Vera Historia de Morte Arthuri*', *Arthurian Literature* 1 (1981), 79–93 (p. 81).

[51] *The Latin Texts of the Welsh Laws*, ed. H. D. Emanuel (Cardiff, 1967); see also 'The Latin Texts', *Cyfraith Hywel*, S. E. Roberts et al., http://cyfraith-hywel.cymru.ac.uk/en/canllaw-testunau-lladin.php, accessed 4 September 2016.

[52] *The Acts of Welsh Rulers, 1120–1283*, ed. H. Pryce, with the assistance of C. Insley (Cardiff, 2005).

[53] D. Huws, *Medieval Welsh Manuscripts* (Cardiff, 2000), p. 3, estimates that fewer than

the output of Sulien, bishop of St Davids, and his sons, Rhygyfarch and Ieuan, who flourished in the late eleventh century at the *clas* house of Llanbadarn Fawr, an autonomous, non-celibate ecclesiastical centre whose abbots were appointed hereditarily.[54] Michael Lapidge argues that they must have received a standard Latin education, which involved the careful study and memorization of poetry.[55] He finds evidence of formal Latin training in their references and allusions, conscious and unconscious, to many authors: Ovid, Virgil, Lucan, Juvencus, Prudentius, Martianus Capella, Caelius Sedulius, Boethius, Aldhelm, and possibly Statius, Horace and Juvenal.[56] These are all fairly standard authors for the Latin educational curriculum in the medieval period, indicating that Llanbadarn Fawr owned a library of some size.[57] As very little library catalogue evidence survives from medieval Wales, this is a rich list of authors alluded to.[58] Five manuscripts were produced by this family, the

one in one hundred Latin manuscripts from medieval Wales have survived.

[54] Sulien was first appointed bishop of St Davids in 1073. For a comprehensive discussion of this ecclesiastical family and the texts and manuscripts they produced, see Zeiser, 'Latinity, Manuscripts, and the Rhetoric of Conquest'; also D. R. Howlett, 'Rhygyfarch ap Sulien and Ieuan ap Sulien', in *The Cambridge History of the Book, Vol. 1 c.400–1100*, ed. R. Gameson (Cambridge, 2012), pp. 701–5; G. Conway, 'Towards a Cultural Context for the Eleventh-Century Llanbadarn Manuscripts', *Ceredigion* 13:1 (1997), 9–28; T. Graham, 'The Poetic, Scribal and Artistic Work of Ieuan ap Sulien in Corpus Christi College, Cambridge, MS 199: Addenda and Assessment', *National Library of Wales Journal* 29 (1996), 241–56; N. K. Chadwick, 'Intellectual Life in West Wales in the Last Days of the Celtic Church', in *Studies in the Early British Church*, ed. N. K. Chadwick, K. Hughes, C. Brooke and K. Jackson (Cambridge, 1958), pp. 121–82. For the *clas* system in pre-Norman Wales, see W. Davies, Wales in the Early Middle Ages (Leicester, 1982).

[55] Lapidge, 'The Welsh-Latin Poetry of Sulien's Family', p. 69: 'medieval literary education consisted for the most part in the minute examination and memorization of certain curriculum authors ... the style of a medieval Latin poet almost invariably bears traces of the process of memorization'. For general discussion and lists of curriculum authors, see E. R. Curtius, *European Literature and the Latin Middle Ages*, trans. W. R. Trask, Bollingen Series 36 (Princeton, 1953), 49; S. C. Ferruolo, *The Origins of the University: The Schools of Paris and their Critics, 1100–1215* (Stanford, 1985); S. Reynolds, *Medieval Reading: Grammar, Rhetoric, and the Classical Text* (Cambridge and New York, 1996); B. M. Olsen, 'La popularité des textes classiques entre le IXe et le XIIe siècle', in *La réception de la littérature classique au Moyen Age*, ed. K. Friis-Jensen (Copenhagen, 1995), pp. 21–34 (p. 29); J. J. Contreni, *Education and Culture in the Barbarian West: From the Sixth Through the Eighth Century* (Columbia, SC, 1976).

[56] Lapidge, 'The Welsh-Latin Poetry of Sulien's Family', pp. 69–70; for further discussion of the Latin curriculum in Welsh schools, see Charles-Edwards, *Wales and the Britons*, pp. 637–40; for a study of Ovid in medieval Wales, see P. Russell, *Reading Ovid in Medieval Wales* (Columbus, OH, forthcoming).

[57] Ferruolo, *Origins of the University*, p. 146.

[58] Catalogues from monastic libraries in Wales that survive are from Marcher houses; these are from Margam (listing 242 volumes), Llanthony (12 volumes), Goldcliff (38)

contents of which include other texts by Latin authors (Augustine's *De Trinitate*, Cicero's *Somnium Scipionis*, Macrobius' *Commentarium*, the passions of Saints Erasmus, Ciricius, Iulitta, Peter and Paul, Bede's *De temporum ratione*), as well as their own compositions (lives of St Padarn and St David, eighteen Latin *disticha* and three poems written in Latin by Rhygyfarch ap Sulien).[59] Together, Rhygyfarch and Ieuan 'have been credited with some 313 lines of Latin poetry'.[60] These works attest to a deeply involved, productive and pervasive practice of Latin composition in a Welsh religious house, with an intimate knowledge of the Latin curriculum as its base.[61]

Lapidge has also discussed the extant evidence for Latin texts in Wales dating from the sixth to the eleventh centuries, a period when Latin education in Wales was strongly connected to Irish teachers and curricula and, it has been argued, took place in ecclesiastical schools.[62] Surviving texts from this period include the *Liber Commonei* and Book I of Ovid's *Ars amatoria* in St Dunstan's Classbook (Oxford, Bodleian Library, Auct. F. 4. 32, s. ix), *De raris fabulis* (Oxford, Bodleian Library, Bodley 572, s. x²), the *Hisperica Famina* (s. vii, written in Ireland but possibly kept in Wales at a later date)[63] and a poem by Juvencus glossed by Welsh scholars (Cambridge

and Brecon (4); see *Registrum Anglie de libris doctorum et auctorum veterum*, 289–91, 293 and 319–21, ed. R. H. Rouse and M. A. Rouse, Corpus of British Medieval Library Catalogues 1 (London, 1991), xiii.

[59] For a complete list of these manuscripts and their contents, see Zeiser, 'Latinity, Manuscripts, and the Rhetoric of Conquest', p. 25.

[60] Zeiser, 'Latinity, Manuscripts, and the Rhetoric of Conquest', pp. 26 and 23: 'Both Ieuan and Rhygyfarch produced saints' lives and Latin poetry, with Ieuan's authorship attributed to the *Vita Sancti Paterni*, 18 short blessings, a seven-line invocation for aid while copying a manuscript, a 160-line biography of Sulien and an Old Welsh *englyn* on Saint Padarn's staff Cyrwen. Rhygyfarch is named as the author of the *Vita Sancti Dauid* and three Latin poems: a 25-line reflection on the Psalter, a 90-line lament regarding the Norman presence in Wales, and a short quatrain discussing a bad harvest.'

[61] On the subject of the possibility of access to these texts through *florilegia*, Lapidge, 'The Welsh-Latin Poetry of Sulien's Family', p. 70, writes, 'we have no difficulty in supposing that a reasonably well-stocked library would have contained copies of the complete works'.

[62] Charles-Edwards, *Wales and the Britons*, pp. 637–41 (p. 637): following the withdrawal of the Roman Empire, 'if the British Church were to retain a Christianity that was part of Latin Christendom, it had to have its own schools in which Latin was taught. In the British Isles the Church had to take the place of the *civitates* of Late Antiquity – one reason among others why the principal churches were called *civitates*.'

[63] The *Hisperica Famina* is extant in four recensions: (A) Vatican City, Biblioteca Apostolica Vaticana, Reg. lat. 81 (s. x, ff. 1–12); (B) Luxembourg, Bibliothèque Nationale, 89 (s. xi²) and Paris, Bibliothèque nationale de France, lat. 11411 (s. ix, fols. 99–100); (C) Luxembourg 89; (D) BNF lat. 11411 (fols. 101–102). For more information, see

University Library, Ff. 4. 42, s. ix).[64] The Book of Llandaf, a twelfth-century compilation of saints' lives, charters and privileges, containing both Latin and Welsh-language texts, is also of note, as are the five Welsh law books in Latin redacted from the thirteenth century onwards.[65]

Several Latin chronicles written in Wales are extant (see Table 1). These are the Harleian, Breviate and Cottonian chronicles, formerly known as the A-, B- and C-texts of the *Annales Cambriae*.[66] They indicate record-keeping in Latin from an early period, collectively displaying a reliance on annals kept at St Davids (specifically from 795–954).[67] Another important example of Latin historical writing from Wales is the *Cronica de Wallia*, a short chronicle found in the final pages of Exeter 3514, a manuscript written in the closing decades of the thirteenth century.[68] This chronicle contains passages which, together with several Latin elegiac poems, are part of a body of Latin writing dedicated to the Lord Rhys ap Gruffudd (d. 1197), ruler of Deheubarth. Taken together with several other localizing details, emphasis in the *Cronica de Wallia* on the Lord Rhys and his family indicate that those sections of the chronicle were most likely written at the Cistercian house of Strata Florida, of which he was patron.[69]

The Hisperica Famina, ed. and trans. M. W. Herren, 2 vols., Pontifical Institute of Mediaeval Studies, Studies and Texts 31 and 85 (Toronto, 1974–87).

[64] For discussion, see P. Russell, '*An habes linguam Latinam? Non tam bene sapio*: Views of Multilingualism from the Early Medieval West', in *Multilingualism in the Greco-Roman Worlds*, ed. A. Mullen and P. James (Cambridge, 2012), pp. 193–224; H. McKee, 'Scribes and glosses from Dark Age Wales: the Cambridge Juvencus MS', *Cambrian Medieval Celtic Studies* 39 (2000), 1–22.

[65] J. R. Davies, *The Book of Llandaf and the Norman Church in Wales*, Studies in Celtic History 2 (Woodbridge, 2003); Russell, '"Go and look in the Latin books"' (forthcoming), and *Welsh Law in Medieval Anglesey: British Library Harleian MS 1796 (Latin C)*, Texts and Studies in Medieval Welsh Law 2 (Cambridge, 2011).

[66] The umbrella title *Annales Cambriae* conflates what are actually quite distinct texts.

[67] K. Hughes, 'The Welsh Latin Chronicles: *Annales Cambriae* and Related Texts', *Proceedings of the British Academy* 59 (1973), 234–5 (p. 235): 'there are strong reasons for thinking that the chronicle was started at St. Davids in the late eighth century, for a year-by-year chronicle nearly always shows signs of localization, and the Harleian annals point to St. Davids only from the late eighth century. ... There is nothing in the form of the names which requires us to assume compilation before the late eighth century'.

[68] Note that the title in the manuscript is abbreviated (*cron.*) and could be expanded to *cronica* or *cronicon*; for present purposes I use *Cronica* because it is already in use by T. Jones, '"Cronica de Wallia" and Other Documents from Exeter Cathedral Library MS. 3514', *Bulletin of the Board of Celtic Studies* 12 (1946), 27–44. This chronicle is accompanied by another unique text, the *Cronica ante aduentum domini*, a composite of Welsh and English sources; for discussion see G. Henley, 'The Use of English Annalistic Sources in Welsh Chronicles', *Haskins Society Journal* 26 (2015), 229–47 (pp. 241–3).

[69] Hughes, 'The Welsh Latin Chronicles', pp. 247–9.

Sections of the *Cronica de Wallia* stand out from the more laconic portions of the Welsh Latin annals for their Latinity, indicating a high level of Latin education on the part of the chronicler. The elegy to the Lord Rhys in the entry for the year 1197, the year of his death, is of particular note, as it contains verbal allusions to no fewer than eleven classical and biblical heroes (marked in bold) in markedly complex syntactical constructions. It is quoted here in full to illustrate the rhetorical capacities of its author:

[1] Hoc enim anno pestifero Atropos, sororum seuissima que nemeni parcere gnara, cunctis mortalibus inuisa, magni uiri, scilicet Resi, exicium[70] ausa est demoliri, quem instabilitatis mater Fortuna, nature condicionem hoc solo oblita, iugi[ter][71] celsitudine rote passa est permanere suoque ab etatis sue exordio benigno refouerat gremio.[72] Ad tanti ergo obitum uiri accedens [h]aut sine lacrimis enarrandum, utpote planctu dignum, [h]aut cuique sine dolore recordandum, quia omnibus dampnosum, [h]aut sine merore audiendum, quia cunctis lugubrem, deficio, uox silet, lingua stupet. [2] Tanti uiri probitates quas ille magnanimus historiographus Thebanus, si temporis uicissitudo concessisset, Tebaide so[s]pita[73] pertractante gauderet, uerum ille historiographus Troianus poetarum nobilissimus, si misera fata dedissent, grandiloquo stilo in longum diffunderet euum.

[3] Letifer hic annus[74] et cunctis lamentabilis annus, cuius iiii. Kalendas Maii Resus Griffini filius, Suthwallie princeps, uerum tocius Wallie capud insuperabile,[75] fato occubuit importune. [4] Hic namque nobilissima regum ortus prosapia, uerum ipse clarus genearcha, mentis probitatem generi coequauit, et sic geminans animum nobilitate generis, consolator procerum, forcium debellator, subditorum benignus tutator, urbium ualidus expugnator, bella mouens,[76] turmas instaurans, hostiles cateruas obruens, [h]aut secus quam aper frendens audacia, seu leo rugiens caude uerbere stimulatus in iras, ferritate deseuiebat in hostes. O belli gloria, milicie decus ac clipeus, nobile tutamen patriae, armorum decus, brachium fortitudinis, largitatis manus, rationis occulus, honestatis splendor, animositatis apex, [5] probitatis **Hercule**, secundus **Achillis** asperitatem pectore gerens, **Nestoris** modestiam, **Tidei** audaciam, **Sampsonis** fortitudinem, **Hectoris** grauitatem,

---

[70] MS: ex*er*icium.
[71] MS: iugi.
[72] Fortune's wheel is described in conceptually similar terms in Boethius, *Consolatio* 2p1.19 and 2m1, noted and discussed by Russell in '"Go and look in the Latin books"' (forthcoming).
[73] MS: sopita.
[74] 'arboribusque satisque lues et letifer annus', Virgil, *Aeneid* III.139.
[75] 'Iam timor ille Phrygum, decus et tutela Pelasgi / nominis, Aeacides, caput insuperabile bello, / arserat: armarat deus idem, idem que cremabat.', Ovid, *Metamorphoses* XII.612–14.
[76] 'bella movens', Virgil, *Aeneid* XII.333.

Euriali agilitatem, **Paridis** formam, **Vlixis** facundiam, **Salomonis** sapienciam, **Aiacis** animositatem, iniurie dampna morte recompensantem! [6] O miserorum tutum refugium, nudorum indumentum, esuriencium morsus, siciencium potus! O omnium postulancium prompta satisfactio donorum! [7] O dulcis eloquio, comis obsequio, morum honestus, sermone modestus, uultu hilaris, facie decorus, cunctis benignus, omnibus equus, simplicitatis [h]aut ficte pietas, humilitatis [h]aut fabricate sublimitas! Heu! heu! iam Wallia uiduata dolet ruitura dolore.

([1] For in this pestilential year Atropos, the most savage of the sisters, knowing how to spare nobody, and hated by all mortals, brought about the destruction of a great man, Rhys. Fortune, the mother of instability, forgetting the circumstances of nature with regard to this person alone, allowed him to remain on the height of the wheel perpetually, and from the beginning of his life had gathered him into her kindly lap. Therefore, to approach the death of so great a man, which is not to be narrated without tears, as is worthy of lament, not to be remembered by each person without sorrow, because it caused the loss of all things, not to be heard without grief, because it is mournful for all, I am insufficient; the voice is silent; the tongue is numb. [2] The honesty of such a man, which that great-hearted Theban historiographer would have celebrated, as the *Thebaid* reliably relates, if the vicissitudes of time had granted it; then that Trojan historian, most noble of poets, if the wretched fates had allowed, would have praised with his eloquent pen for a long time.

[3] This death-bearing year and a lamentable year for all: on the fourth day before the Calends of May Rhys, son of Gruffudd, prince of South Wales, but also the unconquered head of all Wales, succumbed to fate inopportunely. [4] For this man, descended from the most noble line of kings, himself indeed a leader of his race, the honesty of his mind was equal to that of his ancestors [lit. he made level the honesty of his mind with his lineage], and thus doubling his spirit by the nobility of his lineage, a consoler of nobles, a fighter against the brave, a kindly protector of the subjected, a powerful destroyer of cities, starting wars, preparing battalions, destroying enemy columns, snarling with courage like a boar, or a roaring lion lashing its tail roused to anger, he would rage with ferocity at the enemy. O glory of war, honour and shield of soldiers, noble protector of his country, honour of arms, arm of bravery, hand of generosity, eye of reason, splendour of honour, peak of fierceness, [5] a **Hercules** of honesty, a second **Achilles** bearing harshness in his heart, the modesty of **Nestor**, the daring of **Tydeus**, the strength of **Samson**, the dignity of **Hector**, the agility of **Euryalus**, the beauty of **Paris**, the eloquence of **Ulysses**, the wisdom of **Solomon**, the spirit of **Ajax**, repaying the damage of insult with death! [6] O safe refuge for the wretched, clothing for the naked, food for the hungry, drink for the thirsty. O ready provider of gifts for all who petition! [7] O sweet in speech, agreeable in behaviour, honourable in his customs, modest of speech, cheerful of expression, decorous of appearance, kind in all things, fair to all, a dutifulness of unfeigned simplicity,

a loftiness of genuine humility! Alas! Alas! Wales mourns, now widowed and doomed to be destroyed by grief.[77])

The Lord Rhys is compared to Hector, Achilles, Paris, Hercules and several other notable classical heroes. The chronicle's readers were meant to understand these references. The chronicler also implies that one would need a Statius or a Virgil to compose a proper elegy for Rhys in epic fashion (see item [2] in the passage just quoted). His elegy contains verbal echoes of Virgil, Ovid and Boethius. Paul Russell has observed that this passage is 'notable not only for its high rhetoric but also in its context ... this was not a one-off nor an insertion composed by someone else. Glimpses of the same rhetorical devices resurface elsewhere.'[78] The flowing Latinity of this chronicle is not shared by its companion text in the Exeter manuscript, the *Cronica ante aduentum domini*, which is more laconic in style.[79]

An additional 36-line Latin elegy for Rhys ap Gruffudd, this one in verse rather than prose, survives in Peniarth 20, the earliest copy of the Welsh vernacular chronicle *Brut y Tywysogion* (*History of the Princes*).[80] It appears in the entry for the year 1197 and contains references to both Galfridian and classical heroes:

Camber Locrinus Reso rex Albaque nactus. 25
Nominis et laudis inferioris erant

---

[77] I am very grateful to Paul Russell and Rosalind Love for assisting me with this translation. *Cronica de Wallia* is in Exeter 3514, pp. 507–19; a transcription by H. W. Gough-Cooper is online, 'Annales Cambriae: The E-text From Exeter Cathedral Library MS 3514, pp. 507–19', http://croniclau.bangor.ac.uk/documents/AC_E_First_Edition%20%20.pdf, accessed 16 March 2016; a partial edition is available in T. Jones, '"Cronica de Wallia" and Other Documents from Exeter Cathedral Library MS. 3514', *Bulletin of the Board of Celtic Studies* 12 (1946), 27–44 (pp. 30–1).

[78] Russell, '"Go and look in the Latin books"' (forthcoming).

[79] Exeter 3514, pp. 523–8; for a transcription by H. W. Gough-Cooper see 'Annales Cambriae: The D text, From Exeter Cathedral Library MS 3514, pp. 523–8', http://croniclau.bangor.ac.uk/documents/AC%20D%20first%20edition.pdf, accessed 16 March 2016.

[80] *Brut y Tywysogion* is a chronicle in Welsh that continues Geoffrey's history to AD 1282, detailing the activities of the Welsh princes and their dealings with English kings. It survives in two main versions, known as the Peniarth 20 version and the Red Book version, and may have been compiled at the Welsh Cistercian monastery of Strata Florida in Ceredigion; for discussion, editions and translations, see *Brut y Tywysogyon, Peniarth MS. 20*, ed. T. Jones; *Brut y Tywysogyon, or The Chronicle of the Princes, Peniarth MS. 20 Version*, trans. T. Jones (Cardiff, 1952); *Brut y Tywysogyon, or The Chronicle of the Princes, Red Book of Hergest Version*, ed. and trans. T. Jones (Cardiff, 1955); T. Jones, 'Historical Writing in Medieval Welsh', *Scottish Studies* 12 (1968), 15–27; O. W. Jones, 'Historical Writing in Medieval Wales', pp. 19–57; and below, pp. 22–3.

> Cesar et Arthurus leo fortis vterque sub armis.
> Vel par vel similis Resus vtrique fuit
> Resus Alexander in velle pari fuit alter
> Mundum substerni gliscit vterque sibi 30
> Occasus solis tritus Resi fuit armis
> Sensit Alexandri solis in orbe manum
> Laus canitur cineri sancto; cantetur ab omni
> Celi laus regi debita spiritui
> Penna madet lacrimis quod scribit thema doloris 35
> Ne careat forma, littera cesset ea.
>
> (Camber, King Locrinus and Albanactus 25
> Were inferior in name and repute to Rhys.
> Caesar and Arthur, both strong (as) lions in arms,
> Rhys was their equal or similar to both.
> Rhys was a second Alexander of like desire,
> Both yearned for the world to stretch out beneath them 30
> The west was beaten down by the arms of Rhys;
> He felt the hand of Alexander in the sun's orbit.
> Praises are sung to holy ashes; let due
> Praises be sung by everyone to the king of heaven (and)
>   the holy spirit.
> My pen grows wet with tears for it writes on a theme of grief. 35
> Let it not lack beauty, let not the writing cease.[81])

The elegy contains both verbal echoes of Welsh praise poetry and numerous references to classical heroes such as Hector, Achilles and Alexander, as well as to the seminal Galfridian characters Arthur, Locrinus, Camber and Albanactus.[82] This Latin poem embedded in a Welsh-language text, in what is probably a monastic manuscript (produced at Strata Florida in Ceredigion), is an important example of the hybrid, bilingual Latin and Welsh literary culture which existed in twelfth-century Wales. Its references to Geoffrey's heroes indicate that

---

[81] Full text and translation in Henley, 'Rhetoric', p. 121; the poem is also printed in *Brut y Tywysogyon, Peniarth MS. 20*, ed. T. Jones, pp. 140–1; translated into English by R. Turvey, *The Lord Rhys: Prince of Deheubarth* (Llandysul, 1997), pp. 117–18, and Russell, '"Go and look in the Latin books"' (forthcoming); translated into modern Welsh by H. Pryce, 'Y Canu Lladin er cof am yr Arglwydd Rhys', in *Yr Arglwydd Rhys*, ed. N. A. Jones and H. Pryce (Cardiff, 1996), pp. 212–23 (pp. 212–15).

[82] Such as, for example, describing Rhys as 'y gwr a oed ben a thar[y]an a chedernit y Deheu a holl Gymry' (the man who was the head and the shield and the strength of the South and all Wales), a common metaphor of praise in Welsh bardic poetry; see N. A. Jones, 'Hengerdd in the Age of the Poets of the Princes', in *Beyond the Gododdin: Dark Age Scotland in Medieval Wales. The Proceedings of a Day Conference held on 19 February 2005*, ed. A. Woolf (St Andrews, 2013), pp. 41–80 (pp. 53–4); Henley, 'Rhetoric', p. 96.

in an environment predating the earliest extant versions of *Brut y Brenhinedd* by up to fifty years – late twelfth-century Ceredigion – Geoffrey's text was known.[83] A work in the Galfridian corpus with a comparable classicizing effect is the *Gesta regum Britanniae*, a versification of Geoffrey's *Historia* from the first half of the thirteenth century, thought to be written by a Breton author.[84] It compares Arthur to Achilles and suggests that Homer, Virgil and Lucan would have preferred Arthur to their own heroes had they known about him.[85] A 10-line Latin epitaph for the Lord Rhys in the Breviate Chronicle contains similar classical references to those in the texts discussed above.[86] It compares Rhys to Busiris, Phaleris, Antiphates and Ulysses. Though these heroes are Egyptian and Greek, they would have been known to Welsh readers through the medium of Latin, probably by way of Ovid's *Ars amatoria*, Book I.647–54, known in Wales in the ninth and probably still in the twelfth century.[87]

Another important item of Welsh Latin verse composition is the 48-line poem *Trucidare Saxone soliti Cambrenses*, dated to *c*. 1200–15, which calls the Welsh to arms against the Saxons with the help of the French, Cornish and Bretons.[88] Sarah Zeiser has argued that this poem was written during, and with purposeful allusion to, Llywelyn ap Gruffudd's diplo-

---

[83] Further indications that Geoffrey's history was known in Wales in the twelfth century are references to Galfridian characters in the praise poetry of Cynddelw Brydydd Mawr and Elidir Sais to the princes Owain Cyfeiliog and Llywelyn ap Iorwerth, respectively; for discussion see Sims-Williams, *Rhai Addasiadau*, p. 8; for the poems see *Cyfres Beirdd y Tywysogion*, ed. R. G. Gruffydd et al. (Cardiff, 1991–6), I, 17.40; III, 16.80.

[84] Attribution to a Breton author is based on the work's dedication to Cadioc, bishop of Vannes: see A. Putter, 'Latin Historiography after Geoffrey of Monmouth', in *The Arthur of Medieval Latin Literature: The Development and Dissemination of the Arthurian Legend in Medieval Latin*, ed. Siân Echard (Cardiff, 2011), pp. 85–108 (p. 97); for the text see *Gesta regum Britanniae*, ed. N. Wright (Cambridge, 1991); for discussion see also Echard, *Arthurian Narrative*, pp. 93–106.

[85] Another comparison of Arthur to Achilles ('alter Achilles, Arthurus') can be found in Johannes de Hauvilla's *Architrenius*, a Latin hexameter work written in 1184, ed. and trans. W. Wetherbee (Cambridge, 1994), p. 143; discussed by Echard, *Arthurian Narrative*, pp. 108–12.

[86] For discussion and translation, see Russell, '"Go and look in the Latin books"' (forthcoming).

[87] Russell, '"Go and look in the Latin books"' and *Reading Ovid in Medieval Wales* (both forthcoming).

[88] The poem survives in two manuscripts, Leiden, Universiteitsbibliothek, Vossius Lat. F. 77, fol. 144ra–vb and Cambridge, Corpus Christi College 181, p. 277; for discussion see Zeiser, 'Latinity, Manuscripts, and the Rhetoric of Conquest', p. 12; cf. A. Breeze, 'The Date and Politics of "The Song of the Welsh",' *The Antiquaries Journal* 88 (2008), 190–7.

matic communications with France *c*. 1215.[89] Latin was the language which served Llywelyn's diplomatic and bureaucratic needs: as Zeiser notes, it was the 'language of record' in Wales.[90] Intriguingly, the poem constructs its pro-Welsh political message by making use of Geoffrey's history, an interesting instance of political reception of the *Historia* in Wales:

> Virtuosos filii patres imitantur. 25
> Sic Arthurum Britones uirtute sequantur.
> Quam probo quam strenuo monstrant procreantur.
> Ut fuit Arthurus sic uictores habeantur.
> ...
> Ex hac gente quatuor sunt imperatores:
> Arthurus Broinsius fortes bellatores 35
> Constantius Brennius fere fortiores.
> Hii monarchiam tenuerunt ut probiores.
>
> (Sons imitate virtuous fathers. 25
> So let Britons follow Arthur in virtue.
> They show by how upright, by how vigorous a man they are begotten.
> As Arthur was, so let them be held victors.
> ...
> From this race are four emperors:
> Arthur, Broinsius, strong warriors, 35
> Constantine, Brennius, almost stronger.
> They kept the monarchy as more upright men.[91])

These allusions to Geoffrey not only indicate that the *Historia regum Britanniae* was known in Wales at this date, just over a generation prior to the earliest known version of *Brut y Brenhinedd*, but also that it was politically favourable for a writer to use the information in his text to aid Welsh interests.[92] This poem's use of Arthur and other royal figures from Geoffrey's history to make pro-Welsh political arguments is a precursor to the use of Arthur as the *mab darogan* (son of prophecy) in Welsh prophetic poetry of the fourteenth and fifteenth centuries.[93]

---

[89] Zeiser, '"Let the Parisian island be witness": Political Alliance and the Poem *Trucidare Saxones* in Thirteenth-Century Wales', a paper presented at the 15th International Congress of Celtic Studies, University of Glasgow, 16 July 2015.
[90] Zeiser, 'Latinity, Manuscripts, and the Rhetoric of Conquest', p. 51.
[91] D. R. Howlett, 'A Triad of Texts about Saint David', in *St David of Wales*, ed. Evans and Wooding, pp. 268–71.
[92] This usage would support the case that Geoffrey's history was received favourably in Wales and was not considered to be a pro-Norman work at that time.
[93] For discussion see A. L. Jones, *Darogan: Prophecy, Lament and Absent Heroes in Medieval Welsh Literature* (Cardiff, 2013); H. Fulton, *Welsh Prophecy and English Politics in the Late Middle Ages* (Aberystwyth, 2008).

Another instance of poetic reception of Geoffrey's history in a Welsh context is the unique poem written in the mid-thirteenth century in praise of Geoffrey and Galfridian heroes in Cardiff, Central Library, 2.611 (s. xiii[ex], no. 55, provenance Wales), a manuscript also containing the C-text of the First Variant.[94] This poem, as well as the compilation of the C-text itself, is attributed to the Franciscan 'Frater Walensis Madocus Edeirnianensis', who uses the praise poem to introduce the *Historia*.[95] Madocus has been identified as Madog ap Gwallter, a poet who also worked in the Welsh vernacular; three of these poems survive.[96] He is an important example of someone adept at composing verse in both Latin and Welsh. Comparable to these examples of Geoffrey's reception into Welsh Latin literature is the curious text *De vera historia de morte Arthuri*.[97] It has been suggested that its primary aim was to place the death of Arthur at the northern Welsh Cistercian house of Aberconwy rather than the better known burial site at Glastonbury.[98] If this text was written in Aberconwy, it would be valuable evidence of Geoffrey's reception in Latin in Wales.

The Welsh chronicle *Brut y Tywysogion* (*History of the Princes*) is also worthy of discussion here because it is demonstrably based on a Latin exemplar. Spanning the arrival of the Anglo-Saxons down to the final conquest of Wales in 1282, *Brut y Tywysogion* is a continuation of Geoffrey's history, detailing the activities of the Welsh princes.[99] Its Latin exemplar does not survive but seems to have been closely related to the *Cronica*

---

[94] The poem is printed in *Historia regum Britanniae*, ed. J. Hammer, p. 18. J. B. Smith takes Madocus' choice of Latin as an indication that he expected a clerical audience for his work: see 'Literary Encounters in the Anglo-Welsh Borderlands', p. 49.

[95] D. N. Dumville argues that Madocus is responsible for combining versions of the *Historia* into this mixed version of the First Variant: see 'The Origin of the C-Text of the Variant Version of the *Historia Regum Britanniae*', *Bulletin of the Board of Celtic Studies* 26 (1974–6), 315–22.

[96] For identification of Madog ap Gwallter with Frater Madocus, see *Gwaith Bleddyn Fardd a Beirdd Eraill Ail Hanner y Drydedd Ganrif*, ed. R. M. Andrews et al. (Cardiff, 1996), pp. 347–50.

[97] This text is edited by M. Lapidge from two fourteenth-century manuscripts with Aberconwy associations (London, Gray's Inn 7, c. 1340 and London, British Library, Cotton Cleopatra D i, c. 1314): 'An Edition of *De vera historia de morte Arthuri*', *Arthurian Literature* 1 (1981), 79–93. Additional manuscripts are listed in M. Lapidge, 'Additional manuscript evidence for *De vera historia de morte Arthuri*', *Arthurian Literature* 2 (1982), 163–8; for discussion see Echard, *Arthurian Narrative*, pp. 80–5, and Putter, 'Latin Historiography', p. 97.

[98] Putter, 'Latin Historiography', p. 97.

[99] It survives in two main versions (represented by Peniarth 20, s. xiv[1], and the Red Book of Hergest version, named after Jesus College 111, 1382×1405, though this is not the best manuscript witness) and thirty-nine total manuscripts. For discussion of the text see O. W. Jones, 'Historical Writing in Medieval Wales', pp. 19–57.

de Wallia discussed above.[100] Similarly, *Brenhinedd y Saesson* (*History of the English*), a Welsh-language chronicle concerned with the activities of the kings of Anglo-Saxon England, is based on a now-lost Latin exemplar.[101] Given that Latin-educated historiographers in Wales were crafting their own histories in Latin and then at some point later translating these histories – as well as Geoffrey's *Historia* – into Welsh, it is difficult to characterize their translations as acts of reclamation, rehabilitating a loss of language during conquest. Latin was already a medium for historical writing in Wales from an early period. Geoffrey's history filled a perceived gap in historical information for the Welsh just as much as it would have filled that gap for Geoffrey's patron Robert of Gloucester and for historians interested in the British past. Though evidence for the educational system in Wales in this period is scarce, these texts demonstrate that Latin books were known, used and written in Wales, for education, poetry, charters, law and historical narrative. Furthermore, it is possible that a Welsh Latin writer, exposed to the classics at length through standard Latin education, would have felt part of the Western inheritance of classical culture just as much as someone in Normandy.

This evidence suggests a closer relationship between vernacular and Latin writing in Wales than has previously been appreciated. Original Latin poetic compositions, following vernacular models, such as the elegy to the Lord Rhys ap Gruffudd in Peniarth 20, exist in manuscripts produced in monastic scriptoria. The Franciscan author of a Latin panegyric to Geoffrey of Monmouth in Cardiff 2.611 was also the author of several Welsh vernacular poems. The Book of Llandaf, which contains both Latin and Welsh, the Latin elegy to Rhys ap Gruffudd in a Welsh vernacular chronicle and Ieuan ap Sulien's Welsh-language poem on St Padarn in the *Llanbadarn Augustine* (Cambridge, Corpus Christi College 199, fol. 11r) suggest a greater intermingling of languages, and less of a linguistic divide between Welsh and Latin, than has previously been assumed.[102] This matter is discussed further below.

The linguistic legacy of Latin in Wales also pertains to this discussion. It is difficult to gauge whether spoken knowledge of Latin was contin-

---

[100] Hughes, 'The Welsh Latin Chronicles', pp. 247–50.
[101] It survives in thirteen manuscripts. The standard edition is based on Cotton Cleopatra B v (s. xiv^{med}) and the Black Book of Basingwerk (Aberystwyth, National Library of Wales, 7006D, s. xv^2); the Cotton Cleopatra B v text continues to AD 1197, Basingwerk to AD 1461. For details see *Brenhinedd y Saesson or the Kings of the Saxons. BM Cotton MS Cleopatra B v and the Black Book of Basingwerk, NLW MS 7006*, ed. and trans. T. Jones (Cardiff, 1971), p. ix.
[102] For discussion of this Welsh poem and its manuscript context, see Zeiser, 'Latinity, Manuscripts, and the Rhetoric of Conquest', pp. 245–6, and P. Russell, 'The *englyn* to Saint Padarn revisited', *Cambrian Medieval Celtic Studies* 63 (2012), 1–14.

uous in Britain, and the present study does not aim to address this thorny topic head-on.[103] Suffice it to say that patterns of interruption and return to spoken British Latin were possible, and probably varied by region: Thomas Charles-Edwards observes that 'the end of the old native British Latin will have varied in date between different groups in society and different eras, but by *c.* 700 it is likely to have been complete'.[104] Latin continued to be spoken and read in schools, where it was influenced by Welsh pronunciation.[105] In the sixth century we have the example of Gildas who, Lapidge argues, had first-hand knowledge of Latin as a living language.[106] As Wales was subject to various invasions and raids in the subsequent centuries by the Vikings and the Irish, who burned monastic centres, interruptions in regularized systems of learning are likely, and evidence is unevenly distributed across the centuries.[107]

Evidence for awareness of a Romano-British past and classical inheritance in Wales: the case of Breudwyt Maxen Wledic

Rather than assessing the continuity of Latin language and education from the Roman period to the central Middle Ages, for which arguments would be built upon shaky evidence, it is more useful to ask to what extent an educated Welsh person in the twelfth and thirteenth centuries would have been conscious of their Romano-British past. Precedent for this kind of approach is found in Brynley Roberts' study of the Welsh prose tale *Breudwyt Maxen Wledic* (*The Dream of Maxen*

---

[103] Charles-Edwards, *Wales and the Britons*, pp. 89–115 and 625–43; Russell, '*An habes linguam Latinam?*', pp. 193–224.

[104] Charles-Edwards, *Wales and the Britons*, p. 631.

[105] Charles-Edwards, *Wales and the Britons*, p. 631.

[106] Classical education survived in Britain in his day, and Gildas was probably educated in the home, not in a monastic centre, receiving traditional Roman rhetorical training in preparation for a secular administrative career: for discussion see M. Lapidge, 'Gildas's Education and the Latin Culture of Sub-Roman Britain', in *Gildas: New Approaches*, ed. M. Lapidge and D. N. Dumville (Woodbridge, 1984), pp. 27–50, and also N. Wright, 'Gildas's Prose Style and Its Origins', in *Gildas: New Approaches*, ed. Lapidge and Dumville, pp. 107–28. In contrast to the authors of the *Historia Brittonum* and the life of St Samson, Gildas's Latin does not exhibit British Celtic influences; for discussion see Charles-Edwards, *Wales and the Britons*, p. 625, and F. Kerlouégan, 'Le Latin du De Excidio Britanniae de Gildas', in *Christianity in Britain, 300–700: Papers Presented to the Conference on Christianity in Roman and Sub-Roman Britain, Held at the University of Nottingham, 17–20 April 1967*, ed. M. W. Barley and R. P. C. Hanson (Leicester, 1968), pp. 151–76 (p. 172).

[107] The Anglo-Saxons also had a devastating effect, as we can see in Rhygyfarch ap Sulien's lament.

Wledic) which, he argues, illustrates one of the three central themes in medieval Welsh historiography: the relationship between Wales and Rome.[108] The author of this tale was well aware of the Roman past and interested in exploring the place of Emperor Maximus within British history. Roberts argues for a composition date in the second half of the twelfth century.[109] As the text post-dates Geoffrey's *Historia*, analyses of it are never outside the realm of Geoffrey's influence; nevertheless the text provides clues as to the reception of Geoffrey's history in the sense that it demonstrates interest in the Romano-British past and a sense of classical inheritance in Wales.

The main character, 'Maxen', is based on the historical figure Magnus Maximus, the fourth-century Romano-British official who declared himself emperor, rebelled against Gratian and usurped his throne. In the Middle Welsh work he is already emperor at the time of his arrival in Britain, where he must marry the Welsh princess Elen Luyddawg and solidify an alliance with her and her brothers in order to gain control over all of Britain. With the help of Elen's brothers, Maxen reconquers Gaul and Rome before settling in Brittany, thus becoming part of a popular origin legend of the Breton people.[110] *Breudwyt Maxen Wledic*'s account differs from Geoffrey's story of Magnus Maximus to the extent that, Roberts argues, the two may be 'literary compositions drawing on parallel versions of the same legend ... this author, too, is clear that the Welsh should be seen as the dominant partners in the relationship'.[111] It is possible that an independent version of this story circulated, serving as the basis for both Geoffrey's account and the Welsh text. The tale indicates interest in the placement of Maxen / Maximus in British history, which 'develops further as the significance of the relationship of Wales and Rome becomes one of the central themes of medieval Welsh historiography'.[112] This desire extended to the Welsh genealogies, wherein a great many Welsh princes, including Rhodri Mawr, sought

---

[108] The other two themes are loss and prophesied restoration; overall these themes reinforce the concept of the unity of the island of Britain. For further discussion, see Roberts, 'Geoffrey', pp. 100–2.

[109] For discussion see *Breudwyt Maxen Wledic*, ed. B. F. Roberts, Mediaeval and Modern Welsh Series 11 (Dublin, 2005), lxxxv; see also B. F. Roberts, '*Breuddwyd Maxen Wledig*: Why? When?', in *Heroic Poets and Poetic Heroes in Celtic Tradition: A Festschrift for Patrick K. Ford*, ed. J. F. Nagy and L. E. Jones, CSANA Yearbook 8/9 (2011), 303–14.

[110] For the portrayal of Elen Luyddawg and Maxen in the Cotton Cleopatra version of the *Brut*, and their role in the Breton origin legend, see Lambert, 'À propos de la traduction galloise', pp. 89–92.

[111] *Breudwyt Maxen Wledic*, ed. Roberts, pp. lxi–lxii.

[112] *Breudwyt Maxen Wledic*, ed. Roberts, p. xlvii.

descent from the Emperor Maximus. The Harleian genealogies, in a manuscript written c. 1100, also list lines of descent from Maximus.[113] 'Given the importance of concepts of continuity and succession', Roberts argues, 'these political genealogies would have done a great deal to legitimize royal claims'.[114] The theme of 'Wales and Rome' can indeed be extended to Geoffrey's history itself, in which Arthur makes an attempt at conquering Rome. In this historiographical scheme Rome could very much be considered his birthright.

Taken together with the evidence of Welsh genealogies, *Breudwyt Maxen Wledic* demonstrates an awareness of Roman heritage in medieval Welsh culture. Genealogists and historians artificially tried to strengthen rulers' links to Rome: 'native Welsh historians sought a continuity of history from Roman Britain to dark-age Wales with all that that implied in terms of civilised origins and long-standing *Romanitas*'.[115] Given these connections, it is possible to suggest that Latin actually had a special status in Wales, the result of a consciousness on the part of the Welsh literati of their classical inheritance. Geoffrey is not solely responsible for creating these links between Wales and the classical world; his work may have had the effect of strengthening existing themes in Welsh historical and pseudo-historical writing.[116]

This discussion demonstrates that Latin was not a language imposed upon the Welsh by a foreign power, but rather one with deep roots within the culture since the Roman period (or at least perceived to have deep roots by medieval Welsh writers of history). The assumption that working outside the geographic and cultural centre of a given region limits access to the dominant language of the élite (in this case the Anglo-Normans and their use of Latin) does not fit the evidence from within Wales. In evaluating Geoffrey's position with regard to the Welsh and his creation of their history, it is important to consider the texts which survive from Wales as part of the equation.

---

[113] For the Harleian genealogies, see B. Guy, 'A Second Witness to the Welsh Exemplar of Harley 3859', *Quaestio Insularis: Selected Proceedings of the Cambridge Colloquium in Anglo-Saxon, Norse and Celtic* 15 (2014), 72–91.
[114] *Breudwyt Maxen Wledic*, ed. Roberts, p. xlvii.
[115] *Breudwyt Maxen Wledic*, ed. Roberts, p. xlvii.
[116] Indeed, the concept of Trojan ancestry precedes Geoffrey – it is found in the *Historia Brittonum*, written in Gwynedd in 829/30, and these links to the classical world may have been felt prior to his influence on Welsh historical writing.

Conclusion

Throughout this study I have alluded to the false distinction between Latin and the vernacular in the study of medieval Welsh literary and historical productions.[117] In discussing translation, it is far too easy to reduce Latin and the vernacular to a binary opposition. The evidence on the ground suggests a more complicated scenario: Latin was one aspect of 'Welsh learning', part of a multilingual, literate culture in medieval Wales that was active in both languages. This literary culture was abundant, interested in its links to the classical world and *Romanitas* and inseparable from vernacular literary productions. The high status of Latin, recognizable within Wales, very likely would have been recognized outside Wales as well; Geoffrey's audiences would have had no reason to assume Latin learning did not exist there.

One final point for consideration is Geoffrey's own perception of the linguistic environment in Wales. Did he think he was appropriating history and replacing the Welsh language with a dominant foreign one? We can in fact take Geoffrey's purported *liber vetustissimus* as evidence that book-learning in Wales in the twelfth century was respected outside that country and considered authoritative by external audiences: the Welsh language must have had authority for Geoffrey's intended readership or he would not have mentioned it. It is not far-fetched to imagine that Geoffrey was aware of Latin libraries in Welsh monastic houses and Welsh Latin annalistic record-keeping.

In the fourteenth century, an increase in the numbers of texts translated from Latin into Welsh can be attributed to factors other than cultural re-appropriation: shifts in education and patronage in the generations following conquest, an increase in lay readership and the shift of the bulk of manuscript production out of the monasteries and into private enterprise.[118] All of this contributed to the flowering of Welsh translations

---

[117] In so doing, I am echoing previous arguments such as those by J. Blacker, *The Faces of Time: Portrayal of the Past in Old French and Latin Historical Narrative of the Anglo-Norman Regnum* (Austin, 1994); Echard, *Arthurian Narrative*, pp. 195–6; and P. Sims-Williams, 'The Early Welsh Arthurian Poems', in *The Arthur of the Welsh*, ed. Bromwich, Jarman and Roberts, pp. 33–73 (pp. 33–5).

[118] M. B. Parkes, 'The Literacy of the Laity', in *Literature and Civilization: The Medieval World*, ed. D. Daiches and A. Thorlby (London, 1973), pp. 555–77; C. Given-Wilson argues that the increased use of the vernacular was due to chronicle writing moving out of monasteries (*Chronicles: The Writing of History in Medieval England* [London, 2004], p. xix); see also, for example, the arguments for the rise of vernacular histories in A. McColl, 'Rhetoric, Narrative, and Conceptions of History in the French Prose *Brut*', *Medium Ævum* 74.2 (2005), 288–310 (pp. 291–2), citing M. Lynde-

of Latin texts in post-conquest Wales, translations which continued to assume ancestral links to Rome, Roman culture and Latinity, Geoffrey's text included.

Recchia, *Prose, Verse and Truth Telling in the Thirteenth Century: An Essay on Form and Function in Selected Texts* (Lexington, KY, 2000), p. 19: 'the emergence in thirteenth-century France of a large body of writing in French prose, often translated from Latin originals, testifies to the growth of the ability to read texts in the vernacular ... the relatively sudden increase in the use of vernacular prose in the early thirteenth century is linked to the rise in lay vernacular literacy. Lynde-Recchia sees this as an aristocratic development, suggesting that the widening of literacy "created a need for a form"'. Thus Wales can be seen as part of an overall British / French trend rather than an exotic, unique example.

II

CHRÉTIEN'S BRITISH YVAIN IN ENGLAND AND WALES*

Erich Poppe

Introduction:
British elements in a literary text in the English language

The relevance of British and Celtic elements to the literature written in the English language has been highlighted by Peter Clemoes: 'To read Medieval Welsh literature alongside that of Middle English is to understand for oneself the nature of the debt which English literature owes to the Celtic countries for the inspiration of the Arthurian legend.'[1] Here, I examine the presence of British Arthur and Owein in a Middle English romance, namely in *Ywain and Gawain*. Chrétien comes into my title because the Middle English *Ywain and Gawain* is derived by a process of transfer and adaptation from Chrétien's *Yvain*, and it is of course a critical commonplace that 'Chrétien's romances draw on already existing materials, notably motifs of Celtic origin assimilated to an essentially Latin culture.'[2] In *Yvain*, for example, Chrétien acknowledges that Arthur was

---

* I wish to thank the Board of Electors to the O'Donnell Lectureship in Celtic Studies of the University of Oxford for appointing me as the O'Donnell Lecturer for the academic year 2015–16, from which this essay, an extended and referenced version of my O'Donnell Lecture given in May 2016, results. I am grateful to the Faculty of English Language and Literature of the University of Oxford, Thomas Charles-Edwards and Alderik Blom for their generous hospitality while I was in Oxford. I owe thanks to Cora Dietl, Ceridwen Lloyd-Morgan and Regine Reck for their helpful discussions of, and comments on, earlier versions of this paper. Needless to say, I alone bear responsibility for the views presented in it and for any remaining errors.

[1] P. Clemoes, *Rhythm and Cosmic Order in Old English Christian Literature* (Cambridge, 1970), p. 4.
[2] T. Hunt, *Chrétien de Troyes. Yvain (Le Chevalier au Lion)*, Critical Guides to French Texts 55 (London, 1986), p. 10. See also C. Lloyd-Morgan, 'Crossing the Borders:

'li buens rois de Bretaingne' (the good King of Britain) and locates his court 'a Carduel an Gales' (at Carlisle in Wales)[3] – 'Gales' here including Strathclyde, the British kingdom of north-west England and south-west Scotland, the 'Old North' from a Welsh perspective.[4]

Ywain and Gawain, Owein and Chrétien's Yvain

Among Arthurian narratives in Middle English, *Ywain and Gawain* has a special position, as it is 'the only surviving romance in Middle English that was quite certainly translated directly from an original by Chrétien de Troyes'.[5] For all the freedom with which the translator treated his source, as we will see, it is still much closer to *Yvain* than the other Middle English adaptation of a work by Chrétien, *Sir Perceval of Galles*, is to *Perceval*.[6] The reference to Gawain in the title has been explained in terms of the romance's celebration of the close companionship between Ywain and Gawain,[7] as well as by Gawain's appeal for Middle English

---

Literary Borrowings in Medieval Wales and England', in *Authority and Subjugation in Writing of Medieval Wales*, ed. R. Kennedy and S. Meecham-Jones (New York, 2008), pp. 159–173; she notes that 'we cannot ignore the supposedly Welsh setting of many French and English romances, and the high incidence of names of Welsh or Breton origin in such texts, most especially Arthurian narratives from Marie de France and Chrétien de Troyes to Thomas Malory'(p. 159), but also cautions against the 'temptation to characterize certain elements in Old French or Middle English romances and tales as "Celtic"'.

[3] *Chrestien de Troyes,* Yvain (Le Chevalier au Lion), *the critical text of Wendelin Foerster with introduction, notes and glossary by T. B. W. Reid* (Manchester, 1967), lines 1 and 7; quotations from this edition will be identified by the abbreviation Y and line number.

[4] Morfydd Owen kindly reminds me that in *Erec*, Chrétien locates Arthur's court in Cardigan; for a detailed discussion of Chrétien's preoccupation with Wales and Welshness, and the specific relevance of Cardigan, see M. Faletra, *Wales and the Medieval Colonial Imagination: The Matter of Britain in the Twelfth Century* (New York, 2015), pp. 99–133. I wish to thank Victoria Flood for bringing Faletra's book to my attention.

[5] M. Mills et al., 'Chivalric Romance', in *The Arthur of the English. The Arthurian Legend in Medieval English Life and Literature*, ed. W. R. J. Barron (Cardiff, 1999), pp. 113–83 (p. 117); see also *Ywain and Gawain*, ed. A. B. Friedman and N. T. Harrington, EETS OS 254 (London, New York and Toronto, 1964), p. xvi: 'That the English poet ... worked directly from a manuscript of *Yvain* ... is established beyond doubt by the almost identical conduct of the narrative'. Quotations from this edition will be identified by the abbreviation YG and line number.

[6] On this text see, for example, K. Busby, 'Chrétien de Troyes English'd', *Neophilologus* 71 (1987), 596–613; W. R. J. Barron, *English Medieval Romance* (London and New York, 1987), pp. 155–8; Mills et al., 'Chivalric Romance', pp. 136–41.

[7] Mills et al., 'Chivalric Romance', p. 117.

authors and audiences more generally, culminating in the late-fourteenth-century *Sir Gawain and the Green Knight*.[8]

Ywain and Gawain is thought to have been composed in the fourteenth century, perhaps between 1325 and 1350, in a 'Northern [dialect] with some admixture of North-East Midland forms'; it is extant in only one manuscript, London, British Library, Cotton Galba E ix, written in a hand 'belonging to the first quarter of the fifteenth century'.[9] The immediate contexts of the composition of the poem and of its single surviving manuscript remain difficult to historicize.[10] In the light of Peter Clemoes' observation, *Ywain and Gawain* is a particularly rewarding text since it can be read alongside a close medieval Welsh analogue, a narrative called either *Owein*, after the character whom modern critical readings regard as its protagonist, or *Chwedyl Iarlles y Ffynnawn* (*The Tale of the Lady of the Well / Countess of the Spring*), after the designation given in the colophon in the Red Book of Hergest (Oxford, Jesus College 111, between 1382 and *c.* 1400), which transmits the only complete text.[11] For

---

[8] Barron, *English Medieval Romance*, pp. 158–76, see also R. Dalrymple, 'Sir Gawain in Middle English Romance', in *A Companion to Arthurian Literature*, ed. H. Fulton (Chichester, 2009), pp. 265–77. For Gwalchmai, the character corresponding to Gawain in medieval Welsh literature, see R. Bromwich, *Trioedd Ynys Prydein. The Triads of the Island of Britain*, 3rd edn (Cardiff, 2006), pp. 367–71, and N. Petrovskaia, 'Le personnage de Gauvain dans la littérature médiévale galloise', in *Le Personnage de Gauvain dans la littérature européene du Moyen Âge. Actes du colloque international des 6, 7, et 8 mars 2014 à l'Université Paris Est (Marne-la-Vallée)*, ed. M.-F. Alamichel, Medievales 58 (Amiens, 2015), pp. 229–37.

[9] Friedman and Harrington, YG, pp. lviii, xxxvi and xi; for other editions of the text see M. Mills, *Ywain and Gawain, Sir Percyvell of Gales, The Anturs of Arther* (London, 1992) and M. F. Braswell, *Sir Perceval of Galles and Ywain and Gawain*, TEAMS (Kalamazoo, MI, 1995). A Modern English translation-paraphrase is available electronically in the special edition *Harken to Me* of the *Medieval Forum*, http://www.sfsu.edu/~medieval/romances/table_of_contents.html, accessed 10 March 2016.

[10] Compare, for example, J. Breulmann, *Erzählstruktur und Hofkultur. Weibliches Agieren in den europäischen Iweinstoff-Bearbeitungen des 12. bis 14. Jahrhunderts* (Münster, 2009), pp. 430–3, and S. Rikhardsdottir, *Medieval Translations and Cultural Discourse. The Movement of Texts in England, France and Scandinavia* (Cambridge, 2012), pp. 94–5; for some more general historical background, see U. Dirscherl, *Ritterliche Ideale in Chrétiens 'Yvain' und im mittelenglischen 'Ywain and Gawain'. Von 'amour courtois' zu 'trew luf', vom 'frans chevaliers deboneire' zum 'man of mekyl myght'* (Frankfurt, Bern, New York and Paris, 1991), pp. 153–73, and G. Barnes, *Counsel and Strategy in Middle English Romance* (Cambridge, 1993), pp. 1–28.

[11] For an edition of the text, see *Owein or Chwedyl Iarlles y Ffynnawn*, ed. R. L. Thomson (Dublin, 1968); quotations from this edition will be identified by the abbreviation O and line number. For the most recent translations, see S. Davies, *The Mabinogion* (Oxford, 2007), pp. 116–38, and J. K. Bollard and A. Griffiths, *Tales of Arthur. Legend and Landscape of Wales* (Llandysul, 2010), pp. 65–91. Quotations from Davies' translation will be identified by the abbreviation OE and page number; note that she

the sake of brevity, I will use *Owein*. The date of the text's composition remains uncertain; most scholars would currently opt for a date in the first half of the thirteenth century.[12] The Welsh *Owein* thus pre-dates the Middle English *Ywain and Gawain* by no more than a hundred years. The Welsh text is transmitted in three early manuscripts: the two huge compendia of medieval Welsh literature, the White Book of Rhydderch (Aberystwyth, National Library of Wales, Peniarth 4, about 1350)[13] and the Red Book of Hergest, as well as Oxford, Jesus College 20 (dating to the end of the fourteenth or the beginning of the fifteenth century).[14] *Ywain*

> uses Modern Welsh spellings in her translation of the text, thus 'Owain', whereas I use Middle Welsh spellings, thus 'Owein'. For introductions to the text, see B. F. Roberts, 'The Welsh Romance of the *Lady of the Fountain (Owein)*', in *The Legend of Arthur in the Middle Ages*, ed. P. B. Grout et al. (Cambridge, 1983), pp. 170–82; R. L. Thomson, '*Owain: Chwedl Iarlles y Ffynnon*', in *The Arthur of the Welsh. The Arthurian Legend in Medieval Welsh Literature*, ed. R. Bromwich, A. O. H. Jarman, B. F. Roberts (Cardiff, 1991), pp. 159–69; R. Reck, 'Owain', forthcoming in *Arthur in the Celtic Literatures*, ed. C. Lloyd-Morgan and E. Poppe (Cardiff, 2017). The label *Chwedyl Iarlles y Ffynnawn* makes the lady, who otherwise remains nameless, a focus of narrative interest; she would appear to function mainly as a catalyst for Owein's development, but see Reck, 'Owain', for some further comments on her role.
>
> [12] For a survey of dates suggested for *Owein*, and for a date about 1220 or 1230, see A. Breeze, 'Spurs, Horse-armour, and the Date of *Owein*', in *Lochlann. Festskrift til Jan Erik Rekdal på 60-Årsdagen*, ed. M. Hambro and L. I. Widerøe (Oslo, 2013), pp. 105–10. C. Lloyd-Morgan, 'Migrating Narratives: *Peredur*, *Owain*, and *Gereint*', in *A Companion to Arthurian Literature*, ed. H. Fulton (Chichester, 2009), pp. 128–41 (p. 139), thinks that the 'second or third decade of the thirteenth century might still be a reasonable guess at present'; S. Rodway, 'The Where, Who, When and Why of Medieval Welsh Prose Texts: Some Methodological Considerations', *Studia Celtica* 41 (2007), 47–89, suggests a broad dating before the middle of the thirteenth century on linguistic grounds (p.73). Any date for *Owein* also depends on one's assessment of its relation to Chrétien's *Yvain*; see further below.
>
> [13] For the literary interests and social milieu of Rhydderch, see D. Huws, *Medieval Welsh Manuscripts* (Cardiff and Aberystwyth, 2000), pp. 249–54, and C. McKenna, 'Reading with Rhydderch: Mabinogion Texts in Manuscript Context', in *Language and Power in the Celtic World. Papers from the Seventh Australian Conference of Celtic Studies*, ed. A. Ahlqvist and P. O'Neill (Sidney, 2011), pp. 205–30.
>
> [14] Of the seven later medieval or early modern manuscripts, three 'do not contain any of those episodes of the story in which the lion plays a part ... except for that of the Du Traws. ... [T]here may once have existed an older manuscript, now represented only by these three later ones, in which the lion episodes were not present'; furthermore, '[a]ll the later manuscripts agree in ending at our line 819, omitting any reference to Owein's ever leaving Arthur's court again' (Thomson, O, p. x). The two episodes with the lion concern the rescue of Lunet and the killing of a giant, which may be important for the development of the meaning of the story, if we consider Owein to be the all-important protagonist. See below n.96 on Hunt's suggestion that Yvain's 'exemplariness' is already re-established after the successful defence of the Dame de Noroison and that the introduction of the lion only 'serves the *elaboration* of the chivalric ideal'(*Chrétien*, p. 74, his emphasis).

and Gawain was 'quite certainly translated directly from an original by Chrétien' and has been characterized as '*Yvain*, written in fourteenth-century [English] words'.[15] The relation between the Welsh *Owein* and Chrétien's *Yvain*, on the other hand, is more difficult to define. Ignoring for the time being the numerous and significant differences in detail, on which more anon, the two narratives proceed in tandem with regard to their major narrative units.[16]

While Arthur holds court, Calogrenant tells a story about his unsuccessful adventure at a spring. Yvain sets out to undertake the same task, mortally wounds the knight guarding the spring, follows him to his castle and is hidden by a maiden, Lunete. The knight dies, Yvain sees the knight's widow and falls in love with her, and Lunete persuades the lady to marry Yvain. Arthur with his host arrives at the spring; Yvain successfully defends it and invites Arthur to a feast. Yvain returns with Arthur to his court, having been set a strict date for his return. He misses the date and, reminded of his lapse by a maiden sent by the lady, he goes mad and retires to the wilderness. He is found by a lady and her maid, brought back to sanity with the help of a magic ointment and successfully defends this lady's realm against an aggressive neighbour. He rescues a lion, finds Lunete in danger of being killed, kills a giant for the benefit of another castle-owner and finally saves Lunete (this is at about line 4575 of *Yvain* and at line 778 of *Owein*). The main differences so far are that in the Middle Welsh version Owein fights at the spring not only with Kei, but also with other knights of Arthur's host

---

[15] D. Matthews, 'Translation and Ideology: The Case of *Ywain and Gawain*', *Neophilologus* 76 (1992), 452–63 (p. 454). Matthews here applies John Frow's reading of Borges' short story 'Pierre Menard, Author of *Don Quixote*' to *Ywain and Gawain*: 'Menard's version of the Quixote is not a translation or a transcription, simply a verbally identical rewriting' (Matthews, 'Translation', p. 454), but in the eye of Borges' narrator, 'The archaic style of Menard – quite foreign, after all – suffers from a certain affectation. Not so that of his forerunner, who handles with ease the current Spanish of his time' (Frow quoted by Matthews, 'Translation', p. 454). Matthews refers to Frow's suggestion that 'intrinsic structures are not given but are variably constructed in accordance with changing intertextual relations' and concludes: '*Ywain and Gawain* is *Yvain*, written in fourteenth-century words. The lesson of Menard is that the later text must have its own distinct ideological function, and Frow's concept of the text's multiple temporality allows a consideration of *Ywain and Gawain* as an ideological moment in itself, along with its ideological relation to *Yvain*' ('Translation', pp. 454–5).

[16] In the following summary, I use the French names of protagonists in order to avoid the juxtaposition of French and Welsh names. For a tabular comparison between *Yvain* and *Owein* which focuses on the differences between the versions, see Thomson, O, pp. xxix–lvi; for a helpful summary of *Ywain and Gawain*, see J. Finlayson, '*Ywain and Gawain* and the Meaning of Adventure', *Anglia* 87 (1969), 312–37 (pp. 314–16).

and finally with Gwalchmei, and that in the Middle English version Yvain, in a highly charged emotional scene, returns to the spring after having rescued the lion and before meeting Lunete.

From this point onwards, the two narratives develop along different lines. The Welsh narrative is very brief, even sparse, and covers only about forty lines of prose: Lunet and Owein return to the Lady of the Well, who is quickly and unceremoniously reconciled with Owein, and they proceed to Arthur's court. As an epilogue, the Du-Traws (or Black-Oppressor) episode follows, being a variant of Chrétien's Pesme Aventure, and Owein returns to his own domain after spending some time at Arthur's court. The continuation of the French narrative is not only much more complex but also much longer, with over another 2,200 lines of verse: Lunete and Yvain return to Laudine, who does not recognize Yvain, now calling himself the Knight with the Lion. There is no reconciliation, and Yvain leaves again. Next follows a story about two sisters and a legal ordeal, in the course of which Yvain and Gauvain fight against each other; into this story the Pesme Aventure is inserted. Yvain again returns to the spring where he conjures up another destructive storm, and Lunete tricks Laudine into reconciliation with Yvain.

The obvious structural similarities between the French and Welsh narratives have resulted in long and complex scholarly debates about the relationship between the two texts. Three main hypotheses have been discussed: (1) Chrétien's romance derives from a proto-form of the Welsh tale,[17] (2) the Welsh tale in its surviving form derives from Chrétien's romance as its main or only source or (3) the Welsh tale and Chrétien's romance both independently derive from a common source.[18] As Thomson points out, 'the invariable initial *L-* [of the name Lunet in *Owein*] ... suggests a loan-word never fully assimilated in Welsh'.[19]

---

[17] This would appear to have been the position of Thomson (O, p. lxxxiv), but later, in his edition of *Gereint*, he shows himself more agnostic: see *Ystorya Gereint uab Erbin*, ed. R. L. Thomson (Dublin, 1997), p. lxxiv.

[18] For a summary of the main recent strands of the discussion, with further references, see J. T. Koch, 'Tair Rhamant', in *Celtic Culture. A Historical Encyclopedia*, ed. J. T. Koch (Santa Barbara, Denver and Oxford, 2006), pp. 1647–51; for discussions of ways in which British materials might have been transmitted to Old French authors, see R. Bromwich, 'First Transmission to Britain and France', in *The Arthur of the Welsh*, ed. Bromwich et al., pp. 273–98, and P. Sims-Williams, 'Did Itinerant Breton *Conteurs* Transmit the *Matière de Bretagne*?', *Romania* 116 (1998), 72–111. For a scenario that allows for the cross-fertilization of Welsh traditions with Chrétien's text, see T. Hunt, 'The Art of *Iarlles y Ffynnawn* and the European *Volksmärchen*', *Studia Celtica* 8/9 (1973–4), 107–20 (pp. 111–12).

[19] Thomson, O, p. lxii.

The current scholarly consensus favours the view that the main source of *Owein* was Chrétien's *Yvain*.[20]

In the following discussion, I will ignore this controversial question and instead take a comparative literary approach by exploring the semantic structures of *Ywain and Gawain* and *Owein* as representatives of what might be termed the Matter of Yvain, and as works of literature in their own right. But before I embark on the textual analyses, I will briefly survey the British and early medieval Welsh background of the figure of Owein.

British and early medieval Welsh Owein

Unfortunately, available information about the British and early-medieval Welsh Owein is scanty and inconclusive. He is the son of Urien of Rheged and belongs to an early stratum of characters hailing from north Britain, the 'Old North'. He is mentioned in the corpus of poetry conventionally attributed to the 'historical' Taliesin,[21] as well as in another poem in the Book of Taliesin, dated by its editor

---

[20] See for example Lloyd-Morgan, 'Migrating Narratives', pp. 133 and 131: 'Comparative readings of both *Geraint* and *Owain* suggest that the main source of the medieval Welsh texts was the corresponding romance by Chrétien' and 'in the case of these two tales the surviving medieval manuscript witnesses all descend ultimately from a single adaptation of French romance into Welsh'. See further O. Padel, *Arthur in Medieval Welsh Literature* (Cardiff, 2000), p. 78; C. Lindahl, 'Yvain's Return to Wales', *Arthuriana* 10.3 (2000), 44–56; E. Poppe, '*Owein*, *Ystorya Bown*, and the Problem of "Relative Distance": Some Methodological Considerations and Speculations', in *Arthurian Literature* 21 [*Celtic Arthurian Material*], ed. C. Lloyd-Morgan (2004), 73–94.

[21] See *The Poems of Taliesin*, ed. I. Williams and J. E. C. Williams (Dublin, 1968), pp. 6–7 and 12, for the texts, and M. Pennar, *Taliesin Poems* (Felinfach, 1988), pp. 75 and 105–6, for translations. Most scholars would no longer assign this corpus to the second half of the sixth century, but rather to the ninth to eleventh centuries. For some discussion of the problems surrounding the date and historicity of Taliesin, see, for example, J. T. Koch, 'Taliesin [1] the Historical Taliesin', in *Celtic Culture. A Historical Encyclopedia*, pp. 1652–3; G. Isaac, 'Gweith Gwen Ystrat and the Northern Heroic Age of the Sixth Century', *Cambrian Medieval Celtic Studies* 36 (1998), 61–70; O. Padel, 'Aneirin and Taliesin: Sceptical Speculations', in *Beyond the Gododdin. Dark Age Scotland in Medieval Wales: The Proceedings of a Day Conference Held on 19 February 2005*, ed. A. Woolf (St Andrews, 2013), pp. 115–52. Urien's father was Cynfarch, and the name of Owein's troops given in *Owein*, 'trychant cledyf Kenuerchyn' (O 820, 'the Three Hundred Swords of Cenferchyn'), refers to the descendents of Cynfarch. Owein's ravens ('branhes', O 820, 'Flight of Ravens'), mentioned in the same context, appear in *Breudwyt Ronabwy*, a prose narrative that has been assigned dates between the mid-twelfth and the late fourteenth century, and in the works of twelfth-century Poets of the Princes; compare Bromwich, *Trioedd*, pp. 469–70.

Marged Haycock broadly to between the tenth and thirteenth centuries.[22] Haycock places this poem in a north Wales/Gwynedd context and suggests that it celebrates the 'glamorous Old North' and presents the men of Gwynedd 'as the true heirs of the northern heroic age'.[23] According to her, the 'historical' Taliesin's 'Marwnat Owein' (or 'Elegy for Owein') has its closest counterpart in what may be an elegy for Caradog of Gruffudd, slain in battle in 1082, and she notes increasing interest in Owein from the ninth century onwards.[24] In the twelfth century, the Poets of the Princes use the figure of Owein son of Urien as a comparator for the contemporary Gwynedd ruler Owain Gwynedd.[25] The poem 'Sharp is the wind' ('Llym awel', perhaps tenth-century) probably contains a reference to Owein's imprisonment and to his warband's expedition to free him.[26] In these early literary references to Owein he is a martial hero of the Old North, unconnected to Arthur, and there is no hint of a story related to the plot of *Owein*.[27] There are three references to Owein in what Bromwich has reconstructed as the 'Early Version' of the corpus of *The Triads of the Island of Britain* (or *Trioedd Ynys Prydein*), which she believes predate the influence of Geoffrey of Monmouth. These describe Owein as one of the 'Three Fortunate Princes of the Island of Britain' and mention his bard and his horse respectively, but again, no narrative emerges.[28]

The first extant source that links Urien, and Owein, with Arthur is Geoffrey, according to whom Arthur established Urien as king of Moray ('Murefenses').[29] He also mentions briefly Urien's son Hiwenus, that is Owein, who became king of Scotland after the death of his uncle Auguselus in a battle against Modred and 'who later distinguished himself through his many brave deeds in these battles', probably against Modred.[30] Impor-

---

[22] See M. Haycock, *Prophecies from the Book of Taliesin* (Aberystwyth, 2013), pp. 16 and 61–82 for text, translation, discussion and date.
[23] Haycock, *Prophecies*, p. 63.
[24] M. Haycock, 'Early Welsh Poets Look North', in *Beyond the Gododdin*, ed. Woolf, pp. 7–39 (pp. 39 and 18).
[25] See Bromwich, *Trioedd*, pp. lxi and lxiii.
[26] See J. Rowland, *Early Welsh Saga Poetry. Study and Edition of the Englynion* (Cambridge, 1990), pp. 454–7, 501–3, 238–40, 97 and 102 for text, translation and discussion.
[27] For these and further references in genealogies, see P. C. Bartrum, *A Welsh Classical Dictionary: People in History and Legend up to about A.D. 1000* (Aberystwyth, 1993), pp. 518–20, and Bromwich, *Trioedd*, pp. 467–72. The only connection between these earlier traditions and *Owein* is the passing reference to Owein's flight of ravens.
[28] See Bromwich, *Trioedd*, pp. lxv, lxxviii, 8, 20 and 107.
[29] This is (mistakenly) equated with Rheged in the Welsh translations of the *Historia*; see Haycock, 'Early Welsh Poets Look North', p. 10.
[30] See M. D. Reeve (ed.) and N. Wright (trans.), *Geoffrey of Monmouth. The History*

tantly, Owein is not mentioned among the members of Arthur's court in the periods of peace. *Culhwch ac Olwen*, the oldest Arthurian tale, placed by Rodway in the mid-to-late twelfth century, which mentions a great number of Arthurian characters, does not reference either Urien or Owein, only Morfydd, daughter of Urien Rheged.[31]

Textual micro-perspectives I: in the castle of the friendly host

I will begin the textual analyses by taking a micro-perspective and looking at Colgrevance's and Cynon's first sojourn on their journeys, in the castle of a friendly and hospitable owner. This episode features in both narratives and presents many of their themes and concerns in a nutshell. It links the young knights' departure from Arthur's court to their meeting with the monstrous herdsman. Colgrevance describes the motivation for his journey as 'forto seke aventurs' (YG 155); Cynon sets out more specifically to find someone who will overcome him in feats of arms, since so far he has been able to overcome everybody (O 32–3). Both episodes agree in their basic elements, namely description of the host, welcome, reception, entertainment and conversation, and departure in the morning (see Table 1). But, as the following analysis will show, the details and the narrative perspectives are different, while the narrative functions of the episode will turn out to be both similar and different in the two texts – similar with regard to the introduction and definition of an ideal courtly setting and different with regard to the focus in *Owein* on a characterization of Cynon.

---

of the Kings of Britain. An Edition and Translation of De gestis Britonum *(Historia Regum Britanniae)*, Arthurian Studies 69 (Woodbridge, 2007), pp. 202–5, 210–11 and 250–1; for a Welsh version see *Brut Dingestow*, ed. H. Lewis (Aberystwyth, 1942), pp. 152 ('Reget'), 158 and 183 ('Owein'). Bromwich cautions that Owein may well have been drawn into Arthur's orbit in Welsh sources before Geoffrey (*Trioedd*, p. 469).

[31] See S. Rodway, *Dating Medieval Welsh Literature: Evidence from the Verbal System* (Aberystwyth, 2013), p. 169; R. Bromwich and D. S. Evans, *Culhwch ac Olwen. An Edition and Study of the Oldest Arthurian Tale* (Cardiff, 1992), pp. 13 and 109. For Owein in the later tale *Breudwyt Ronabwy (The Dream of Rhonabwy)*, see C. Lloyd-Morgan, 'Breuddwyd Rhonabwy and Later Arthurian Literature', in *The Arthur of the Welsh*, ed. Bromwich, pp. 183–208, and C. McKenna, 'Breuddwyd Rhonabwy', forthcoming in *Arthur in the Celtic Literatures*, ed. Lloyd-Morgan and Poppe. In *Peredur*, Owein is one of Arthur's knights whom Peredur meets in the wilderness (compare *Historia Peredur vab Efrawc*, ed. G. W. Goetinck [Caerdydd, 1976], p. 8, ll.13–14) and who remains nameless at this point in Chrétien's *Perceval* (I wish to thank Ceridwen Lloyd-Morgan for pointing this out to me).

Table 1: Comparison of narrative elements in first-sojourn epiodes in
Ywain and Gawain and *Owein*

narrative element	*Ywain and Gawain*	*Owein*
arrival	Colgrevance sees a castle	Cynon sees a castle
		two lads at a game with bow and arrows
host	'knight with fawkon on his hand' (YG 168)	richly dressed man
welcome	'He answerd me mildeli with mowth. / Mi sterap toke þat hende knight / And kindly cumanded me to lyght' (YG 172–4)	'he was so courteous that he greeted me before I could greet him' (OE 117)
reception	'Curtayse men in worde and dede' (YG 193) bring the horse to a stable; a beautiful and courteous / gracious maiden changes Colgrevance's clothes	twenty-four beautiful maidens receive Cynon and his horse, change his clothes, prepare the table
entertainment	the maiden converses with Colgrevance	
entertainment	supper of excellent quality; the maiden serves Colgrevance 'Curtaisly' (YG 220)	equipment and supper of excellent quality
conversation	the host invites Colgrevance to come back	Cynon complains of a lack of conversation; the host explains the reason; Cynon explains the motivation of his journey, to find someone to get the better of him; the host, after some hesitation, points him to the herdsman
departure	after a restful night, Colgrevance departs	Cynon is anxious to resume his journey and departs in the morning

In relation to Chrétien's text (Y 175–277), on the narrative surface *Ywain and Gawain* follows it quite faithfully. It omits the reference to the castle's location close to the enchanted (and continental) forest of Broceliande. It upgrades the social standing of the host – who in Chrétien is a 'vavasour' (Y 211), a minor noble, a vassal of another vassal – and makes him a 'knight' (YG 168, 169) and the 'lord and keper of þat halde' (YG 170).[32]

---

[32] Matthews, 'Translation and Ideology', p. 460, points out that 'the host is potentially Colgrevance's equal, but for the fact that he already has the sovereignty which Colgrevance, the young landless knight, seeks'.

More importantly, the Middle English text spells out positive characterizations of the host, the maiden and the inhabitants of the castle as courteous, polite, well-mannered ('hende', 'curtayse', 'hendly', 'curtaisly'), and thus flags the qualities of the castle for the audience:[33] 'Mi sterap toke þat hende knight' (YG 173); 'Curtayse men in worde and dede' (YG 193); 'Hendly scho toke me by þe hand' (YG 198); 'Byfor me sat þe lady bright / Curtaisly my mete to dyght' (YG 219–20). Particularly significant in this context is the description of the maiden who takes Colgrevance by the hand, converses with him in a chamber and then takes him to the evening meal:[34]

> Scho served me hendely te hend:
> Hir maners might no man amend.
> Of tong sho was trew and renable
> And of hir semblant soft and stabile. (YG 207–10)

The descriptor 'trew' (with a wide range of meanings, including 'steadfast [in fidelity], loyal; noble; courteous, mild [of speech]'[35]) has no analogue in Chrétien, who characterizes the maiden with regard to her conversation as 'bien parlant et anseigniee' (Y 242, 'well spoken and taught'). It is no coincidence that 'trew', next to 'wise', is already part of the first brief characterization of Arthur in the narrative's introduction:[36]

> Of al knightes he [Arthur] bare þe pryse.
> In werld was none so war ne wise.
> Trew he was in alkyn thing. (YG 11–13)

In this introduction and its description of the feast at Arthur's court, the English redactor introduced some significant innovations and changes. During this feast, Chrétien's knights and ladies speak of 'love, of the torments and sorrows and of the great blessings that often come on the

---

[33] Compare T. Hunt, 'Beginnings, Middles, and Ends: Some Interpretative Problems in Chrétien's *Yvain* and its Medieval Adaptations', in *The Craft of Fiction: Essays in Medieval Poetics*, ed. L. A. Arrathoon (Rochester, MI, 1984), pp. 83–117, who notes the 'directness of expression which characterises the [Middle English] poet's revelations of his interests' (p. 91). On the importance of the notion of *hende* see J. Bollard, '*Hende Wordes*: The Theme of Courtesy in *Ywain and Gawain*', *Neophilologus* 78 (1994), 655–70, and below.

[34] Breulmann, *Erzählstruktur und Hofkultur*, p. 445, suggests that this chamber has fewer erotic connotations than Chrétien's lawn.

[35] See eMED, *The Electronic Middle English Dictionary*: http://quod.lib.umich.edu/m/med/, s.v. *treu(e)*.

[36] Chrétien says that Arthur's example should teach his audience to become 'preu et cortois' (Y 3, 'honourable and courtly').

members of its [love's] order'[37] ('Li autre parloient d'amors, / Des angoisses et des dolors / Et de granz biens, qu'ant ont sovant / Li deciple de son covant', Y 13–16), and the narrator then reflects on the status of love in his own time and its decline since Arthur's. In *Ywain and Gawain*, the conversation of the knights and ladies concentrates on past feats of martial prowess and hunting:

> Fast þai carped and curtaysly
> Of dedes of armes and of veneri
> And of gude knightes þat lyfed þen
> And how men might þem kyndeli ken
> By doghtiness of þaire gude ded. (YG 25–9)

The Middle English narrator also draws a contrast between the past and his present, to the disadvantage of the present. A brief reference to the status of 'luf' indicates that his reflections are triggered by Chrétien's text.[38] His focus, however, is on a different value here, on '(trew) trowth' ([true] fidelity, loyalty; integrity, honesty):[39]

> Þai told of more trewth þam bitw[e]ne
> Þan now omang men here es sene,
> For trowth and luf es al bylaft;
> Men uses now anoþer craft.
> With worde men makes it trew and stabil,
> Bot in þaire faith es noght bot fabil;
> With þe mowth men makes it hale,
> Bot trew trowth is nane in þe tale. (YG 33–40)

Thus a contrast is constructed between Arthur and the maiden on the one hand, who are both 'trew', and the narrator's contemporaries on the other, who are 'trew' only in words. I will come back to the notion of 'trew trowth', which is a central conceptual concern of the Middle English narrative.

---

[37] Chrétien de Troyes, *Arthurian Romances*, trans. with introduction and notes by D. D. R. Owen (London and Vermont, 1993), p. 281; quotations from this translation will be identified by the abbreviation YE and page-number.
[38] Compare G. K. Hamilton, 'The Breaking of the Troth in *Ywain and Gawain*', *Mediaevalia* 2 (1976), 111–35 (p. 113); Busby, 'Chrétien de Troyes English'd', p. 600; Dirscherl, *Ritterliche Ideale*, pp. 88–9. In the Norse *Ívens saga*, the scene with the knights and ladies and the narrator's reflections are omitted altogether; see Rikkhardsdottir, *Medieval Translations*, pp. 91–2.
[39] For the range of meanings of *trowth*, see eMED, s.v. *treuth*. For the importantance of *trowth* in Middle English literature of the thirteenth and fourteenth centuries, see already K. Lippmann, 'Das ritterliche Persönlichkeitsideal in der mittelenglischen Literatur des 13. und 14. Jahrhunderts' (Meerane, 1933), pp. 11–12.

There is one further pervasive, and decisive, difference between Chrétien's *Yvain* and *Ywain and Gawain*, and also its Middle High German and Norse descendants, and this concerns narratorial attitude and tone. Hunt suggests that 'Chrétien's introduction to *Yvain* ... sets the tone for the whole romance: it is oblique, ironic, and, above all, auto-reflective' and that he is 'already moving in the direction of literary burlesque'.[40] The tone of the narrator of *Ywain and Gawain*, on the other hand, in the introduction and the remainder of the romance, is direct and unironic; in the words of Harrington, it is geared towards the 'sober, practical, realistic tastes of a fourteenth-century English audience',[41] and Matthews observes the replacement of Chrétien's paradox, the figure 'in which two apparently opposite "truths" can coexist', by 'trowth', which 'asserts without contradiction'.[42] I will address this issue again later.

To come back now to the message of Colgrevance's sojourn in the castle of the friendly host: it introduces and defines a courtly setting and a mode of polite and courteous interaction between the sexes, but without any of the hints of dalliance present in the French text.[43] This is encapsulated in a small, but significant difference: Chrétien juxtaposes Calogrenant's individual desires and regard for social conventions when the host interrupts his conversation with the maiden in order to announce the evening meal:

> Que mout m'i delitoit a estre,
> Ne ja mes por nul estovoir
> Ne m'an queïsse removoir;
> Mes tant me fist la nuit de guerre
> Li vavassors, qu'il me vint querre,
> Quant de soper fu tans et ore. (Y 244–9)

---

[40] Hunt, 'Beginnings, Middles, and Ends', pp. 88 and 90; see, for example, also Hunt, *Chrétien de Troyes*, pp. 16–21, and D. Kelly, 'Chrétien de Troyes', in *The Arthur of the French. The Arthurian Legend in Medieval French and Occitan Literature*, ed. G. S. Burgess and K. Pratt (Cardiff, 2006), pp. 135–85 (pp. 144–8 and 152–6).

[41] N. T. Harrington, 'The Problem of the Lacunae in *Ywain and Gawain*', *Journal of English and Germanic Philology* 69 (1970), 659–65 (pp. 664–5).

[42] Matthews, 'Translation and Ideology', p. 458. See also Busby, 'Chrétien de Troyes English'd', p. 603, who describes it as 'a faster moving, no-nonsense sort of romance, in which the subtle interplay between courtesy, chivalry, and love plays a subordinate role', and Finlayson, '*Ywain and Gawain*', p. 314, who notes the English author's 'avoidance of the main features of Chrétien's style: his love of self-communing dialogue and play upon words'.

[43] See Finlayson, '*Ywain and Gawain*', p. 319, and Breulmann, *Erzählstruktur und Hofkultur*, p. 445; according to J. Bumke, *Höfische Kultur. Literatur und Gesellschaft im hohen Mittelalter* (München, 1994), pp. 466–8, the maiden serves as the exemplar of the courtly ideal in Hartmann's Middle High German adaptation of Chrétien's *Yvain*.

> (I would never have wished to leave on any account. But that night the vavasour thwarted my wishes by coming to look for me when supper-time came around. [YE 284])

In the Middle English version, on the other hand, there is no such interruption, and therefore no tension between emotions and conventions – and on the syntactic level not even an adversative conjunction (as Chrétien's 'Mes', Y 247). The maiden simply takes Colgrevance to supper at the appropriate time:

> Ful fain I wald, if þat I might,
> Have woned with þat swete sight.
> And, when we sold go to sopere,
> Þat lady with a lufsome chere
> Led me down into the hall. (YG 211–15)

It is time now to leave the Middle English protagonists at their supper and to see how Cynon fares in the castle of the friendly host. As Table 1 shows, the narrative development of his sojourn there is both similar and different. Some important and characteristic courtly elements are missing: the hawk as a marker of the host's status and his leisure activities, the host holding the stirrups of his guest's horse, reminiscent of the *officium strepae*, and, most importantly perhaps, the maiden who entertains and enchants Calogrenant. I will argue that even though these emblematic elements are absent, the Welsh author still constructed an ideal courtly setting.[44]

When Cynon approaches the castle, he first of all sees two richly-clad lads engaged in a game with valuable implements:

> ...two lads with curly yellow hair, and a band of gold on their foreheads, and each wearing a tunic of yellow brocaded silk, and boots of new Cordovan leather on their feet with golden buckles fastening them around the ankle. And each had a bow of elephant ivory in his hand, with strings of deer sinew, and arrows with shafts of walrus ivory, peacock-feathered, and

---

[44] For presentations of Welsh courts in the twelfth- and thirteenth-century poetry of the Poets of the Princes and in legal texts respectively, see M. Owen, 'Literary Convention and Historical Reality: The Court in the Welsh Poetry of the Twelfth and Thirteenth Centuries', *Études celtiques* 29 (1992), 69–85, and D. Stephenson, 'The Laws of Court: Past Reality or Present Ideal', in *The Welsh King and His Court*, ed. T. M. Charles-Edwards, M. E. Owen, P. Russell (Cardiff, 2000), pp. 400–14; for a comparison of the courtly society of *Peredur* with the backward-looking societal images of the Poets of the Princes, see M. Owen, '"Arbennic milwyr a blodeu marchogyon": Cymdeithas *Peredur*', in *Canhwyll marchogyon: Cyd-destunoli* Peredur, ed. S. Davies and P. W. Thomas (Caerdydd, 2000), pp. 91–112.

gold tips on the shafts; and knives with blades of gold and hilts of walrus ivory as targets, and they were aiming at their knives. (OE 117)

These lads never reappear in the narrative, and the only function they have is, I think, to convey an image of leisure and luxury.[45]

The Welsh friendly host does not take the stirrup of Cynon's horse, as a polite and courtly gesture, but his excellent manners show themselves in other ways and are commented on by Cynon: 'When I saw him I approached and greeted him. But he was so courteous that he greeted me before I could greet him' (OE 117).[46] Charles-Edwards has shown that for the definition of status in Middle Welsh narratives it is crucial who greets first, and it should be the guest who does so.[47] Cynon's observation indicates that it is unexpected that the owner of the castle should be the first to greet. The phrase translated as 'he was so courteous' by Sioned Davies is in Welsh 'rac daet y wybot', more literally 'because of the goodness / quality of his courtesy'.[48] *Gwybot*, the verbal noun 'knowing', also had a more specialized meaning of 'knowing how to behave', or an 'acknowledged form of behaviour'.[49] Cynon's comment on the friendly host's 'gwybot' sets the standard for the two audiences' assessment of his court, the audience inside the

---

[45] See also, with a slightly different focus, Lindahl, 'Yvain's Return to Wales', p. 50. A similar vignette of British pre-historic splendour is found in *Breudwyt Maxen* (*The Dream of the Emperor Maxen*), in the first description (admittedly in a dream) of the court of Eudaf son of Caradog, a British ruler located in Anglesey of the late fourth century; see Davies, *The Mabinogion*, p. 104; *Breudwyt Maxen Wledic*, ed. B. F. Roberts (Dublin, 2005), p. 2.52–9. *Breudwyt Maxen* is conventionally dated to the second half of the twelfth century, or somewhat earlier, and is assigned by Rodway to the same wider chronological group of texts as *Owein*; see Rodway, 'The Where, Who, When and Why', pp. 59 and 70–3.

[46] This is repeated when Owein comes to the same castle (O 242–3); later in the narrative, when Owein regains consciousness, the maiden similarly greets him first (O 602–3).

[47] T. Charles-Edwards, 'Honour and Status in Some Irish and Welsh Prose Tales', *Ériu* 29 (1978), 123–41 (pp. 124–7); see also R. Reck, *The Aesthetics of Combat in Medieval Welsh Literature* (Rhaden, 2010), p. 307.

[48] This is the only instance of *gwybot* in this meaning in *Owein*.

[49] M. Phillips, '*Defod a moes y llys*', in *The Welsh King and His Court*, ed. Charles-Edwards et al., pp. 347–61 (p. 354); see also eGPC, *Geiriadur Prifysgol Cymru. A Dictionary of the Welsh Language*: http://www.welsh-dictionary.ac.uk/, s.v. *gwybod*. In a Welsh version of Geoffrey's *Historia Regum Britanniae*, for example, Arthur's court is credited with a number of courtly virtues, unsurprisingly with *gwybot* among them: 'A chymeint oed syberwyt llys Arthur o uoes a gvybot a haelder a daioni a dewred a milwraeth' (And so great was the munificence of Arthur's court of civility, courtesy, generosity, [goodness,] bravery and valour; Phillips, '*Defod a moes*', p. 358).

narrative at Arthur's court, to whom Cynon tells his tale, and the audience of *Owein*.[50]

When Cynon enters the hall of the castle with his host, he sees 'twenty-four maidens embroidering silk at a window' (OE 117); they would seem to mirror the lads playing with bow and arrow outside the castle and are engaged in a courtly activity suitable for women. They are furthermore extremely beautiful, and Cynon describes their beauty with a rhetorical hyperbole, including an extravagant and daring comparison with Gwenhwyfar:

> I am sure that the ugliest one of them was fairer than the fairest maiden that you ever saw in the Island of Britain, the least beautiful was more beautiful than Gwenhwyfar, the wife of Arthur, when she is at her most beautiful ever at the Christmas Day or Easter Day Mass. (OE 117)[51]

The description of these maidens connects with two similar images in the text: Gwenhwyfar and an unquantified number of handmaidens embroidering (with unspecified materials) at a window in the introductory scene at Arthur's court (O 3–4), and twenty-four very handsome but shabbily dressed and sad maidens in the court of the Du Traws, the Black Oppressor, at the end of the text (O 785–7). These maidens' knightly escorts were killed by the Black Oppressor. The maidens are not described as engaged in any handicraft, in contrast to the maidens in Chrétien's analogue, the Pesme Aventure:

> Et par antre les pes leanz
> Vit puceles jusqu'a trois çanz,
> Qui diverses oevres feisoient.
> De fil d'or et do soie ovroient
> Chascune au miaux qu'ele savoit.
> Mes tel povreté i avoit,
> Que desliiees et desçaintes
> An i ot de povreté maintes,
> Et as memeles et as cotes
> Estoient lor cotes derotes
> Et les chemises as cos sales. (Y 5193–203)

---

[50] For discussions of elements of Welsh courtliness, see Phillips, '*Defod a moes*', and R. Reck, '*daet y wybot* "die Exzellenz seiner Maniere": Höfisches Protokoll in den mittelalterlichen kymrischen Prosaerzählungen', in *Akten des 5. Deutschsprachigen Keltologensymposiums*, ed. K. Stüber, T. Zehnder, D. Bachmann (Wien, 2010), pp. 303–15.

[51] Owein encounters the same maidens when he re-enacts Cynon's adventure: 'he could see the maidens in golden chairs, sewing brocaded silk. And Owain thought that they were far more beautiful and attractive than Cynon had described' (OE 122).

(...and looking inside between the stakes he [Yvain] sees up to three hundred maidens engaged in various kinds of work. Each one was sewing as best she could with gold thread and silk. But they were in such poverty that many of them were bare-headed and ungirdled, so poor were they, and their dresses were torn at the breast and elbows, and their smocks were dirty at the neck. [YE 351])

Returning to *Owein*, the numerical specification in the Welsh text of twenty-four maidens in the castles of the friendly host and of the Black Oppressor is too striking to be coincidental.

The descriptions of the three courts echo each other and effect thematic correspondences: in Arthur's court luxury items (Arthur's mantle of yellow-red brocaded silk, the cushion with its cover of red brocaded silk) are balanced by humble furnishing (the pile of fresh rushes on which Arthur sits);[52] the castle of the friendly host presents a consistent image of idealized leisured luxury; the court of the Black Oppressor is troubled and in need of a redeemer.

The maidens in the castle of the friendly host get up to provide for Cynon in an efficient and stylized way, in groups of six:

And they rose to meet me; and six of them took my horse and removed my boots; and another six took my weapons and polished them in a burnisher until they were as bright as bright could be; and the third six of them laid a cloth on the table and set out food; and the fourth six removed my travel-stained clothes and dressed me in other garments, namely a shirt and breeches of fine linen, and a tunic and surcoat and cloak of yellow brocaded silk with a wide border. (OE 117–18)

The table arrangements are similarly lavish and luxurious – among other things, 'there was not a single vessel served at table except ones of gold or silver or buffalo horn' (OE 118). The castle of the friendly host represents an ideal court, in which women embellish and serve ('schmücken und dienen') in the background, to take up Joachim Bumke's characterization of the function of women in this court's equivalent in Hartmann's Middle High German *Iwein*.[53] However, a central courtly element in both Chrétien and Hartmann is missing from *Owein*, as well as from

---

[52] Reck observes that it is 'this domestic sedateness which will be Owain's downfall when instead of three months he stays for three years "among his people and drinking companions..."'; whereas Yvain leaves his wife to pursue his chivalric fame, the *peripeteia* of Owain lies in his neglecting his duties for a highly questionable form of companionship at the Arthurian court' ('Owain', forthcoming).

[53] Bumke, *Höfische Kultur*, pp. 466–8.

Ywain and Gawain, namely the maiden introducing the protagonist to the complexities of courtly love, a love that was perceived to ennoble the lover in the service of his loved one.[54] The Welsh narrative and Arthur's Welsh court are male-dominated: Calogrenant's erotic dalliance with the maiden is replaced by a serious educational conversation between Cynon and the host. Furthermore, Gwenhwyfar has no role in the introductory scene at Arthur's court, beyond sitting at a window and embroidering with her handmaidens; Arthur goes to sleep alone, and there is no discussion between the knights and the queen, as there is in Chrétien.

In Cynon's encounter with the friendly host, the Welsh author pursues a second narrative concern besides the presentation of an ideal court, namely the characterization and education of his protagonist. This is not meant to imply that Colgrevance returns unchanged from his adventure. Bollard points out that his 'account of his adventure is an exemplum demonstrating courteous behaviour and the insufficiency of seeking adventure for its own sake'.[55] Having told his tale, Colgrevance comments: 'I fand þe folies þat I soght' (YG 456), whereas the French Calogrenant, as Hamilton observes, 'calls himself foolish for telling the story, not for his motives therein'.[56] The Welsh Cynon describes his story as a 'profitless tale', that is, profitless with regard to his own role in it.[57] It is certainly significant in this context that Cynon self-critically characterizes himself as having been 'high-spirited, and extremely arrogant' when he set out looking for adventures and for someone to show him his limits:[58] 'I was looking for someone to get the better of me' (OE 118). He sought adventures for their own sake, and his motivation was utterly self-centred.

The friendly host is instrumental in Cynon's education; he points out his lack of table manners and then actively directs him to the next stage on his quest for adventure, the encounter with the monstrous herdsman – he does not do this in Chrétien's *Yvain* and its direct derivatives. Half-way through the meal, the host displays excellent courtesy, as is acknowledged by Cynon: 'when the man thought that I would prefer to talk rather than

---

[54] For helpful introductions to the concept of 'courtly love', see for example Bumke, *Höfische Kultur*, pp. 503–29, and Hunt, *Chrétien de Troyes*, p. 13.

[55] Bollard, '*Hende Wordes*', p. 666, where he also notes that the story Colgrevance tells 'prefigures the thematic development of Ywain's adventures, outlining in miniature the narrative and thematic concerns of the whole'; the same holds true for Cynon's in-tale; compare Reck, *The Aesthetics*, p. 96.

[56] Hamilton,'The Breaking of the Troth', p. 127.

[57] 'nat adeuawd dyn arnaw e hun chwedyl vethedigach no hwnn eiryoet' (O 213–14), lit. 'that nobody ever admitted a more profitless / futile tale / account than that about himself'.

[58] 'a drythyll oedwn, a mawr oed vy ryvig' (O 31–2); *trythyll* 'lively, spirited', appears to be positive or neutral in this context, associated with youthful enthusiasm.

eat, he asked me where I was going and who I was' (OE 118). Cynon's response is gratuitously rude or, to use his own earlier words, 'high-spirited, and extremely arrogant': 'And I said it was high time I had someone to talk with, and that the greatest fault of the court was that they were such poor conversationalists' (OE 118). The host gently but firmly sets him straight: 'we would have talked with you a long time ago except it would have interfered with your eating' (OE 118). Owein, replicating Cynon's adventure, also has a meal with the friendly host, and 'halfway through his meal the yellow-haired man asked Owain where he was going' (OE 122). Reck provides telling analogues from the native Welsh *Four Branches of the Mabinogi* which show that it was good practice for a conversation to start only after the guests have eaten.[59]

Cynon's rudeness is echoed by Owein's later similar insensitivity in the castle which is besieged by a giant. Owein senses a pervading unhappiness – 'The greatest failing Owain saw there was the men's sadness' (OE 135) – but is well served. When he is welcomed by his host halfway through the meal, he retorts 'It's high time to be more cheerful' (OE 135), and the host then patiently explains his court's reasons for sadness and grief. There is no such rudeness in *Yvain*, and no reference to the question being asked halfway through the meal:

> 'Por De!', fet il, 'biaus douz chiers sire!
> Ice vos pleiroit il a dire,
> Por quoi m'avez tant enoré
> Et tant fet joie et tant ploré?' (Y 3835–8)[60]
>
> ('In God's name, kind, dear sir, would you be willing to tell me why you've done me such honour amid so much rejoicing and so many tears.' [YE 332])

The reasons for Owein's rudeness remain puzzling, but there is an obvious echo here of Cynon's lack of table manners in the castle of the friendly host.[61]

The courtly atmosphere of the castle of the friendly host invites comparison with another courtly event, the festivities for Arthur at Laudine's court later in the narrative, when Yvain has replicated Calogrenant's adventure with greater success and become Laudine's husband. Without being recognized, he defends the spring against Arthur and his men and afterwards invites them to partake in a feast at the court.

---

[59] See further Reck, '*daet y wybot*', pp. 311–12, for a passage from *Chwedlau Seith Doethon Rufein*, the Welsh version of the *Seven Sages of Rome*.
[60] Compare YG 2229–44.
[61] See Reck, '*daet y wybot*', p. 312.

Textual micro-perspectives II: festivities for Arthur

Chrétien provides a lavish description of this feast (Y 2400–75), with a focus on the developing friendship between Gawain and Lunete, flirtations between the ladies of Laudine's court and Arthur's men, and Laudine's courteous behaviour towards them.[62] The flirtations are described thus:

> Car dames i ot tes nonante,
> Don chascune estoit bele at jante
> Et noble et cointe, preuz et sage,
> Dameisele de haut parage;
> Si s'i pooient solacier
> Et d'acoler et de beisier
> Et de parler et de veoir
> Et de delez eles seoir:
> Itant an orent il au mains. (Y 2443–51)

> (There were some ninety ladies there, every one beautiful and attractive, noble, intelligent, prudent, sensible and a damsel of high breeding. So the men could enjoy themselves by embracing and kissing them, talking to them, looking at them and sitting by their side: they had at least that satisfaction from them! [YE 314])

There is also a reference to sports and sightseeing:

> Deduit de bois et de riviere
> I ot mout, qui le vost avoir.
> Et qui vost la terre veoir,
> Que mes sire Yvains ot conquise
> An la dame, que il ot prise,
> Si se repot aler esbatre
> Ou deus liues ou trois ou quatre
> Par les chastiaus d'iluec antor. (Y 2468–75)

> (The forests and rivers offered plenty of sport for all who wished. And as for anyone who wanted to get to know that land that had come into my lord Yvain's possession through the lady he had married, he could enjoy himself visiting the nearby castles within a radius of two, three, or four leagues. [YE 314])

---

[62] Laudine's behaviour has some potential for misunderstanding that the narrator comments on. See for example Breulmann, *Erzählstruktur und Hofkultur*, pp. 164–70, on these festivities.

In the Middle English text, not only is the description of the feast much shorter (YG 1427–49), but there is no reference to a friendship developing between Gawain and Lunet, and the flirtations between Alundyne's ladies and Arthur's men are given short shrift, mentioned on a par with courtly sports, hunting and hawking:[63]

> Of maidens was þare so gude wane,
> Þat ilka knight myght tak ane. (YG 1429–30)
> And ilk day had þai solace sere
> Of huntyng and also of revere. (YG 1443–4)

This provides further support for the critical consensus that the English author was not interested in the rules and the practice of courtly love.[64] In the Middle Welsh *Owein* the description of the feast is even shorter. Its material glories are implied in Owein's statement that he prepared a feast for Arthur for three years, and the narrator simply says, without even hinting at any erotic dalliances: 'the feast that had taken three years to prepare was consumed within just three months, and they never had a more pleasant or better feast than that' (OE 130).

The three texts thus show very different foci in their depiction of a feast for Arthur. Chrétien highlights the opportunities for the development of courtly and erotic relations between Arthur's men and the ladies of Laudine's court. The Middle English author mentions the erotic element of the feast, but only very briefly and on a par with hunting and hawking – the key terms characterizing the feast are 'joy' and 'myrth' (used four times between lines 1427 and 1440). In the Middle Welsh narrative, the feast is described as better and more pleasant than any other, without further details beyond a reference to the amount of preparation that went into it and the lavish provisions; this may reflect the economic challenges of comparable festivities for the Welsh nobility of the Middle Ages.[65]

The micro-textual analyses of the episodes about the sojourn in the castle of the friendly host and the festivities for Arthur in *Yvain*, *Ywain and Gawain* and *Owein* reveal some significant differences between the

---

[63] Alundyne simply partakes in these festivities – 'The lady omang them al samen / Made ful mekyl joy and gamen' (YG 1433–4) – without any erotic implications; see also Breulmann, *Erzählstruktur und Hofkultur*, pp. 438 and 443–5, and Friedman and Harrington, YG, p. xx.
[64] Compare, for example, Hamilton, 'The Breaking of the Troth', p. 112; Hunt, 'Beginnings, Middles, and Ends', p. 110 ('the love element is entirely subordinated to the theme of chivalric trowthe'); Busby, 'Chrétien de Troyes English'd', p. 600; Breulmann, *Erzählstruktur und Hofkultur*, p. 496.
[65] For the festivities in Hartmann's *Iwein* and in *Ívens saga*, compare, for example, Breulmann, *Erzählstruktur und Hofkultur*, pp. 254–5 and 340–5.

texts. Chrétien's emphasis on love relations and erotic dalliances between a knight and a lady finds no echo in *Ywain and Gawain* or *Owein*:[66] the festivities for Arthur are characterized by enjoyment in the English poem and by material effort and splendour in the Welsh narrative. The sojourn in the castle of the friendly host provides an opportunity to develop an image of an ideal courtly setting. In *Ywain and Gawain* this is conveyed by description and flagged by evaluative lexis. The time at the court provides no specific educational experiences for Calogrenant, whereas deficits in Cynon's character and education are revealed, to him and to the audience, by his own behaviour and the host's gentle correction.

The next passage selected for analysis, which gives Lunete's / Lunet's motivations for helping the hero, is concerned with courteous behaviour, particularly in *Ywain and Gawain*, but is also instructive with regard to narrative presentation.

Textual micro-perspectives III: motivations for helping the hero

Chrétien's Lunete has a good rational reason for helping Yvain: her gratitude for his earlier courteous behaviour towards her at Arthur's court:

>'Et sachiez bien, se je pooie,
>Servise et enor vos feroie;
>Que vos le feïstes ja moi.
>Une foiz a la cort le roi
>M'anvoia ma dame an message.
>Espoir si ne fui pas si sage,
>Si cortoise ne de tel estre,
>Come pucele deüst estre;
>Mes onques chevalier n'i ot,
>Qu'a moi deignast parler un mot,
>Fors vos tot seul, qui estes ci;
>Mes vos, la vostre grant merci,
>M'i enorastes et servistes.
>De l'enor, que la me feïstes,
>Vos randrai ci le guerredon.' (Y 1001–15)

---

[66] This is not to say that medieval Welsh writers and their patrons and audiences were not interested in love as a topic of literary works; compare, for example, the importance of love in the poetry of Dafydd ap Gwilym (*c.* 1315–*c.* 1350), who is roughly contemporary with the White Book of Rhydderch and whose work reflects 'some of the more widespread commonplaces of the courtly love movement' (H. M. Edwards, *Dafydd ap Gwilym: Influences and Analogues* [Oxford, 1996], p. 283), but also in the prose-tales of the Mabinogion-corpus. This question requires further research.

('I would serve and honour you because you, indeed, did the same for me. My lady once sent me on an errand to the king's court. Perhaps I wasn't as prudent, courtly or well behaved as a maiden should be; but there was not a single knight there who deigned to speak a word to me except you alone who stand here. But you, thanks to your great kindness, honoured and served me there. For that honour you did me there I shall reward you here.' [YE 294])

The same reason is given in *Ywain and Gawain*:

'I aw þe honore and servyse;
I was in message at þe king
Before þis time, whils I was ȝing.
I was noght þan savese,
Als a damysel aght to be;
For þe tyme þat I was lyght
I cowrt was none so hend knyght,
Þat unto me þan walde take hede,
Bot þou allane, God do þe mede.
Grete honore þou did to me,
And þat sal I now quite þe.' (YG 720–30)

The Welsh Lunet explains her reasons for helping Owein in a very different way:

'God knows', said the maiden, 'it's a great shame that you cannot be rescued; and it would only be right for a woman to help you. God knows I have never seen a better young man for a woman than you. If you had a woman friend, you would be the best friend ['kar'] a woman could have; if you had a mistress, you would be the best lover ['gorderch']. And because of that,' she said, 'whatever I can do to rescue you, I will.' (OE 123)

Her description of, and claims for, Owein's qualities in interaction with women could stem from gratitude resulting from earlier positive experiences with him, as in the French and English versions, but no previous meeting of Lunet and Owein is mentioned in the Welsh narrative. Mac Cana argues that 'there are clear indications in her words and actions that she is deeply in love with him'.[67] Unexplained love in absence, that is love without prior knowledge of the other person, is not unheard of in medieval Welsh literature, the prime example being Rhiannon's love for Pwyll in the *Four Branches of the Mabinogi*.[68] Be that as it

---

[67] P. Mac Cana, *The Mabinogi* (Cardiff, 1992), p. 116.
[68] Compare Davies, *The Mabinogion*, p. 11: 'I am Rhiannon, daughter of Hyfaidd Hen,

may, Lunet's speech builds up considerable expectations for Owein on the part of the audience, who have not met him in great detail. But her claims for him are dramatically discredited by the following events, during which he proves that he is neither the best friend nor the best lover a woman could have.

When Owein later meets Lunet in the forest, where she is imprisoned by the Lady of the Well's two chamberlains, and she does not recognize him, she explains that Owein was the 'friend' ('kedymdeith', O 689) she 'loved best in the whole world'.[69] Lunet's affection and confidence have remained constant, to her own disadvantage, since she defended Owein against the chamberlain's accusation of being 'a cheat and a traitor' ('yn dwyllwr bradwr', O 692–3). But this time Owein fulfils the expectations and saves Lunet's life. Lunet's initial expression of affection and, perhaps, love may appear unmotivated, but is appropriate in relation to the tale's narrative and thematic structure, perhaps even more so than Chrétien's at first convincing and rational explanation. Even without stating anything explicitly himself, the Welsh narrator here subtly highlights Owein's lapse and his later growth, allowing characters and events to speak for themselves. I will come back to the events surrounding his growth and rehabilitation, but before rehabilitation, there needs to be a fall – and I will now turn to perceptions and evaluations of the hero's lapse.

Textual micro-perspectives IV: confronting the hero with his lapse

Owein is made aware of his lapse in a key passage in which he is confronted by a messenger sent by his wife and is publicly accused in Arthur's court of having overstayed his leave of absence.[70] The account is brief:

> One day as Owain was eating at table in the Emperor Arthur's court in Caerllion ar Wysg, behold, a maiden approaching on a bay horse with a

---

and I am to be given to a husband against my will. But I have never wanted any man, because of my love for you'.

[69] Note use of *kedymdeith* here, which indicates a less personal and intimate relationship than *kar* and *gorderch*.

[70] Note that it is Arthur who 'sent messengers to the countess, asking her to allow Owain to accompany him so that the noblemen of the Island of Britain and their ladies could see him for just three months' (OE 130). F. Salisbury suggests that Arthur has partial responsibility for Owein's lapse since Owein's 'negligence is not corrected by Arthur'; this is within the context of her larger argument that Arthur in *Owein* is weak and incompetent, 'incapable of exercising proper control over his men or even taking action to fulfil his own desires', in 'The figure of Arthur in *Chwedyl Iarlles y Ffynnawn* and *Ystorya Gereint uab Erbin*', *Quaestio Insularis* 7 (2006), 161–79 (pp. 172–3 and 178).

curly mane that reached the ground; she was dressed in yellow brocaded silk, and the bridle and what could be seen of the saddle were all of gold. And she rode up to Owain and grabbed the ring that was on his finger. 'This', she said, 'is what we do to a deceitful cheat and traitor [y dwyllwr aghywir bradwr] – shame on your beard!' And she turned her horse's head and away she went. And then Owain remembered his journey, and he grew sad [a thristau a oruc]. And when he had finished eating, he went to his lodging; and he was very uneasy that night [a goualu yn vawr a wnaeth]. (OE 131)

The messenger removes a ring from Owein's finger and explains this as befitting a 'deceitful cheat and traitor', referring to the promise he gave to the Lady of the Well and broke. Two details may be noted here. The only ring mentioned in the Welsh narrative so far is the one which Lunet gave Owein and which concealed him from the Black Knight's men when they searched for him; the Lady of the Well did not give Owein a ring as a token when he departed, as Laudine does in *Yvain*.[71] 'Cheat and traitor' ('twyllwr bradwr') are the exact terms of the accusation that will be levied against Owein by the two chamberlains of the Lady of the Well later, against which Lunet defends him to her own disadvantage (already mentioned). The phrase 'shame on your beard' appears to be a formula to dishonour a man: Welsh law texts mention a woman's 'shameful words to her husband, such as wishing a blemish on his beard'.[72]

It is only after this confrontation that Owein remembers his promise and realizes his lapse. This is different from Chrétien and *Ywain and Gawain*: here the hero suddenly and privately recalls his promise before he is publicly accused by the messenger of having broken it. Finally, Owein's reaction is briefly outlined: he grows sad, retreats to his room and is uneasy and worried for the rest of the night. The narrator, to whom I will return later, grants the audience a glimpse of the protagonist's emotional state.

---

[71] Compare Y 2600–13 for Laudine's ring and Y 1023–5 for Lunete's ring, which she asks Yvain to return when she has rescued him; see also Thomson, O, pp. 48 and 56. It is unlikely that the removal of Lunet's ring would have any significance in the context of Owein's having broken the promise he gave to the Lady of the Well. Is the motif of the ring therefore small-scale evidence for *Owein*'s dependence on *Yvain*, or another source? For a similar incidence, compare Yvain wiping his sword after having killed the venomous serpent, Y 3408–10; Owein too wipes his sword, for no obvious reason, since there is no previous mention of the serpent being venomous. See O 664–70, noted by L. M. Cordo Russo, 'The Reception of Medieval French Narrative in Medieval Wales: The Case of *Chwedyl Iarlles y Ffynnawn* and *Cân Rolant*', (unpublished Ph.D. dissertation, Universidad de Buenos Aires, 2014), pp. 182–3.

[72] D. Jenkins, *The Law of Hywel Dda. Law Texts from Medieval Wales* (Llandysul, 1986), p. 52; see also Thomson, O, p. 56, 'apparently a deadly insult'.

The corresponding episode in Chrétien is much longer, slightly over a hundred lines (Y 2694–797). Yvain suddenly realizes that 'he had broken his pledge to her [Laudine] and that the time-limit had passed' (YE 317),[73] but he keeps back his tears for shame. By a strange narrative coincidence, his wife's messenger arrives at that moment and publicly characterizes him as 'the disloyal traitor, liar and deceiver, who has abandoned and duped her' (YE 317–18; 'Le desleal, le traïtor, / Le mançongier, le jeingleor, / Qui l'a leissiee et deceüe', Y 2719–21). A central thread in her accusations concerns his failings as a lover, 'pretending as he did to be a true lover, though he is a false, treacherous thief' of Laudine's heart (YE 318; 'Bien a sa jangle aparceüe, / Qui se feisoit verais amerre, / S'estoit fel, soduianz et lerre', Y 2722–4).[74] But, as Cheyette and Chickering argue, there is a further layer too:

> These terms of invective [a liar, a trickster, unfaithful, false, a thief and a seducer] point specifically to the injury he has done to Laudine's honor: by not keeping the agreement, he has tricked and deceived her and thus diminished her good name. In an aristocratic world where fidelity to one's companions and one's lord was the primary virtue, no offense could be greater than this. ... an offense to fidelity was also an offense to love. In its routine use in political contexts, 'love' signified political and personal loyalty.[75]

Yvain is described as being 'an grant enui' (Y 2780; 'in great distress') after the messenger's departure, and the narrator provides a lengthy and complex introspective analysis of his mental turmoil.[76]

In *Ywain and Gawain*, the episode is shorter than in *Yvain*, by about twenty lines (YG 1583–650), mainly due to the omission of the French messenger's discourse on love dialectics, which provides a 'detailed distinction between the false lover, who steals hearts treacherously, and the true lover, who, wherever he goes, cherishes the heart of his lady and takes care to restore it to its proper place'.[77] As in *Yvain*, Ywain is condemned by the messenger 'for trayture' and is called a 'fals and lither losenjoure' ('false and wicked, deceiving rascal') who 'has bytrayed my lady' (YG 1601–3). His reported assertion 'of al he lufed hir moste' has

---

[73] 'car bien savoit, / Que covant manti li avoit / Et trespassez estoit li termes' (Y 2699–701).

[74] Compare on this passage, for example, Hunt, *Chrétien de Troyes*, pp. 62–3, and Breulmann, *Erzählstruktur und Hofkultur*, pp. 206–7.

[75] F. L. Cheyette and H. Chickering, 'Love, Anger, and Peace: Social Practice and Poetic Play in the Ending of *Yvain*', *Speculum* 80.1 (2005), 75–117 (p. 84).

[76] Compare Y 2781–801.

[77] Friedman and Harrington, YG, p. xix; compare Y 2722–41.

turned out to be (alliterating) 'treson and trechery' (YG 1608–9). But compared to Chrétien, Alundyne's perspective as lover recedes into the background. The Middle English messenger furthermore prefixes her order to return the ring with another direct address to Ywain, which has no parallel in Chrétien: 'þou es / Traytur untrew and trowthles / And also an unkind cumlyng' (YG 1625–7).[78] This repetition of the reproach and the emotional impact of the adjectival doublet 'untrew and trowthles' brings home the focus of her message, Ywain's breaking of the *trowth*.[79]

Interestingly, Ywain's emotions after the messenger has departed are given a slightly different narrative space. There is not only a seven-line narratorial description of the extent of his sorrow, 'Þat nere for murni[n]g wex he mad' (YG 1640),[80] but he also directly voices his despair in a five-line monologue, which has no analogue in Chrétien:

> 'Allas, I am myne owin bane;
> Allas' he sayd, 'þat I was born,
> Have I my leman þus forlorn,
> And al es for myne owen foly.
> Allas, þis dole wil mak me dy.' (YG 1643–8)

All three versions necessarily agree on the importance of the protagonist's disloyalty and self-centredness which made him forget his promise. The very short Welsh episode focuses on Owein and his lapse; the emotions of the Lady of the Well are only implied, in that Owein is described as a traitor, but they otherwise play no overt role. *Ywain and Gawain* follows Chrétien, but significantly reduces Alundyne's role as lover and the discussion of the paradoxes of love, and emphasizes Ywain's 'treson and trechery'. The Welsh and Middle English texts both highlight the protagonist's betrayal and its repercussions for him.

The second part of each narrative is then concerned with his attempts to atone for his failure, in order to achieve reconciliation with his wife and to re-establish his social position within Arthurian society, which he left on the morning after the confrontation with the messenger, receding into mental and social isolation. The steps necessary for the protagonist's eventual rehabilitation reflect the narratives' positive values and contain

---

[78] This refers back to YG 1607–12, 1621–2.
[79] Compare also Breulmann, *Erzählstruktur und Hofkultur*, pp. 469–71, for this episode.
[80] For an insightful analysis of Ywain's madness as 'the moral consequence of his breach of truth', within the context of the poem's 'emphasis on the crucial importance of truth', see P. B. R. Doob, *Nebuchadnezzar's Children: Conventions of Madness in Middle English Literature* (New Haven and London, 1974), pp. 139–53, quotations pp. 141 and 145.

conceptual (moral and social) messages; before I turn to these, I will discuss briefly the respective manners of narrating, since they are relevant for the ways in which the narrator constructs the unfolding of meaning.

Textual macro-perspectives I: manners of narrating

Critics agree that the Middle English *Ywain and Gawain* is action-driven rather than introspective or exegetical.[81] Friedman and Harrington observe that the English author is '[a]lways eager to get on with the story',[82] and Barron accounts for the reduced length of the English version with similar reasoning:

> Chrétien is as much concerned with meaning as with matter and his narrative is interspersed with lengthy analyses of sentiment, rhetorical expositions of courtly values undercut by pervasive irony and humour, and a whole dialectics of thematic and verbal oppositions which direct the reader's response to events. It is principally this extra-narrative material which has disappeared in the reduction of the 6800 lines of the original to some 4000 [of *Ywain and Gawain*].[83]

But as Finlayson emphasizes, this does not result in a tale without themes or messages: 'the themes are expressed in action rather than through the narrator's comments, though the import of these themes is in no way lessened'. It is, as he appropriately characterizes it, a 'dramatic rather than explicit revelation'.[84] Invisible as the narrator may appear to be, he still has subtle means at his disposal in order to intervene and to steer his (contemporary and modern) audiences' perception. This point has been made forcefully by Bollard with regard to the theme of courtesy in *Ywain and Gawain*n which, he says, 'can be traced throughout the tale, not merely as a theme implicit in the action but as one made explicit by the

---

[81] For the absence of exegesis – 'the constant analysis of ideas and feelings' – in *Peredur*, the Welsh tale related in complex ways to Chrétien's *Perceval*, see C. Lloyd-Morgan, 'Medieval Welsh Tales or Romances? Problems of Genre and Terminology', *Cambrian Medieval Celtic Studies* 47 (2004), 41–58 (p. 56).

[82] Friedman and Harrington, YG, p. xxii; compare also Harrington, 'The Problem of the Lacunae'.

[83] Barron, *English Medieval Romance*, p. 160; Hunt, *Chrétien de Troyes*, p. 89, observes that narratorial observations take up about 500 lines of Chrétien's *Yvain*.

[84] Finlayson, '*Ywain and Gawain*', p. 314. Compare also J. Frey, *Spielräume des Erzählens. Zur Rolle der Figuren in den Erzählkonzeptionen von* Yvain, Îwein, Ywain and Ívens saga (Stuttgart, 2008), p. 177, and Bollard, '*Hende Wordes*', p. 659: 'The meaning of the tale is not made explicit by the author, as it is in *Yvain*. It is implicit in the narrative, however, and can be extracted from it.'

author's use of vocabulary and the careful balancing of the poem's narrative and thematic structures'.[85] His analysis of the employment in *Ywain and Gawain* of the word *hend(e)*, and of its antonym *unhende*, reveals that the narrator uses it in order to foreground a positive and desirable quality, namely 'courtesy' / 'courteous speech or actions', which emerges as one of the social ideals celebrated in the romance. The repeated references to *trew* and *troth* already mentioned serve a similar purpose. On a different, structural level, actions and events described by the narrator develop a semantic message when they establish thematic structures and correspondences; for example, Ywain's combats in the second part, after he has been cured of his madness, emerge from the narrator's descriptions as 'exclusively concerned with the righting of wrongs' of others, in contrast to Calogrenant's and Ywain's initial series of adventures, which is 'an end in itself, or at most a means to test prowess'.[86]

The Welsh narrator of *Owein* is similarly inaudible, in that he does not intrude with narratorial digressions, explanations or assessments; Roberts comments that 'for him ... the essence of narrative lay in an account of a series or sequence of events and actions rather than in an analysis of motives and emotions or descriptions of character'.[87] He is omniscient and at times provides descriptive insights into the protagonist's mind and emotions, but he does not step outside and explain or evaluate Owein's reasons or behaviour on a meta-level, as the following examples demonstrate:

Ac ny welas eiryoet lle kyn amlet anrec odidawc o vwyt a llynn ac yno (O 327–8)

(And he [Owain] had never seen anywhere so many wonderful courses of food and drink as there [OE 124])

Ac ef a tebygei Owein bot yr awyr yn edrinawt rac meint y gweidi (O 346–7)

(And Owain felt that the sky was ringing because of all the wailing [OE 125])[88]

---

[85] Bollard, '*Hende Wordes*', p. 669.
[86] Finlayson, '*Ywain and Gawain*', pp. 321–2.
[87] Roberts, 'The Welsh Romance', p. 172. He also notes (pp. 180–1) that 'There are no authorial comments [in *Owein*] on the significance of events or situations, there are no formal rhetorical passages to amplify the material or to explore the emotions. It follows that there are no soliloquies, descriptive monologues or imaginary debates. The only narrator is the anonymous author who never intrudes or intervenes'.
[88] 'rac meint y gweidi' ('because of all the wailing') qualifies the preceding phrase, 'bot yr awyr yn edrinawt' ('was ringing'), not 'tebygei' ('felt').

a diheu oed gan Owein na welas eiryoet vn vorwyn delediwach no honno (O 720–2)

(And Owain was certain that he had never seen such a beautiful girl [OE 135])

A thruan uu gan Owein hynny, a mynet a oruc y orymdeith allann (O 797–8)

(And Owain was sad to hear that, and went out to walk [OE 137])

Furthermore, thematic and structural correspondences steer the audience's perception and understanding: for example, by the references to (twenty-four) maidens in Arthur's court and in the castles of the friendly host and the Black Oppressor respectively, and the two expressions of Lunet's affection for, and confidence in, Owein, already discussed earlier. The narrator similarly connects several episodes by verbal repetition: Owein's departure the morning after the confrontation with his wife's messenger, to 'the remote regions of the world and desolate mountains' (OE 131, O 575); his earlier departure from Arthur's court after Cynon's narrative, also to 'the remote regions of the world and desolate mountains' (OE 122, O 234–5); his later departure from the castle of the widowed countess, again to 'the remote and uninhabited regions of the world' (OE 133, O 659–60); and Cynon's departure to 'the remote and uninhabited regions of the world' (OE 117, O 35) at the beginning of the tale. On a structural level, these phrases signal the beginning of new narrative units,[89] and, on a thematic level, they invite the audience to compare the adventures and their respective outcomes. Reck therefore suggests that the issue of promises and obligations resulting from them, at the heart of Owein's lapse, is already raised in a dramatic form in the tale's opening scene at Arthur's court.[90]

As in *Ywain and Gawain*, meaning remains implicit in the narrative events of *Owein* – even more so than in the Middle English romance, since in the latter a conspicuous use of lexical items, such as *hend(e)* and *troth*, flags up narratorial concerns and evaluations.[91] The revelation of meaning in *Owein* is 'dramatic', and in the final part of my textual

---

[89] On uses of verbal repetition in *Yvain* see Hunt, *Chrétien de Troyes*, p. 85.
[90] According to Reck, *The Aesthetics*, p. 92, 'Owein's words demonstrate his propensity for shying his obligations and he is later mocked by Kei as a person who speaks instead of acting. This, at first sight light-hearted, verbal interplay is mirrored tragically by Owein's failure to keep his promise to the Lady of the Fountain.'
[91] For the lexical flagging of narratorial concerns in *Gereint*, see my forthcoming paper 'The Theme of Counsel in *Ystoria Gereint uab Erbin*', *Cambrian Medieval Celtic Studies* 72 (2016).

analyses I will survey what the narrative events tell us about the narrators' conceptual concerns.

Textual macro-perspectives II: meanings and messages

In my reading of the second part of the Welsh narrative I privilege an approach that focuses on Owein, considered by modern critics to be the tale's protagonist,[92] and on the immediate textual information about his actions, along the lines suggested, for example, by Roberts and Reck.[93] In this part of the narrative Owein's rehabilitation is enacted, but the conditions on which it will depend are never spelled out. The brief descriptions of his reconciliation with his wife and his re-integration into Arthur's court provide the only evidence of his successful return:

> And then Owain, accompanied by Lunet, went to the kingdom of the Lady of the Well, and when he left there he took the countess with him to Arthur's court, and she was his wife as long as she lived. ... [after the Du Traws episode] And Arthur had been happy to see him before he was lost, but he was even happier now. ... And Owain remained at Arthur's court from then on as captain of the retinue, and was dear to Arthur, until he went to his own people. (OE 136–8)

---

[92] See for example Thomson, O, p. 163: 'Owain is the central character of the tale and his rise, fall and rehabilitation are its theme', but note the medieval designation 'Chwedyl Iarlles y Ffynnawn' in the colophon in the Red Book. Later copyists, however, privilege Owein in their titles and colophons; compare S. Davies, 'O Gaer Llion i Benybenglog: Testun Llanstephan 58 o "Iarlles y Ffynnon"', in *Cyfoeth y Testun. Ysgrifau ar Lenyddiaeth Gymraeg yr Oesoedd Canol*, ed. I. Daniel et al. (Caerdydd, 2003), pp. 326–48 (p. 327).

[93] See Roberts, 'The Welsh Romance', pp. 177–9, and Reck, *The Aesthetics*, pp. 90–7. For other approaches, which privilege the narrative's response to social and historical conditions, see H. Fulton, 'Individual and Society in *Owein/Yvain* and *Gereint/Erec*', in *The Individual in Celtic Literatures*, ed. J. F. Nagy, CSANA Yearbook 1 (Dublin and Portland, 2001), 15–50, and K. L. Over, *Kingship, Kingship, Conquest, and Patria. Literary and Cultural Identities in Medieval French and Welsh Arthurian Romance* (New York and London, 2005), and, for a succinct summary of these, Reck, 'Owein' (forthcoming). I would agree, however, with Fulton, 'Individual and Society', p. 49, that a development ascribed to fictional characters in medieval texts such as *Owein* is first of all a social and discursive construct. Compare, with a slightly different perspective, Sif Rikhardsdottir, *Medieval Translations*, p. 106, on Ywain in the Middle English poem: 'By removing the internal complexities of the characters the audience's attention is diverted from the elaboration of individualistic psychological insight to generalised traits of gendered and socially prescribed behavioural patterns. Ywain is cast in a role that is immediately recognisable and can therefore be used to represent the narratorial concerns of the author.'

Owein faces three main adventures in the second part, that is, during his stay with the widowed countess, then when he meets Lunet in the forest and finally in the castle of the earl whose sons have been abducted by a giant. Each time, Owein hears about sad predicaments and hardly reacts, twice with the same non-committal phrase 'truan yw hynny' ('that is sad') and once non-verbally. In particular he shows no emotion or involvement and makes no offers to help, as one might expect of an Arthurian knight, even though in two passages the conversations are said to have continued.

> [At the castle of the widowed countess:] 'God knows', said the maiden, 'a widowed countess owns the castle over there, and when her lord and husband died he left her two earldoms, but tonight all she has left is just that one house over there which has not been taken by the young earl, her neighbour, because she would not marry him.' 'That is a sad story ['Truan yw hynny']', said Owain. And Owain and the maiden went to the castle... (OE 132, O 604–10)

> [With Lunet in the forest:] 'Are you sure', said Owain, 'that if the young man knew this he would come to defend you?' 'I am certain, between me and God', she said. And when the chops were cooked through, Owain divided them in half between himself and the maiden, and they ate. And after that they conversed until it was light the next day. (OE 134, O 697–702)

> [In the castle of the earl:] 'I had two sons, and yesterday they went to the mountain to hunt. And there is a monster there, and he kills men and devours them. And he has captured my sons, and tomorrow is the day set between us to hand over this maiden, or else he will kill my sons in front of me. And although he looks like a human, he is as big as a giant.' 'God knows', said Owain, 'that is a tragedy ['truan yw hynny']. And which one of those things will you do?' 'God knows', said the earl, 'I find it more honourable for him to kill my sons whom he got against my will than to give him my daughter willingly, to be raped and killed.' And they talked of other matters. (OE 135, O 728–37)

The narrator offers no insights into Owein's state of mind at these crucial moments; he remains the 'silent hero'.[94] Hunt links the absence in these episodes of 'psychological study or analysis as there is in the courtly romance' to *Owein*'s closeness to the *Märchen*. Owein's lack of reaction leaves a distinct and conspicuous narrative and verbal void, which complements his refusal to say anything about his intentions, even though

---

[94] Reck, *The Aesthetics*, p. 90.

the following events show that in each case Owein is prepared to provide the necessary help in due course.[95]

Let me digress briefly and look at these three scenes in Chrétien and *Ywain and Gawain* respectively: In the case of the widowed countess, her predicament is not mentioned explicitly before Count Alier attacks her castle, and Yvain has no occasion to comment or to commit himself. However, when Yvain regains consciousness and calls out to the maiden of the countess for help, he at the same time offers her his help in an automatic, but situationally incongruous, knightly reaction: 'Dameisele! or me dites donc, / Se vos avez mestier de moi?' (Y 3078–9; 'Tell me, then, young lady, if you have need of me', YE 322). Understandably, given his condition, the maiden answers curtly, even if her affirmative 'Oïl' acknowledges her lady's precarious state:

> 'Oïl', fet ele, 'mes je croi,
> Que vos n'estes mie bien sains.
> Jusqu'a quinzainne a tot le mains,
> Vos covandroit a sejor estre.' (Y 3080–3)
> ('Yes', she says; 'but I think you're not at all in a fit state. You ought to rest for at least a fortnight.' [YE 322])[96]

Chrétien's playful and paradoxical tone is, unsurprisingly, not taken up by the Middle English author, who does not have his Ywain make this offer.[97]

In the conversation with Lunete, Yvain identifies himself to her and promises his help, as does Ywain in the Middle English version, which adds the characteristic and telling self-characterization 'trew':

---

[95] Hunt, 'The Art of *Iarlles y Ffynnawn*', p. 113. Compare also Reck, *The Aesthetics*, p. 90: 'Throughout the second part of the tale Owein is shown to be reluctant to promise chivalric help in words but nevertheless willing to assist the weak and oppressed in deeds'. Thomson, '*Owain: Chwedl Iarlles y Ffynnon*', p. 165, similarly observes that Owein repays the widowed countess 'without making any promise and without even declaring his intention' and that he later 'does not reveal himself [to Lunet] or make any promise'.

[96] I wish to thank Regine Reck for pointing out to me the importance of this scene. Hunt, *Chrétien de Troyes*, p. 74, takes the underlying message of this passage seriously and observes that it establishes 'the principle of reciprocity and gratitude' which is constitutive for Yvain's restoration. He also argues that Yvain's 'exemplariness' is already re-established after the successful defence of the Dame de Noroison and that the introduction of the lion 'serves the *elaboration* of the chivalric ideal, pursued, not in respect of a personal relationship, but as a public demonstration in which the hero is cast, not in the role of lover, but of ruler'. In this context it is interesting to remember that three of the later manuscripts of *Owein* 'do not contain any of those episodes of the story in which the lion plays a part, ... except for that of the Du Traws' (Thomson, O, p. x); compare also Reck, 'Owain' (forthcoming).

[97] Compare YG 1819–32.

> 'Tant que je vive, n'i morroiz!
> Demain atandre me porroiz
> Apareillié lonc ma puissance,
> De metre an vostre delivrance
> Mon cors, si con je le doi feire.' (Y 3723–7)

('You'll not die so long as I'm alive! Tomorrow you may expect me prepared to the best of my ability to commit myself to your deliverance, as is my duty.' [YE 331])

> 'Als I am trew knyght,
> I sal be redy forto fyght
> To-morn with þam al thre,
> Leman, for þe luf of þe ...' (YG 2189–92)

Similarly, Yvain offers to fight with the giant, in *Ywain and Gawain* with the addition that Ywain does so for Gawain's sake, highlighting his bonds with him and his own reliability and fidelity:[98]

> 'Je m'an metroie volantiers
> An l'avlanture et el peril,
> Se li jaianz et vostre fil
> Venoient demain a tel ore,
> Que n'i face trop grant demore...' (Y 3944–8)

('I'd happily undertake the adventure with its perils if the giant and your sons came tomorrow early enough for me not to have to wait too long for them...' [YE 334])

> 'Syr', he sayd, 'for Gawayn sake
> Þis batayl wil I undertake
> Forto fyght with þe geant;
> And þat opon swilk a covenant,
> Yif he cum at swilk a time,
> So þat we may fight by prime.' (YG 2299–304)

But to come back now to Owein's silence and its possible meaning, in a convincing reading of the narrative Reck concludes that:

---

[98] Both Yvain and Ywain offer their help in the two episodes that have no equivalent in *Owein*, namely to the messenger of the younger sister (YE 349–50; YG 2923–30), and to the oppressed maidens in the Pesme Aventure (YE 351–2 and 353; YG 3003–4 and 3068–71).

[t]he second part of the tale then seems to illustrate how Owein learns to be more thoughtful about what he says and promises and that in certain situations, it is best not to talk at all but to act. ... [T]he characters in the Welsh tale of *Owein* clearly respond to and learn from their own actions and the effect which they have upon others. Therefore, it is possible to imagine Owein maturing within the tale and learning to be more prudent with promises.[99]

Reck furthermore draws attention to similar implicit learning processes presented in native Welsh tales, the most obvious example perhaps being Pwyll in the first branch of the *Four Branches*.[100]

Owein's learning process is first of all an individual one, but may reflect the norms and expectations of a society that places great emphasis on in-group reliability and fidelity, along the lines of Fulton's interpretation of the possible historical and social dimension of the narrative: 'the Welsh tales [i.e. *Owein* and *Gereint*] demonstrate the duties and responsibilities of the contemporary nobility, the *uchelwyr*, part of a hierarchy of lordship with ultimate authority residing in an Arthur-like prince or regional chieftain', and thus represent 'discourses of *uchelwyr* loyalty and service'.[101]

Critical responses to *Ywain and Gawain* would appear to agree on the individual and social dimensions of its message, which is intimately linked to the concept of *trowth* (loyalty, constancy). Hunt, for instance, describes it as a 'poem which commends true chivalry and identifies it with the possession of *trowthe*: reliability in keeping one's word'.[102] It

---

[99] Reck, *The Aesthetics*, pp. 92 and 96.
[100] Reck, *The Aesthetics*, pp. 92–4; see also C. E. Byfield, 'Character and Conflict in the Four Branches of the Mabinogi', *Bulletin of the Board of Celtic Studies* 40 (1993), 51–73 (p. 55), who says that Pwyll gains 'both a measure of circumspection and a recognition of the consequences of his words and actions'. For further examples of similar learning processes, see C. McKenna, 'Learning Lordship: The Education of Manawydan', in *Ildánach, Ildírech. A Festschrift for Proinsias Mac Cana*, ed. J. Carey, J. T. Koch, P.-Y. Lambert (Andover and Aberystwyth, 1999), pp. 101–20; C. McKenna, 'Revising Math: Kingship in the Fourth Branch of the Mabinogi', *Cambrian Medieval Celtic Studies*, 46 (2003), 95–117; H. Fulton, 'The Mabinogi and the Education of Princes in Medieval Wales', in *Medieval Celtic Literature and Society*, ed. H. Fulton (Dublin and Portland, 2005), pp. 230–47.
[101] Fulton, 'Individual and Society', pp. 48–9. See also p. 45: 'The Welsh Arthur [in *Owein* and *Gereint*] is constructed as a native prince, modelled on the rulers of the three main Welsh provinces, who supports a warband of nobles and functions as the overlord of a local area. His relationship with his men corresponds to that between a Welsh prince and his *teulu*, based on traditional kin-group loyalties.'
[102] Hunt, 'Beginnings, Middles, and Ends', p. 92, and see also pp. 101 and 110: 'the central action of the hero is ... his negligence in forgetting the term set by Alundyne which is an offence against the poet's ideal of knightly *trowthe*'; 'the love element is entirely subordinated to the theme of chivalric *trowthe*, in which the keeping of

is perhaps appropriate at this point to quote Hamilton's juxtaposition of Chrétien's focus on love with the Middle English author's on *trowth*:

> The switch in concern from love to *trowth* is at the core of the English poem. Of particular importance in both passages [in the poems' prologues[103]] is the stress placed on trustworthiness in word. For Chrétien, a central problem is that false lovers may feign truth in speech. The English author instead concerns himself with truth in all human relationships. ... Contemporary hypocrisy in love is only a subset of a general falseness: 'for trowth and luf es al bylaft' ([YG] 35).[104]

According to Hamilton, the English author's 'major concern certainly lies in the growth of his hero Ywain', who from the beginning knows 'the power of an oath and the shame which will result from breaking it; he learns the meaning of these things anew from personal experience'.[105] Sif Rikhardsdottir would concur with this reading of the poem's underlying concerns, but takes a more radical position with regard to the construction of its characters:

> In the English text the focus has thus shifted from the psychological maturing of the protagonist (needed for him to become worthy of Love and of the reputation as 'the Knight with Lion'), to the narratorial depiction

---

one's word is all-important. The coordination of love and chivalry is not made to appear problematic. Ywain's mistake in the amatory sphere is merely a symptom of his chivalric immaturity'. Barnes, *Counsel and Strategy*, p. 41, draws attention to embedded thematic relations between *Ywain* and *Ywain and Gawain*: 'this "no-frills" English re-telling of Yvain throws into relief the motif, embedded in the infrastructure of Chrétien's narrative, of conflict and accord. ... the unresolved "courtly dilemma" of *Yvain* becomes, instead, a story of broken *trawþe*, rehabilitation, and reconciliation, achieved through *red* as both "counsel" and "remedy"'.

[103] Compare Y 24–8 and YG 33–6.
[104] Hamilton, 'The Breaking of the Troth', pp. 113–14, who furthermore relates the importance of truthfulness in word to its being an 'integral part of a feudal society' (p. 114): 'Community order depends upon men who fulfil their oaths of fealty to their lord and lords who support and protects their retainers as they promised. Faithlessness in word eats away such a society at its roots.' For significant problems regarding the historical contextualization of *Owein* in its transmission, see Lloyd-Morgan, 'Migrating Narratives', p. 139: 'It is hard to believe that in the mid-fourteenth century, when *Geraint*, *Owain*, and *Peredur* were set down in the White Book, Rhydderch and his circle would read these narratives in the same way as those who had originally received them. Major changes had occurred in Welsh life since the Edwardian conquest of 1282, and Rhydderch himself, as a deputy justiciar, belonged to the new world of compromise and collaboration with the English crown, while still being immersed in traditional Welsh learning and culture.'
[105] Hamilton, 'The Breaking of the Troth', p. 124; see also p. 128 for a summary of Ywain's learning experience: 'he never aims at self-aggrandisement. He instead learns to bear the responsibilities of an honorable man in the relationships given him.'

of the social obligations of giving one's word. The characters do not signify in themselves, but function as vessels of potential meaning that assume significance as the reader proceeds through the narrative.[106]

The social value that motivates keeping one's word is *trowth*. The general critical emphasis on *trowth* can usefully be complemented by taking into account the importance of the concept of *hende* (having the approved courtly or knightly qualities). As already mentioned, Bollard convincingly shows that this word, and the contexts and collocations in which it is used, establish in the poem a lexical and thematic concern with 'courtesy' as one of the 'ideals toward which the hero is striving'.[107] The Middle English Ywain not only gives promises, but also keeps them, and this 'dramatic' revelation of meaning, to use Finlayson's characterization again,[108] together with a lexical flagging of values and qualities (*trowth*, *hende*), makes the second part of *Ywain and Gawain* conceptually less opaque than the second part of *Owein*. In both *Ywain and Gawain* and *Owein*, the protagonists are construed as undergoing learning processes as individuals (whatever their psychological reality and status) and as (re-)learning from personal experiences the proper meaning of social values which are, as it were, the glue of their societies.

Comparative and methodological conclusions

In the comparative perspective of my discussion, Chrétien's elaboration of the Matter of British Owein emerges as very special. The main differences between his *Yvain*, on the one side, and the Middle English *Ywain and Gawain* and the Middle Welsh *Owein*, on the other, reside in the form of presentation and in the concomitant literary and social values.[109] The form of *Yvain* is crucially defined by its narrator's voice and its author's

---

[106] Rikhardsdottir, *Medieval Translations*, p. 105. Compare also Fulton, 'Individual and Society', and see Rikhardsdottir, *Medieval Translations*, p. 104: 'Rather than focusing on the moral enlightenment of a single character, the author of *Ywain and Gawain* explores various social conceptualisations by stringing together recognisable semantic units, which by nature of their relation to each other and to the characters, assume signification. Ywain is moved through the narrative fabric in an effort to foreground the various principles he stands for within the social context of the literary realm. In fact, he does not progress as a character himself, instead his figure assumes signification through the narrative progress not as an individual, but as a semiotic representation.'
[107] Bollard, '*Hende Wordes*', p. 659.
[108] Finlayson, '*Ywain and Gawain*', p. 314.
[109] For the purpose of this conclusion, the literary level of form and values will be kept separate from a consideration of the cultural and historical contexts in which the English and Welsh authors of *Ywain and Gawain* and *Owein* wrote.

tone. Its narrator is present in about 500 lines of the poem,[110] and Chrétien, its author, has been seen as 'a dialectician who juxtaposes rather than harmonises, who is committed to no single belief, and who *experiments* in each of his romances with various combinations of contemporary debating points'.[111] In *Yvain*, voice and tone are self-reflective, exegetical and paradoxical. These games of argumentation and dialectics played by Chrétien with the audience of *Yvain* are absent from both *Ywain and Gawain* and *Owein*. Their tone is sober and straightforward. The two tales are furthermore connected by an interest in basic moral and social values, in *trowth* and *hende*, for example, and in the giving and keeping of promises respectively. Barron remarks on the English poem, contrasting it with Chrétien's, that it focuses on:

> the single standard of *trowth* (loyalty, constancy) governing conduct in love and marriage as well as fellowship between knights. Its celebration of that aspiration places the English text firmly in the romance mode; its expressive means are characteristic of the English genre, basic human values replacing the social codes celebrated and queried in Chrétien's *romans courtois*.[112]

However, Barron's focus on 'basic human values' arguably underestimates the extent to which the moral standards the poem celebrates are firmly embedded in contemporary societal concerns.

The final phrase of this quotation leads on to the vexed question of the three texts' genres.[113] Kelly helpfully summarizes key terms for an

---

[110] Hunt, Chrétien de Troyes, p. 89.

[111] Hunt, *Chrétien de Troyes*, p. 92. He comments on p. 20: 'Uppermost is the notion of game, which embraces the ingenuity of intertextual references, the humorous reslanting of commonplaces, joy in sophistical debate, and a constant under-current of self-mocking irony'. See also Hunt, 'Le Chevalier au Lion: *Yvain Lionheart*', in *A Companion to Chrétien de Troyes*, ed. N. J. Lacy and J. T. Grimbert, Arthurian Studies 63 (Cambridge, 2005), 156–68 (p. 158): 'for Chrétien's ludic, theatrical, interrogatory tone makes it clear that almost everything in *Yvain* is debatable, deliberately so, and that it is a deeply paradoxical work, which tests readers' intelligence and alertness at every turn'.

[112] W. R. J. Barron, 'Arthurian Romances', in C. Saunders (ed.), *A Companion to Romance: From Classical to Contemporary* (Malden, 2007), pp. 65–84 (p. 75).

[113] Another rewarding direction of comparative inquiry, which cannot be pursued here, concerns the texts' didactic potential, which may connect them with the Scandinavian adaptation of *Yvain*, *Ívens saga*, on which see, for example, C. Bornholdt, 'The Old Norse-Icelandic Transmission of Chrétien des Troyes's Romances: *Ívens saga*, *Erex saga*, *Parcevals saga* with *Valvens þáttr*', in *The Arthur of the North. The Arthurian Legend in the Norse and Rus' Realms*, ed. M. E. Kalinke (Cardiff, 2011), pp. 98–122 (esp. pp. 107–12). Another link could be with Barnes' 'discourses of counsel' and her notion of a 'shared seam of ideology in *roman courtois* and translated *riddarasaga*

understanding of the genre of Chrétien's *romans courtois*, his Arthurian courtly romances:

> ...*matiere* and *san* designate, respectively, the source material Chrétien chooses to rewrite and the meaning given to material chosen for its marvellous features. Applying his critical intelligence (*sans*) and artistic effort (*painne*) to rewriting, Chrétien realises a purpose (*antancion*) by moulding *matiere* and *san* into a coherent, intelligible whole. This whole, which he calls a *bele conjointure*, comes to be known as a *roman*, a word that for him seems to connote a coherent amalgam of marvellous adventures in a sophisticated narrative.[114]

Chrétien's *bele conjointure* results from his specific combination of *matière* and *san*, as well as his specific format of 'Arthurian (courtly) romance'; Busby, for example, suggests that 'Chrétien de Troyes was the first author to produce what we generally recognise as an Arthurian romance, indeed that it is he who determines our expectations of the genre'.[115] Chrétien's British *matière* is replicated, as we have seen, in *Ywain and Gawain*, and to some extent also in *Owein*; but the *san*, the meaning, of the English and Welsh texts is dramatically different, as well as the mode of rewriting the plot, the purpose and the resulting English or Welsh *bele conjointure*, the narrative whole. If, therefore, genre is understood as the outcome of a specific combination of all these various elements, neither *Ywain and Gawain* nor *Owein* is an 'Arthurian romance' in the same sense as is Chrétien's *Yvain*. *Ywain and Gawain* is conventionally classified as a 'Middle English Arthurian / chivalric romance', with the important modifier 'Middle English'. Lloyd-Morgan has shown that 'the romances' as a generic umbrella term for the Welsh Chrétien-related tales *Owein*, *Gereint* and *Peredur* is unsatisfactory, as is 'romance' for each of them on its own. She suggests calling *Peredur*, a Welsh narrative related in complex

---

which goes beyond the rituals and conceits of courtly love to the fundamental principles of ideal rulership and of chivalry: generosity, justice, the heeding of beneficent counsel': see G. Barnes, 'The 'discourse of counsel' and the 'translated' *riddarasögur*', in *Learning and Understanding in the Old Norse World. Essays in Honour of Margaret Clunies Ross*, ed. J. Quinn, K. Heslop, T. Willis (Turnhout, 2007), pp. 375–97 (pp. 396–7), and also Barnes, *Counsel and Strategy*, p. 41.

[114] Kelly, 'Chrétien de Troyes', p. 149.
[115] K. Busby, 'The Characters and the Setting', in *The Legacy of Chrétien de Troyes*, ed. N. J. Lacy, D. Kelly, K. Busby, 2 vols. (Amsterdam, 1987), I, 57–89 (p. 65). See similarly R. L. Krueger, 'Chrétien de Troyes and the Invention of Arthurian Courtly Fiction', in *A Companion to Arthurian Literature*, ed. H. Fulton (Chichester, 2009), pp. 160–74, and Faletra, *Wales*, p. 121, for Chrétien's pivotal role in the creation of this genre.

ways to Chrétien's *Perceval*,[116] 'a tale with romance elements', and this designation would, *mutatis mutandis*, fit *Owein* as well. We could therefore label it with good justification a 'Middle Welsh Arthurian tale', if we want to highlight its conceptual distance from Chrétien's romance. If, on the other hand, we want to highlight the similarities with Chrétien's *Yvain* with regard to *matière*, as well as the atmospheric distance to the Welsh Arthurian tales *Culhwch ac Olwen* and *Breudwyt Ronabwy* – which in ways very different from Chrétien approach the burlesque and the self-reflective – we may want to retain the label 'Middle Welsh Arthurian romance'.[117]

But whatever their generic designation, *Ywain and Gawain* and *Owein* have each, I hope, emerged from this discussion as an English respective Welsh narrative whole (a '*bele conjointure*') in its own literary right, rather than as a simplified translation of Chrétien's *Yvain*, in the case of *Ywain and Gawain*, or as a naive form of rewriting its *matière*, in the case of *Owein* (if we accept the proposition that Chrétien's romance is at least an important source for the latter).[118] Both are forms of a 'reception' of *Yvain*,[119] or of the Matter of British Owein. Both attest to the attraction of the Arthurian *matière* for, and its conceptual applicability to, different audiences and different literary, cultural and historical contexts: in England and Wales, where the stories of Arthur and Ywain / Owein were part of the country's own early history, but also in Iceland, and perhaps Norway (with *Ívens saga*) and Germany (with Hartmann's *Iwein*).

The final question to be considered concerns the value of the comparative literary approach exemplified here, which concentrates on an exploration of the semantic structures of two thematically similar texts. This would appear to offer a clearer understanding of the possibilities and

---

[116] Lloyd-Morgan, 'Medieval Welsh Tales or Romances?', p. 58; on *Peredur* compare Lloyd-Morgan, 'Migrating Narratives', pp. 131–5, and C. Lloyd-Morgan, 'Peredur', forthcoming in *Arthur in the Celtic Literatures*, ed. Lloyd-Morgan and Poppe.

[117] On *Culhwch ac Olwen* and *Breuddwyd Ronabwy* compare, for example, Lloyd-Morgan, 'Breuddwyd Rhonabwy', pp. 183–93, Padel, *Arthur*, pp. 14–26, and 94–9, McKenna, 'Breuddwyd Rhonabwy', and S. Rodway, 'Culhwch ac Olwen', forthcoming in *Arthur in the Celtic Literatures*, ed. Lloyd-Morgan and Poppe. Roberts, 'The Welsh Romance', p. 182, B. R. Roberts, *Studies on Middle Welsh Literature* (Lampeter, 1992), pp. 133–45, and Padel, *Arthur*, for example, still favour the designation 'romance'. Roberts, *Studies*, p. 143, suggests the qualification 'romances, albeit in a Welsh form of the genre', and Padel, *Arthur*, p. 79, points to structural similarities and conceptual differences between the Welsh texts and Chrétien's: 'Welsh romances [i.e., *Owein, Gereint* and *Peredur*] are thus structured as if written within the same new genre as Chrétien's romances, but omitting the primary purpose of that genre'.

[118] Lloyd-Morgan, 'Migrating Narratives', p. 131.

[119] Matthews, 'Translation and Ideology', p. 456, describes *Ywain and Gawain* as a 'form of reception of *Yvain*'.

constraints governing the shape of these reception projects,[120] provides a framework for constructing a metric for the purpose of 'defamiliarizing the genre of the Arthurian romance [as created by Chrétien] and allowing us the aesthetic distance to perceive more clearly its underlying tropes and assumptions',[121] as well as, more importantly perhaps, their own underlying tropes and assumptions and their own thematic pre-occupations. Furthermore, and this brings me back to the beginning of my essay and to Peter Clemoes' observation quoted there: to read the Middle English *Ywain and Gawain* alongside the Medieval Welsh *Owein* helps to make it possible to understand the literary appeal and flexibility of the British Arthurian legend.

---

[120] I here rephrase M. Edlich-Muth, *Malory and His European Contemporaries. Adapting Late Arthurian Romance Collections*, Arthurian Studies 81 (Cambridge, 2014), p. 6, who in her analysis of late Arthurian 'chronographies' applies a 'form of historicism based on intratextual comparison, in which an awareness of thematically comparable texts created for similar purposes and at a similar time acts as the primary basis for understanding the possibilities and constraints governing the shape of these compilation projects'.

[121] Faletra, *Wales*, p. 132, in the context of his comparison of the Welsh Arthurian tales with Chrétien's Arthurian romance.

III

EDWARD III'S ABANDONED ORDER OF THE ROUND TABLE REVISITED: POLITICAL ARTHURIANISM AFTER POITIERS*

Christopher Berard

After the capture of Jean II of France (r. 1350–64) at Poitiers on 19 September 1356, Edward III of England (r. 1327–77) found himself in a diplomatic quandary. How could he negotiate a peace treaty with (and demand a kingly ransom for) Jean II without undermining his claim to the throne of France?[1] With reference to the Florentine chronicle of Matteo Villani (d. 1363) and the chronicle of 'Anonymous of Canterbury' (1346–65), I shall demonstrate that Edward's solution was to fashion himself after King Arthur once again and that this course of action is the most probable cause of the historiographical conflation of Edward III's abandoned Order of the Round Table, which had been developed between January and November 1344, and the Order of the Garter, which was established in its place approximately five years later. According to the

---

* For their helpful comments and suggestions, I thank Professor Anthony Esolen, Anthony J. Fredette, Professor Dorothea Kullmann, Dr Rachel Lott and Nicholas Wheeler.

[1] See W. M. Ormrod, *Edward III* (New Haven and London, 2011), p. 385: 'The great challenge that faced Edward III between 1356 and 1360 was to balance his allies' and subjects' inflated expectations of such a settlement against the many practical impediments that still stood in his way ... Edward III tried to formulate a diplomatic strategy based on three firm principles. The first was to secure as large a ransom as possible for the release of David [II] Bruce [king of Scotland] and John [II] of Valois. The second was to effect, as quickly as possible, a territorial settlement in France that would allow England to take control, in full sovereignty, of its ancient rights and new conquests in Aquitaine, Ponthieu and Calais. The third, which proved the trickiest position to sustain, was to reserve Edward's own claims to the thrones of Scotland and France as a means both of guaranteeing the ransoms and of securing promises of further titles and territories to follow.' Also see C. Given-Wilson and F. Bériac, 'Edward III's Prisoners of War: The Battle of Poitiers and its Context', *EHR* 116.468 (2001), 802–33, who argue that Edward III was more interested in the political advantages than the financial gains that could be reaped by holding Jean II and other high noblemen of France as his captives.

Galfridian chronicle tradition, Arthur was a king of kings and France was one of the many realms under his yoke.[2] Edward, by likening himself to Arthur, conveyed that he too should be seen as suzerain of France and that Jean had become his vassal. Moreover, the outcome of the battle of Poitiers presented Edward III with an opportunity to revive his Arthurian image. The victory had been a decisive one in which his army had the opportunity and martial discipline to capture (rather than to kill) forty-two of the leading lords of France (including the king of France himself) and a further 1,933 men-at-arms.[3] If, as I have argued previously, the total-war tactics employed by the English at Crécy in 1346 were contrary to Arthurian ideals and made Arthur a problematic paradigm for Edward III (especially at the time of the institution of the Garter), the outcome of Poitiers made Arthur again an appealing model.[4]

The very idea that Edward III resumed Arthurian self-fashioning after Poitiers is contrary to the prevailing scholarly opinion, which rests uncomfortably on tentative conclusions drawn by Roger Sherman Loomis in 1939. In order to demonstrate the significance of my new findings, I shall begin by explaining the state of scholarship on the matter. Loomis held that Edward ceased explicitly likening himself to Arthur once he instituted the Order of the Garter (1348–9); he was also of the opinion that there was a 'marked decline in the prestige of things Arthurian at the English court and in the metropolis between 1350 and the accession of the Tudors'.[5] He did not hazard an explanation either for Edward's change of plans or for the putative decline in the prestige of Arthurian works. He did, however, justify the latter by commenting that 'Gower, Chaucer, and their disciples felt no attraction to the [Arthurian] cycle, and Chaucer at least evinces some contempt for it.'[6] This is yet another bold and unqualified claim.

---

[2] See, for example, *The Brut or the Chronicles of England*, ed. F. W. D. Brie, EETS OS 131 and 136, 2 vols. (London, 1906–8), I, 78–80.

[3] See Given-Wilson and Bériac, 'Edward III's Prisoners of War', pp. 803–8.

[4] See C. Berard, 'Edward III's Abandoned Order of the Round Table', *Arthurian Literature* 29 (2012), 1–40.

[5] R. S. Loomis, 'Chivalric and Dramatic Imitations of Arthurian Romance', in *Medieval Studies in Memory of A. Kingsley Porter*, ed. W. R. W. Koehler, 2 vols. (Cambridge, MA, 1939), I, 79–97 (p. 81). Also see C. Dean, *Arthur of England: English Attitudes to King Arthur and the Knights of the Round Table in the Middle Ages and the Renaissance* (Toronto, 1987), p. 129, and D. Carlson, 'King Arthur and Court Poems for the Birth of Arthur Tudor in 1486', *Humanistica Lovaniensia* 36 (1987), 147–83 (pp. 164–5).

[6] Loomis, 'Chivalric and Dramatic Imitations', p. 81. For a detailed study of the two poets' respective attitudes towards Arthurian literature, see E. D. Kennedy, 'Gower, Chaucer, and French Prose Arthurian Romance', *Mediaevalia* 16 (1993), 55–87. Also see D. Brewer, 'Chaucer and Chrétien and Arthurian Romance', in *Chaucer and*

Now even if, for the sake of argument, we were to take for granted Loomis' remarks about the two poets, the choice of Chaucer and Gower as bellwethers of Arthurian interest in the critical third quarter of the fourteenth century remains problematic. These poets' literary bloom largely dates from the final quarter of the century. Moreover, if we infer from the paucity of Arthurian content in Chaucer and Gower's surviving writings that they were not enthralled with things Arthurian, of what relevance is this to the question of the reception of the Matter of Britain more broadly speaking in later fourteenth-century England? In point of fact, Chaucer makes passing allusions to Arthurian characters in *The Canterbury Tales* which suggest that he was not unfamiliar with Arthurian tales and that he expected some of his audience to catch his references.[7] In the Tale of Sir Thopas, Chaucer, the pilgrim-narrator, states that 'Men speken of romances of prys' (7.897).[8] What romances does he mean? The pilgrim-author proceeds to list three eponymous heroes from the Matter of England: 'Horn child' (*King Horn*), 'Beves' (*Bevis of Hampton*) and 'sir Gy' (*Guy of Warwick*); next, he names an eponymous hero from an Arthurian romance, 'sir Lybeux' (*Lybeaus Desconus*) (7.898–900). Shortly thereafter he draws a comparison between Sir Thopas and 'the knight sire Percyvell' (7.916). When it comes to the Arthurian names, Chaucer may well have been directly referencing the Middle English romances *Lybeaus Desconus* and *Sir Perceval of Galles*, both of which are thought to date from the mid-to-late fourteenth century.

Another way that Loomis sought to substantiate his claim that Arthurian interest was waning after 1350 was by making a point of the fact that he could not find concrete evidence that a round table festival took place

---

Middle English Studies in Honor of Rossell Hope Robbins, ed. B. Rowland (London, 1974), pp. 255–9.

[7] Kennedy has advanced this line of reasoning. See his 'Gower, Chaucer and French Prose Arthurian Romance', p. 56: 'The brevity of Chaucer's and Gower's allusions to the Arthurian characters, like the brevity of allusions in *Beowulf*, further suggests that the works in which the characters appear would have been as familiar to many at court as some of the biblical, theological, and rhetorical works to which they also alluded.'

[8] All quotations from Chaucer are from *The Riverside Chaucer*, ed. Larry D. Benson, 3rd edn (Boston, 1987). 'Sir Thopas' is a deliberately lacklustre rhyming romance, a parody of its ilk, and the Host puts a stop to the tale, remarking that the poet's 'drasty rymyng is nat worth a toord' (7.930). If we infer that Chaucer is deriding Middle English Arthurian romances such as *Lybeaus Desconus* and *Sir Percyvell of Galles*, then, by the same reasoning, Chaucer was equally contemptuous of the Matter of England. Indeed, he seems to have been dismissive of romances more broadly speaking, with the exception of those set in antiquity (as typified by 'The Knight's Tale').

in England after 1345.[9] He did not claim to have made an exhaustive search and his tentative statement is by no means definitive: the crucial accounts of the Great Wardrobe covering the period between January 1349 and 1361 have been lost.[10] If any round tables were held during these years, the records of the Great Wardrobe would almost certainly have documented them. Loomis did, however, come across one possible exception to his statement. The Issue Roll of the Exchequer for Michaelmas, 1356 (30 Edward III),[11] preserves an entry dated 18 December, revealing that 'a "Round Table", made of oak, was constructed at Windsor some time before December 1356, in which year the Prior of Merton was paid £26 13*s*. 4*d*. in full satisfaction of money due for fifty-two oaks, taken from his woods near Reading, for the Round Table at Windsor.'[12] Loomis dismissed this record on the grounds that it was an outstanding debt from the 1340s. He might be correct. The Crown was notoriously slow in payments, and it is possible that the entry concerns a debt incurred

---

[9] Loomis, 'Chivalric and Dramatic Imitations', p. 81: 'The royal tailor's accounts show that in 1345 a Round Table feast was held there [Windsor], and it was probably about this time that fifty-two oaks were cut in the woods near Reading to furnish the building at Windsor. This is the last festival called a Round Table in medieval England of which I have found record.' Juliet Vale has demonstrated that the royal tailor accounts to which Loomis refers were mislabelled and in actuality reflect the expenses of 1344, specifically the Windsor Round Table of 19–22 January 1344, at which Edward took an oath to restore the Order of the Round Table to the same 'manner and standing' as that of King Arthur. Hence Loomis did not find record of a round table held in England subsequent to the well-known Windsor Round Table of 1344. See J. Vale, *Edward III and Chivalry: Chivalric Society and its Context, 1270–1350* (Woodbridge, 1982), p. 67. Also see D'A. J. D. Boulton, *The Knights of the Crown: The Monarchical Orders of Knighthood in Later Medieval Europe, 1325–1520* (Woodbridge, 2000), p. 111, and Adam Murimuth, *Continuatio Chronicarum*, ed. E. M. Thompson, RS 93 (London, 1889), 155–6 and 231–2.

[10] On this matter, see N. H. Nicolas, 'Observations on the Institution of the Most Noble Order of the Garter', *Archaeologia: or, Miscellaneous Tracts relating to Antiquity Published by the Society of Antiquaries of London* 31 (1846), 1–163 (p. 134).

[11] For a transcription and translation of 'Issue Roll, Michaelmas 30 Edward III, m. 23, PRO E403/378', see 'Appendix C. Building accounts for the House of the Round Table, 6. The Prior of Merton's oaks, 1356' in J. Munby, R. Barber and R. Brown, *Edward III's Round Table at Windsor* (Woodbridge, 2007), pp. 236–7. Also see 'Issue Roll, Michaelmas, 30 Edward III', in *Issues of the Exchequer being a collection of payments made out of His Majesty's revenue from King Henry II to King Henry VI. Inclusive*, ed. and trans. Frederick Devon (London, 1837), p. 164, and W. St John Hope, *Windsor Castle, an Architectural History*, 2 vols. (London, 1913), I, 118 and 127 n. 45. St John Hope understands the concluding statement in the entry to mean that the round table, upon its abandonment, had been sent to Westminster for the king's works there (p. 118).

[12] Nicolas, 'Observations', p. 107.

twelve years earlier.[13] But it is also possible that this record is the first indication of a post-Poitiers Arthurian revival at the English court. I shall return to this possibility below.

In addition to not knowing whether a round table festival took place in England (or more specifically at Windsor) between Edward III's initial announcement of his plans to re-establish the Order of the Round Table on 22 January 1344 and the Garter feast of 23 April 1358, we do not know the state of completion of Edward's *domus tabule rotunde* (House of the Round Table), a massive round structure two hundred feet in diameter that once stood in the Upper Ward of Windsor Castle. Contemporary fourteenth-century building accounts and the discovery in August 2006 of the structure's outer wall line confirm that the structure did exist. We know that work began on it in February 1344 and that the project was halted in November of the same year.[14] Julian Munby, a leading member of the 2006 excavation team and an expert on the construction records of the *domus tabule rotunde*, has called attention to the fact that the walls of the structure had been covered with tile; he has further observed that '[s]ince doors had been made for the building, it may actually have been completed as a shell, even if not fully fitted out'.[15] The structure may have been an open-air stadium with a lean-to roof along the perimeter providing a thin canopy for spectators.[16] Munby allows for the possibility that the 'shell' of the *domus tabule rotunde* was used 'as late as 1358 for the St George's day events of that year'; he suspects that William of Wykeham (*c.* 1324–1404) proceeded to demolish the structure in or shortly after 1359 in order to make room for new works,[17] but no record of the structure's demolition has come to light.[18] Thus it appears that Edward established the Order of the Garter with the Round Table both literally and figuratively standing in the background at Windsor. If this was the case, then the Knights of the Garter possibly made use of the *domus tabule rotunde* from time to time during their Garter festivities.

---

[13] I thank Professor W. Mark Ormrod for his expert opinion on this matter.

[14] See J. Munby, 'The Round Table Building: The Windsor Building Accounts', in Munby, Barber and Brown, *Edward III's Round Table*, pp. 44–52 (p. 45).

[15] Munby, 'Round Table Building', p. 52.

[16] Munby, 'Round Table Building', pp. 51–2.

[17] See J. Munby, 'Carpentry Work for Edward III at Windsor Castle', in *St George's Chapel Windsor in the Fourteenth Century*, ed. N. Saul (Woodbridge, 2005), pp. 225–37 (p. 228). Richard Barber has embraced Munby's theory: see his 'Why did Edward III hold the Round Table? The political background', in Munby, Barber and Brown, *Edward III's Round Table*, pp. 77–83 (p. 82).

[18] See S. Brindle and S. Priestley, 'Edward III's Building Campaigns at Windsor and the Employment of Masons, 1346–1377', in *St George's Chapel Windsor*, ed. Saul, pp. 203–23 (p. 206).

The looming presence of the *domus tabule rotunde* at Windsor might also account in part for the numerous round table / Garter conflations that appear in chronicles beginning in the late 1350s.

Notwithstanding, Loomis had valid grounds for concluding that Edward III, when instituting the Order of the Garter, avoided formally linking it with Arthur's fellowship or giving it 'Arthurian coloring'.[19] There are no references to King Arthur or his Fellowship of the Round Table in the Statutes of the Garter. Admittedly the earliest surviving redaction dates from 22 April 1415.[20] One could speculate that there were Arthurian references in an earlier, lost version. Yet there is no clear reason why this element would have been subsequently eliminated. One might also conclude, as Noël Denholm-Young has done, that the Garter, with its own mystique and unique visual imagery, supplanted the planned renewal of the Order of the Round Table and that Garter festivals 'killed the Round Table in England'.[21]

The Garter supersession hypothesis has not gone wholly unchallenged. Juliet Vale agrees with Loomis that when it came to establishing the Order of the Garter, Edward III 'chose to abandon formal links with Arthur's Round Table', but she is less comfortable with Denholm-Young's idea that Garter pageantry supplanted Arthurian pageantry. Vale has called attention to the aforementioned round table / Garter conflations and, on these grounds, she allows for the possibility that 'the secular and informal aspects of the Garter celebrations may have had an Arthurian theme'.[22] Francis Ingledew, also referencing the round table / Garter conflations in fourteenth-century historical writing, believes that the Order of the Garter was 'saturated' with Arthurian symbolism from its inception and that

---

[19] This point has also been made by M. Prestwich, *Armies and Warfare in the Middle Ages: the English Experience* (New Haven and London, 1996), p. 228. Also see Ormrod, *Edward III*, p. 307: 'The visual imagery of the Order of the Garter included no direct allusions to Arthur'.

[20] See L. Jefferson, 'MS Arundel 48 and the Earliest Statutes of the Order of the Garter', *EHR* 109 (1994), 356–85. Also see Boulton, *Knights of the Crown*, p. 101: 'Evidence for the history of the Order of the Garter in the fourteenth century is extremely scanty. Because of the loss of its official records in or shortly before 1416, historians have been obliged to piece together its history under its first three "Sovereigns" on the less than satisfactory basis of a handful of chronicle accounts, occasional references in the financial records of the royal household, and three Latin redactions of the statutes which seem to have been current before 1416.'

[21] N. Denholm-Young, 'The Tournament in the Thirteenth Century', in *Collected Papers of N. Denholm-Young: Cultural, Textual and Biographical Essays on Medieval Topics* (Cardiff, 1969), pp. 93–120 (p. 119 n. 1).

[22] See J. Vale, 'Arthur in English Society', in *The Arthur of the English: The Arthurian Legend in Medieval English Life and Literature*, ed. W. R. J. Barron (Cardiff, 1999), pp. 185–96 (pp. 193–4).

contemporaries understood the Order of the Garter to be the 'Edwardian Round Table by another name'.[23] In short, the precise nature of the relationship between Edward III's planned Order of the Round Table and the actualized Order of the Garter remains a mystery and has been a heavily trodden field of speculation and contention.

As far as I am aware, all scholars concerned with Edward III's Arthurian activities and the cult of Arthur in fourteenth-century England have missed Matteo Villani's and Anonymous of Canterbury's entries on the St George's Day Garter celebration of 1358.[24] Both sources are almost contemporary with the event. Matteo Villani continued the *Cronica Universale* of his better-known brother Giovanni (d. 1348) until his own untimely death in 1363, which was also caused by plague.[25] He characterized the Windsor Garter feast of 1358 as 'una solenne festa di cavalieri della Tavola Ritonda' (a solemn feast of the Knights of the Round Table).[26] The chronicle of Anonymous of Canterbury covers events in England from 1346 to 1365; its author demonstrates detailed knowledge of the affairs of Canterbury and Rochester and also about the Anglo-French diplomacy of the period.[27] Anonymous of Canterbury referred to the St George's Day event as a 'solempne conuiuium ac etiam rotundam tabulam' (a solemn feast and also a round table).[28] These two accounts indicate that at least one round table was held in England after the establishment of the Order of the Garter, and, even more importantly, the round table happened in the context of a Garter festival. This finding undermines the idea of the Garter supersession theory and confirms Vale's

[23] F. Ingledew, Sir Gawain and the Green Knight *and the Order of the Garter* (Notre Dame, 2006), pp. 99 and 109.
[24] I first shared these findings in my 'Edward III's Abandoned Order', pp. 33–4.
[25] For a classic English-language analysis of the style and concerns of Matteo Villani's *Cronica*, see Louis Green, *Chronicle into History: An Essay on the Interpretation of History in Florentine Fourteenth-Century Chronicles* (Cambridge, 1972), pp. 44–85. Giovanni and Matteo were sons of an affluent Florentine merchant family. Matteo was a partner of the Buonaccorsi company until its bankruptcy in 1342. He served as its representative in Naples (1319–25), in Avignon (1333–5) and then again in Naples (1340–1). In 1337–8, he served Florence by helping to negotiate an alliance with Venice and Lombard states. See Cristian Bratu, 'Villani, Matteo', in *Encyclopedia of the Medieval Chronicle*, ed. Graeme Dunphy, 2 vols. (Leiden, 2010), II, 1479.
[26] Matteo Villani, *Cronica con la continuazione di Filippo Villani*, ed. G. Porta, 3 vols. (Parma, 2007), II, 182; translations are my own.
[27] The chronicler may have been a monk at Christ Church, Canterbury or Rochester or a secular clerk in the company of William Rede, who served as an archdeacon of Rochester (1359–63) and as a provost of Wingham College near Canterbury (1363–8) before becoming bishop of Chichester (r. 1368–85). See *Chronica Anonymi Cantuariensis: The Chronicle of Anonymous of Canterbury 1346–65*, ed. and trans. C. Scott Stokes and C. Given-Wilson (Oxford, 2008), pp. xxxix–xlvii.
[28] *Chronica Anonymi Cantuariensis*, pp. 42–3.

suspicion that an informal Arthurian element was behind at least one of the Garter celebrations. It also opens up new questions. Was the Windsor Round Table of 23 April 1358 a singular Arthurian revival or merely the only surviving documented instance of a larger trend? Were round tables regular occurrences at Garter festivals prior to and / or after the 1358 feast? The surviving historical records do not permit us to resolve these questions conclusively. It is prudent, therefore, to focus attention on determining the character and function of the 1358 Windsor Round Table in its historical moment.

The political symbolism of King Arthur in the Anglo-French peace negotiations of 1358

The more detailed entries on the St George's Day Garter feast of 1358, namely those by Anonymous of Canterbury and Matteo Villani, as well as by Jean le Bel and Henry Knighton, indicate that the event had political significance in the context of the Anglo-French peace negotiations resulting in the First Treaty of London, which the two kings signed a fortnight after the feast on 8 May 1358. The primary sources disagree as to the feast's function in relation to the treaty. Some state that Edward III used the St George's Day Round Table to celebrate a nearly finalized Anglo-French peace while others suggest that the king used it to expedite the peacemaking process.[29] Before comparing the sources, we must take into account what is known about the status of Anglo-French negotiations leading up to Garter feast.

The exact state of affairs on 23 April 1358 is not entirely clear. Only a single draft copy of the First Treaty of London survives (London, British Library, Cotton Caligula D iii, n. 84–8), and we do not know at what stage in the negotiation process it was written.[30] In this document, titled 'Le trattié et la parlaunce de la paix par entre Nostre Sire le Roi et la partie de Ffrance' (The treaty and peace agreement between our lord, the king, and the French party), the English Crown avoids explicitly recognizing Jean of Valois as king of France. Instead Jean is consistently referred to

---

[29] Sumption and Ormrod favour the latter scenario. See J. Sumption, *The Hundred Years War, Volume II: Trial by Fire* (London, 1999), pp. 309–10 (p. 326), and Ormrod, *Edward III*, p. 394.

[30] For an edition, see 'Premier traité de Londres. Minute ou projet', in R. Delachenal, *Histoire de Charles V, vol. 2: 1358–1364* (Paris, 1909), pp. 402–11. Also see 'The First Treaty of London', in *The Wars of Edward III: Sources and Interpretations*, ed. and intro. C. J. Rogers (Woodbridge, 1999), pp. 170–1.

as 'l'adversaire de Ffrance' (the adversary of France).[31] But the document stipulates that 'le dit adversaire [rendra et baillera] pour lui et pour toutes ses heirs rois de Ffrance' (the said adversary [will render and grant] on his own behalf and on behalf of all of his heirs, the kings of France) rights and privileges to 'nostre seigneur le roi et à ses heirs rois d'Engleterre' (our lord, the king, and to his heirs, kings of England).[32] This is a tacit recognition of Jean of Valois as king of France, and presumably Edward would have recognized Jean's sovereign status once the treaty took effect.[33]

According to the *Chronique des règnes de Jean II et de Charles V*, on 27 January 1358 messengers dispatched by King Jean II arrived in Paris in order to inform his son and regent Charles (1338–80) that a treaty of accord had been made in England between the kings of France and England.[34] It is unclear how close this January accord was to the final terms of the treaty, for negotiations were to continue right until the document was signed. In February 1358, Edward III placed what appears to have been the January version of the accord before Parliament.[35] The House of Commons knew that the Pope was desirous of an Anglo-French peace and wanted to use the proposed accord as leverage to obtain papal concessions regarding unrelated grievances with the Curia; it demanded that Edward send a solemn embassy to Avignon to resolve the issues before it would grant its approval to the treaty.[36] The Estates-General, which had also met in February and considered the draft, was more concerned with overcoming the long-standing corruption and with rectifying the mismanagement of the French government than with obtaining the king's release.[37] In spite of these setbacks, Jean II remained optimistic that a settlement would be reached and that his kingdom would provide the required funds and hostages for his release. We have record of an outlay by him (dated 24 March 1358) for a great skin of parchment and for ink 'à escrire le traictié du Roy et du Roy d'Angleterre' (to write the treaty of the king and of the king of England).[38] We can surmise that in April of 1358, Edward III, Jean II, the English Parliament

---

[31] See, for example, 'Premier traité de Londres', p. 403.
[32] 'Premier traité de Londres', p. 405.
[33] The First Treaty of London asks a lot of Jean II and a lot for him. For its stipulations, see 'First Treaty of London', p. 170; John Le Patourel, 'The Treaty of Brétigny, 1360', *Transactions of the Royal Historical Society* Fifth Series 10 (1960), 19–39 (p. 24).
[34] See *Chronique des règnes de Jean II et de Charles V: les grandes chroniques de France*, ed. R. Delachenal, 3 vols. (Paris, 1910–20), I, 143–4.
[35] Ormrod, *Edward III*, p. 393; Delachenal, *Histoire de Charles V*, p. 76.
[36] Sumption, *Trial by Fire*, pp. 309–10.
[37] Sumption, *Trial by Fire*, p. 320.
[38] See the record of the expenses of Jean II in England from 25 December 1358 to 1 July 1359 transcribed in 'Notes et documents relatifs à Jean, roi de France, et à sa

and the French Estates-General all seem to have understood the basic terms of the peace: Edward III would be giving at least tacit recognition to his adversary's sovereign status in exchange for a hefty ransom and substantial allods in France.

The treaty seems to have been acceptable to Edward III, provided he was confident that the terms of the agreement would be kept in good faith.[39] But it was not at all clear that the agreement would – or even could – be honoured. France was suffering depredations from English and Navarrese military companies. In late February and March there was a formidable popular uprising in Paris, and public order was at an all-time low. Jean II's authority in France was slipping away, and the political capital of Edward III's prized captive was depreciating rapidly.[40] Jean II was becoming a king of France in name only, and it was precisely this, Jean's kingly title, that Edward could not readily acknowledge. In the spring of 1358, Jean of Valois was barely the *de facto* king of France, and Edward could not recognize him as the *de jure* king. Edward nevertheless sought to garner as much ideological benefit as possible from his illustrious prisoner, and Arthurianism was a singularly appropriate means to achieve this end.

In the context of the peace negotiations of 1358 Arthurianism was multivalent, and this, I argue, was the true appeal of the figure of King Arthur to Edward III after Poitiers. I have observed three non-mutually exclusive messages behind the English king's use of Arthurian social display in this context. First, there was the interpersonal dynamic that existed between Edward III and Jean II. They shared a common interest in King Arthur, but were rivals for the mantle of *Arthurus redivivus*.[41] By hosting a round table event on St George's Day 1358, Edward seems to have been calling attention to their shared interest. The round table could be seen as a conciliatory nod honouring Jean II's fondness for Arthurian literature. Edward did, however, reserve pride of place for himself at the grand international event, and this conveyed that he – rather than Jean II –

---

captivité en Angleterre', ed. H. E. P. L. d'Orléans, duc d'Aumale, *Miscellanies of the Philobiblon Society* 2 (1855), 1–190 (p. 113).

[39] See C. J. Rogers, 'The Anglo-French Peace Negotiations of 1354–1360 Reconsidered', in *The Age of Edward III*, ed. J. S. Bothwell (York, 2001), pp. 193–213 (p. 201).

[40] See Sumption, *Trial by Fire*, p. 311.

[41] On the spirit of competition and pattern of reciprocal emulation that existed between Edward III and Jean II and how this is reflected in the institution of the Order of the Garter and the Company of the Star (*c.* 1344–52), see Y. Renouard, 'L'Ordre de la Jarretière et l'Ordre de l'Etoile: Etude sur la genèse des Ordres laics de Chevalerie et sur le développement progressif de leur caractère national', *Le Moyen Age* 55 (1949), 281–300.

was the true successor to Arthur.[42] Secondly, the event had significance in terms of domestic politics. As stated above, the imperial aspect of Arthur furnished the English king with an honourable precedent for receiving tribute from his defeated adversary. Edward could obtain a kingly ransom for Jean II without wholly sacrificing his own French royal pretensions, which had been the *raison d'être* for his 'just quarrel' in the first place. By evoking the imperial Arthur, Edward III may have been attempting to allay the concerns of his countrymen that he was 'selling out' his claim to France. Thirdly, the event had a special significance in terms of international relations. Edward's Arthurian self-fashioning implied that in the event of the proposed treaty collapsing, Edward III, like Arthur before him, had the strength of character (bravery, leadership ability and prowess), a righteous claim (based on Galfridian history and prophecy) and the means (political, military and financial) necessary to conquer France once and for all.

Edward, I argue, appreciated the full range and ambiguity of meaning that resumption of the Arthurian mantle entailed; its multivalence was ideal for his complex situation. Did Edward use Arthurian spectacle to call attention to Edward and Jean's shared culture? Was this social display a call for détente and for honest and faithful negotiation? Was Edward mocking Jean II's Arthurian pretensions and revelling in his personal victory over him? Was Edward using these festivities to communicate to an international audience that he had won important military victories in the past and would do so again if necessary? The answer to all of these questions is yes. Edward III aimed to appear magnanimous and intimidating. Arthurianism was the perfect idiom for the agenda and circumstance of the moment.

Edward III, from the hour that he learned of Jean II's capture at Poitiers, does not seem to have wasted any time in resuming his Arthurian mantle. Chandos Herald declares in his *Vie du Prince Noir* (1385) that after the Black Prince's triumphant procession through London with King Jean as his prisoner on 24 May 1357:

> Dauncier et chacier et voler,
> Faire grantz festes et juster,

[42] The Garter feast of 1358 offered Edward a platform to demonstrate that he had a stronger claim than Jean of Valois to the coveted mantle of *Arthurus redivivus*. In addition to his existing Arthurian credentials as a victorious *dux bellorum* and as a gracious captor, Edward, in the words of Michael Bennett, 'was clearly seeking to make Windsor the new Camelot'. See Bennett, 'Isabelle of France, Anglo-French Diplomacy and Cultural Exchange in the Late 1350s', in *The Age of Edward III*, ed. Bothwell, pp. 215–25 (p. 221).

Faisant [com] en regne d'Artus
L'espace de quatre ans ou plus.[43]
(There was dancing, hunting, hawking, feasting and jousting, as in the reign of Arthur, for the space of four years or more.)

Although Chandos Herald's remarks may seem rather generic, the arrival of Jean of Valois did begin, as Mark Ormrod has noted, 'one of the most sustained and purposeful demonstrations of royal magnificence witnessed in medieval England'.[44] It included jousts at Smithfield in September of 1357, attended by Edward III and the two captive kings, Jean II of France and David II of Scotland.[45] The payment to the Prior of Merton for fifty-two oaks may indicate that preparations for an Arthurian round table at Windsor were underway. From 1356 to 1358, Edward III aimed to intimidate both Jean II and the *de facto* government in France through conspicuous displays of his wealth and power, and thereby procure the best possible terms of peace.

Moreover, Arthurianism was a fitting means for Edward III to demonstrate his power as well as his magnanimity in victory because it catered to Jean's literary taste. Jean II's plans for his ill-fated Company of the Star bore resemblance to the code of the Round Table as represented in the Lancelot-Grail Cycle.[46] When in English captivity, Jean is known to have borrowed Arthurian romances. An account book of Isabelle, mother of Edward III, states that a certain 'John of Paris' came from the king of France to the Queen at Hertford on 10 December 1357 in order to return two volumes, of Lancelot and the 'Sang Réal' (possibly Sangreal, viz. Holy Grail), which Isabelle had lent to Jean II.[47] By hosting a round table, Edward was using Jean II's preferred idiom. The chronicler Jean le Bel, it should be noted, characterized Edward's Garter feast of 1358 as a cour-

---

[43] Chandos Herald, *La Vie du Prince Noir*, ed. D. B. Tyson (Tübingen, 1975), p. 189, ll. 1513–6. For the translation provided, see *Life of the Black Prince by the Herald of Sir John Chandos. Edited from the Manuscript in Worcester College, with linguistic and historical notes*, ed. and trans. M. K. Pope and E. C. Lodge (Oxford, 1910), p. 148.

[44] Ormrod, *Edward III*, p. 387.

[45] An account of this appears in *A Chronicle of London, from 1089 to 1483*, ed. N. H. Nicolas, (London, 1827), p. 63; also see *The Brut or the Chronicles of England*, ed. F. Brie, EETS OS 131 and 136, 2 vols. (London, 1906–8), II, 308, and *Chronica Johannis de Reading et Anonymi Cantuariensis, 1346–67*, ed. J. Tait (Manchester, 1914), pp. 129 and 272.

[46] See Berard, 'Edward III's Abandoned Order', pp. 28–33.

[47] See E. A. Bond, 'Notices of the Last Days of Isabella, Queen of Edward II, Drawn from an Account of the Expenses of her Household', *Archaeologia* 35 (1854), 453–69 (p. 468). For the suggestion that we interpret 'Sang Réal' as a misreading of 'sangreal', see R. Barber, 'What Was a Round Table?', in Munby, Barber and Brown, *Edward III's Round Table*, pp. 69–76 (pp. 75–6). Also see Berard, 'Edward III', p. 3 n. 10.

teous gesture designed to 'entertain and honour' Jean of Valois.[48] If the two kings went to the Windsor feast of 1358 having already more or less arrived at terms of peace, then it is possible that the Arthurian elements of the event were meant to build on this reconciliation. Matteo Villani's *Cronica* hints in this direction:

> I·rre Adoardo d'Inghilterra avendo fatta concordia, e lasciato di prigione i·rre Davit di Scozia suo cognato, si pensò di volere far pace co·rre di Francia, la quale avesse principale movimento dalla sua persona. E per fare questo, fece bandire in Francia, in Fiandra, in Brabante, e in Irlanda, e'n Allamagna, e in Iscozia e altri reami, una solenne festa di cavalieri della Tavola Ritonda alla San Giorgio d'aprile del detto anno; faccendo ogni maniera di gente sicura in suo reame, offerendo arme, cavalli, e arnesi a ogni cavaliere che alla festa venisse, e apresso le spese a·cchi fare no·lle potesse; e ancora a tutta gente d'arme per loro, e chi per loro servigi venisse, ogni cosa che loro bisognasse per loro vita, e per far pruove di loro cavallerie. Perché molta gente, udito il bando, si misse in assetto per esservi al tempo, chi per mostrare di sua virtù, chi per vedere. (II, 182)

> (King Edward of England, having made peace and released from prison his brother-in-law, King David of Scotland, decided he wanted to make peace with the king of France, which peace would be made on his own initiative. And to do this, he caused to be proclaimed in France, Flanders, Brabant, Ireland, Germany, Scotland and other realms a solemn feast of the Knights of the Round Table on the feast day of St George in April of said year. He gave assurances of security to every manner of man in his realm, offering arms, horses and riding equipment to every knight who would come to the feast and even the expenses of those who were unable to meet them, and offering all men of arms and those who came in their service everything that they needed for their sustenance and for making proof of their knighthood. And so many people, having heard the proclamation, sent word that they would be there at that time, some in order to demonstrate their virtue, others in order to watch.)

An entry in the Issue Rolls of the Exchequer confirms payment on 9 March 1358 to William Volaunt and four other heralds for proclaiming this tournament in the aforesaid lands.[49] Once again, the international character of this Garter feast must be born in mind. Edward was communicating his power over his 'adversary of France' to Europe's nobility at large.[50] In a subsequent chapter Villani adds:

---

[48] See Jean le Bel, *Chronique* 94, ed. J. Viard and E. Déprez, 2 vols. (Paris, 1904–5), II, 239. All English translations provided for this source are from *The True Chronicles of Jean le Bel, 1290–1360*, trans. N. Bryant (Woodbridge, 2011); see p. 230.
[49] See 'Issue Roll, Michaelmas, 32 Edward III', in *Issues of the Exchequer*, p. 169.
[50] This point has been made by H. E. L. Collins, *The Order of the Garter, 1348–1461: Chivalry and Politics in Late Medieval England* (Oxford, 2000), p. 238.

A dì XIIII d' aprile, essendo bandita la gran festa che i·rre d'Inghilterra dovea fare alla San Giorgio, i·rre mandò inanzi a Guindisora, ove era prigione i·rre di Francia, e 'l figliuolo e altri baroni di Francia, messer Lionello suo figliuolo a dirli che i·rre suo padre volea venire a·ffare co·llui collezione. I· re di Francia i· ricevette a gran festa, e tennelo la mattina con seco a desinare; apresso mangiare i· re d'Inghilterra fu· llà, e i· re di Francia li si fece incontro, e ricevettonsi insieme con molta reverenzia, e dopo molta contesa di mettere inanzi, e onorare l'uno l'altro, i· rre di Francia lo prese di pari, e andarono a·bbere insieme con gran festa e allegrezza; di che uno ministriere festeggiando disse: 'Mala morte possa fare chi di voi sturba la pace'. I· re d'Inghilterra rispuose al motto che· ggià per lui no· rimarrebbe, e·cche coll' aiuto di Dio tra·lloro sarebbe buona pace; e invitò i·rre di Francia alla festa ch'avea ordinata alla San Giorgio, e i·rre di Francia accettò, e fece suo sforzo per potervi comparire magnificamente com' a· llui s'apartenea; dopo ciò i· rre d'Inghilterra preso il congio si tornò al suo ostiere. (II, 192–3)

(On the fourteenth day of April, after having announced the great feast that he was to hold on St George's Day, the king of England sent Sir Lionel, his son, to Windsor, where the king of France, his son and the other barons of France were imprisoned, in order to tell them that King Edward (his father) wished to come and have a meal with the king of France. The king of France received him (Sir Lionel) with great pleasure and kept him at table with them all morning. After eating the meal, the king of England was there, and the king of France came to meet him, and they received one another with much reverence, and after much contention about the initial matter, each one striving to put himself forward in honouring the other, then the king of France took his hand as an equal, and both men went drinking together with great joy and gladness; whereupon one of the ministers said with delight: 'May a wicked death take whichever one of you should disturb the peace.' The king of England responded to that word, saying that as for him there was nothing to add and that with the help of God there would be good peace between them, and he invited the king of France to the event that he had planned on the feast of St George, and the king of France accepted, wishing to appear magnanimous as befitted his station. After that the king of England took his leave and returned to his abode.)

Villani illustrates the posturing on the part of the two kings, but also encourages us to believe that they were on amiable terms – at least superficially – and has Edward express his shared desire for peace. The Florentine writer's remarks do support the idea that Edward intended the event to be pleasing to Jean II. According to Villani, the precise terms of peace had not yet been finalized by the time of the event.

In contrast to his account of the event, other contemporary sources are more obscure as to Edward's intentions for the feast. The chronicle of

John of Reading, a Benedictine monk and chronicler active at Westminster until 1368, offers us one such example. According to this monastic chronicle, Edward saw to it that the feast of St George the Martyr was celebrated in royal fashion, yet too sumptuously, 'tam pro amore militari quam proprio honore ac praesentia domini Johannis regis Franciae, aliorumque nobilium'.[51] The paratactic structure of this sentence is somewhat ambiguous. If one reads *praesentia* as a third, non-correlatively signalled object of 'pro', then purpose is implied: Edward saw to it that the feast of St George was celebrated in royal fashion 'as much for his love of martial splendour as for his own honour, and because of the presence of Lord John, king of France, and of the other nobles'. It was in this way that the author of the Middle English Prose *Brut* understood the passage. He wrote: '[t]he xxxiij. ȝere of his regne þe same King Edward at Wyndesore, as wel for loue of knyȝthood as for his owne worship, & at þe reuerence of þe King of Fraunce & oþer lordeȝ þat were þere at þat tyme, he held a wonder rial and costlow feest of sent Gorge, passyng eny þat was hold euere afore.'[52] The Middle English translator inserts 'at þe reuerence of' into his translation for clarity. If, however, one reads *praesentia* as an ablative of place, then John of Reading was communicating that Edward put on his great show in the face of King Jean and the other nobles in attendance. It is worth noting that the monk adds that the king of France was contemptuous of Edward's prodigality on this occasion.[53] John of Reading's account of the event permits one to conclude that Edward III was aiming to humble Jean of Valois, and Jean certainly seems to have had lingering animosity and was at least scornful of Edward's prodigality.[54]

Before pursuing the possibility that Edward incorporated Arthur into the Garter feast of 1358 to communicate his expanding *imperium* in France, let us consider more closely what our sources say about *when* the two kings arrived at terms of peace. Jean le Bel states that Edward and Jean had reached a settlement prior to the Garter feast, but their efforts were impeded by Étienne Marcel, Provost of the Merchants of Paris, who

---

[51] *Chronica Johannis de Reading*, p. 130.
[52] *Brut*, II, 308–9.
[53] See *Chronica Johannis de Reading*, p. 130: 'Quibus irridens, ipse rex Franciae nunquam tanta solempnia cum talliis absque auri et argenti solutione se audivisse ne vidisse testatur' (Mocking these things, the king of France declared that he had never heard nor seen so much solemnity with tallies without payment of gold and silver). Also see *A Chronicle of London*, pp. 63–4 and *Brut*, II, 309. Ormrod intepets this to mean that Jean was critical of Edward III for 'living off credit while dining from gold and silver plate' (*Edward III*, p. 389). Collins argues that Jean 'is more likely to have resented his role as a pawn in an English propaganda event than the actual expense of the celebrations' (*Order of the Garter*, pp. 238–9).
[54] This point has been made by Ormrod, *Edward III*, p. 389.

opposed giving the French Crown further financial support; Marcel had been conspiring with the third claimant to the throne of France, Carlos of Navarre.[55] Jean le Bel then asserts that it was during the Windsor feast that the kings of England and France finally reached a peace agreement:

> mais toutesfoys, oncques la paix ne fut parfaite jusques à la moitié de l'an mil CCC L VIII, que le noble roy d'Angleterre fist faire un trés noble feste au chastel de Vindessore. Et pour mielx festier et honnourer le roy Jehan, il fist venir dames et damoiselles, des plus belles et mielx habillées d'Angleterre, et jousta lui mesmes et ses III filz aprez en paremens semblables. A celle feste fut parfaitte la paix entre ces II roys, et baiserrent l'ung l'aultre par devant tout ceulx qui le pœurent et voulurent veoir, et jurerent et promirent tous deux de tenir la paix fermement, et qu'ilz seroient bons amis à tousjours, aydans et confortans l'ung l'autre encontre tous. Mais la maniere de la paix et les condicions ne sçavoit on encores communement, quant ce fut escript. Si m'en tairay jusques au point que on le sceut. (II, 240)

> (In any event, peace was not fully concluded until half way through the year 1358, when the noble King of England held a magnificent feast at Windsor Castle. To entertain and honour King John all the more, he invited ladies and damsels, the most beautiful and gorgeously attired in all England, and took part in the jousting himself, followed by his three sons, all in identical arms. It was at this feast that peace was made between the two kings. In the sight of all who wished and were able to see it, they exchanged kisses and promised and vowed to keep the peace securely, and to be good friends forever, giving help and support to each other against all foes. But the exact terms and conditions of the peace were still not generally known when these words were written; I'll say no more about them until they are. [229–30])

On the evidence of these lines, Edward III and Jean II seem to have hoped that a joint declaration of peace and good will on such a notable occasion would oblige the Estates General to muster the requisite funds and sureties. A letter from Jean II to his dear and faithful subjects, the *bourgeois* and the inhabitants of the town of Nîmes, dated 9 July, confirms the substance of Jean le Bel's entry. The king informs the citizens of Nîmes that

> le roy d'Angleterre a tenue une moult bele feste à la sainct George derrenier passé à Windonses, ou nous estans presenz; & la nous fist moult grant honnours; & y furent presentes les roynes, c'est assavoir les roynez Ysabel sa mere, la royne sa fame, la royne d'Escoce, fusent. Et illec nous fu donné bonne esperance par lui & par ces gens, de bonne paiz & accord sur le trai-

---

[55] See Jean le Bel, *Chroniques*, II, 254; *True Chronicles of Jean le Bel*, pp. 234–5.

ctié autre foiz accordé par nous conseaulx, d'une part & d'autre, & après delaié pour certaine chose touchant la cour de Roume, si comme autrefoiz avons mandé par dela par messatger sollempnel, & par lettres signeez de nostre main. Et après la feste, vint à nous le roy d'Angleterre à Windonses le mardi VIII. jour de May, & tant parlames & tractamez enssemblez que le merci Nostre Sire, nous fumez à bonne paiz & accord à l'anour de Dieu & de sancte eglise, & au proffit de noz royames & de toute chrestianeté; & en signe de paiz, nous entresbeasmez plusieurs foiz, & nous entredonnamez noz enneaux que nous avions en nouz doiz, & soupamez enssamblez moult amicablement; & sommes eslargis & venus à Londres ...[56]

(the king of England held a very grand feast on the most recent St George's Day at Windsor, where we were present; and he showed us great honour; and in attendance there were the queens: they were Queen Isabelle, his mother, the queen his wife, and the queen of Scotland. And at that place good hope was given to us by him and by these people, hope of good peace and accord on the treaty previously accorded by our counsellors on both sides, and after having been delayed on account of a certain matter touching the court of Rome, just as previously, we sent word there by solemn messenger and by letters signed by our hand. And after the feast, the king of England came to us at Windsor on Tuesday, the eighth day of May, and we spoke and negotiated together to such an extent that by the mercy of Our Lord we came to good peace and accord to the honour of God and of Holy Church and to the profit of our realms and of all Christendom and as a sign of peace we kissed one another several times and we exchanged our rings that we had on our fingers and we supped together very amicably; and we set out and came to London ...)

Thus, at the feast of St George, Edward III communicated to his subjects and to Jean II that he was ready to reach a settlement and that he would not wait until his envoys secured benefits from Rome. It must be stressed, though, that the absolute final terms of peace were not yet reached.[57] If the precise conditions of the peace had not been settled prior to the feast, then there is cause to infer that Edward, when designing his grand Arthurian spectacle, sought to intimidate Jean II into acceding to terms most favourable to the English king. By promising arms, horses and harnesses to all knights who were in need of them in order to participate in the feast, and by having such notables as the dukes of Brabant and Luxembourg

---

[56] A transcription of this letter is contained in Léon Ménard, *Histoire civile, ecclésiastique et littéraire de la ville de Nismes, avec des notes et les preuves*, 2 vols. (Paris, 1751), II, 204b.

[57] Also see the account of the Augustinian canon Henry Knighton in his chronicle of events from 1337 to 1396: *Knighton's Chronicle, 1337–1396*, ed. and trans. G. H. Martin (Oxford, 2008), pp. 158–61. Both Jean's letter and *Knighton's Chronicle* indicate that there were negotiations in May.

on his guest list, Edward showed that he could match Arthur's legendary magnificence and intimated, both to Jean II and to the Estates General of France, that if his conditions were not met he could and would muster a rather formidable alliance to conquer France once and for all.

Edward did not stop there. He assumed the role of Arthur. Furnishing us with one of the most detailed chronicle accounts of a medieval round table, Villani writes:

> Nella città di Londra era per tutto apparecchiato a ricevere i forestieri onoratamente, ciascuno secondo il grado suo. Quivi rinovellandosi l'antiche favole della Tavola Ritonda, furono fatti XXIIII cavalieri erranti, i quali seguendo i fallaci romanzi che della vecchia parlano, richiedieno, ed erano richiesti di giostra e battaglia per amore di donna. E intorno alla piazza erano levati incastellamenti di legname con panche da sedere, coperti di ricchi drapia a oro, e forniti di dietro di ricche spalliere, dove i·re e· lle reine e altre nobili dame stavano a vedere; e davanti a· rre venieno dame e cavalieri con finti e composti richaimi di gravi oltraggi, e diferenti l'uno dall'altro, domandando l'amenda del misfatto, o battaglia, e i· rre discernea la giostra, e quale era vinto perdeva sua dama: le quali faciono alle loro giostre calcare, quasi come presente premio di colui che vincesse: le conquistate erano di presente menate a corte, e asegnate alla reina come gaggio del vincitore: e altre molte cose simili a queste vane e pompose, e piene di tante inveccerie, che forse a·dDio ne dispiacque. (II, 196–7)[58]
> (In the city of London all were prepared to receive the foreigners honourably, each according to his rank. Here, renewing the ancient fables of the

---

[58] Matteo Villani is dismissive of the Matter of Britain, the chivalric dramatic enactment of it and the overall conspicuous consumption at the Garter feast. This exemplifies the pessimistic and fatalist tone of his chronicle writing. See Green, *Chronicle into History*, p. 46. Villani's dismissal of Arthurian tales as fiction possibly reflects the influence of Petrarch's vernacular poetry. Petrarch writes in his *Triumphus Cupidinis* (Book III, ll. 79–81), a work which was begun either in 1340 or 1352, 'Ecco quei che le carte empion di sogni: / Lancilotto, Tristano, e gli altri erranti, / ove conven che'l vulgo errante agogni' (Here are those who fill the pages with dreams—Lancelot, Tristan and the other knights errant, whom the errant masses naturally crave). See Petrarch, *Trionfi, Rime estravaganti, Codice degli abbozzi*, ed. V. Pacca and L. Paolino (Milan, 1996). For the English translation provided, see C. Kleinhenz, 'The Arthurian Tradition in the Three Crowns', in *The Arthur of the Italians: The Arthurian Legend in Medieval Italian Literature and Culture*, ed. G. Allaire and F. R. Psaki (Cardiff, 2014), pp. 158–75 (p. 158). Also see Kleinhenz's commentary on these lines: 'The word play on *erranti* is both descriptive (the "knights errant" who wandered about in search of adventure) and judgmental (the moral aberrancy of those same individuals). The general populace ("*'l vulgo errante*") is also criticised for their "errant" literary tastes, and this is typical of Petrarch's view of the common folk, who are easily swayed by their enthusiasms rather than their intellect. The passage also emphasises Petrarch's negative view of Arthurian romance, based primarily on the lack of historical foundation for these pleasant but fatuous tales' (pp. 158–9).

Round Table, twenty-four men were made knights-errant, who following the false romances that speak of the Round Table of old, did bid and were being bidden to joust and battle for the love of ladies. And around the square were raised wooden fortifications covered with gold drapery equipped with rich back-rests. There the king and queen and other noble ladies looked on. Then, lords and ladies, with false and made-up laments of great outrages, and disagreeing with one another, demanded amends for the misdeed, or battle. And the king judged the joust, and the one who was defeated lost his lady. The defeated were made to step down from the jousting, as if they were an immediate reward to the victor. The conquered were presented to the court and were handed over to the queen as a gage of the victor and many other silly and pompous things similar to this and full of such foolishness, which perhaps was not displeasing to God.)

This chivalric display must have spoken to the Arthurian penchant of Jean II, but one wonders whether watching Edward's knights parade around as the Knights of the Round Table goaded the French king.[59] The number of knights-errant mentioned by Villani, twenty-four, evokes the membership of the Garter minus its sovereign and the prince of Wales. This number seems to have been a motif at the festival, for Haukin FitzLibbin and his twenty-three fellows, the King's Minstrels, also entertained the guests.[60] Perhaps during this celebration of the Order of the Garter on the feast of St George, the king of France had a chance to reflect on how Edward expropriated his idea of establishing a congregation of knights dedicated to the Blessed Virgin and the dragon-slaying saint.[61] The French king might also have remembered how on the very day that he finally managed to institute his own Arthurian Company of the Star (6 January 1352), an English force seized the castle of Guînes (six miles south of Calais).

[59] Richard Barber, based upon his reading of the passage, does not think that the knights adopted Arthurian personas during this event. See his *Edward III and the Triumph of England: The Battle of Crécy and the Company of the Garter* (London, 2013), p. 281: 'The knights do not seem to have assumed Arthurian identities, but merely to have echoed the proceedings in the romances'. I respectfully disagree. It is clear from Villani's account that Edward III's knights acted out scenarios at least loosely inspired by Arthurian romance.

[60] See 'Issue Roll, Easter, 32 Edward III', quoted in Nicolas, 'Observations', p. 138. Also see C. C. Olson, 'The Minstrels at the Court of Edward III', *PMLA* 56.3 (1941), 601–12 (p. 602): '[t]his was probably the entire group of Edward III's minstrels, for they would doubtless all be present at so splendid an affair.' The same entry in 'Issue Roll, Easter, 32 Edward III' records payment 'To Walter Norman, and his twenty-three fellows, for carrying oats to Windsor about the time of St. George's Feast' (p. 138). After the Garter feast, the number of fellows of Walter Norman dropped from twenty-three to seventeen. See 'Issue Roll, Michaelmas, 32 Edward III', in *Issues of the Exchequer*, p. 168.

[61] See Renouard, 'L'Ordre', pp. 290–1.

And he might also have recalled how forty-five of his Companions of the Star died in an English ambush at Mauron on 14 August 1352 because they had sworn that they would not retreat more than four *arpents* (280 metres) and feared reproach by the Company if they broke their vow.[62] It is also worthy of note that in a letter dated 2 October 1358 the dauphin announced that he was prepared to divert funds from construction work at La Noble-Maison de Saint-Ouen, the seat of the Company of the Star, in order to contribute to the ransom demands set for his father by the king of England.[63] Implementation of the treaty would effectively have been the *coup de grâce* to the Company of the Star.

Not content as judge and spectator at the Windsor Round Table of 1358, Edward, according to Jean le Bel, took part in the jousting together with his three sons – all in identical arms. The anonymous monk of Malmesbury responsible for the *Eulogium historiarum* (*c.* 1365) declares that these were 'hastiludia invisa a tempore regis Arthuri ... ubi equitarunt Angli, Scotti, et captivi Franci' (jousts the likes of which had not been seen since the time of King Arthur ... where the English, Scottish and captive French competed on horseback).[64] Indeed, now that we know that the event was a round table, the monk of Malmesbury's reason for choosing Arthurian times as a point of comparison becomes apparent. Anonymous of Canterbury holds that the jousts lasted for two days and that the English were, on the whole, victorious.[65] During these proceedings, Edward proved to the king of France and all in attendance that his court's mettle matched its majesty.

Lastly, and most importantly, by evoking Arthur, the English king may have been signalling that he would again prosecute his dynastic claim to France with all the military and monetary means at his disposal if his demands were not met. Throughout his reign, Edward fostered the notion that he was the lionhearted Boar from Windsor named in the *Prophecy of the Six Kings to Follow John*, who as successor to Arthur, the boar of Cornwall, would sink his tusks into the gates of Paris and retake the lands his ancestors had lost.[66] Moreover, when Edward's ambassadors,

---

[62] Jean le Bel, *Chronique*, II, 206–7; *True Chronicles of Jean le Bel*, p. 217.
[63] See Léopold Pannier, *La Noble-Maison de Saint-Ouen, la Villa Clippiacum et l'Ordre de Étoile d'après les documents originaux* (Paris, 1872), pp. 135–6.
[64] *Eulogium Historium sive Temporis a Monacho Quodam Malmesburiensi* (*c.* 1365), ed. F. S. Haydon, RS 9, 3 vols. (London, 1858–63), III, 227.
[65] *Chronica Anonymi Cantuariensis*, pp. 42–5.
[66] In the first quarter of the fourteenth century, an anonymous writer drew upon Geoffrey of Monmouth's *Prophetia Merlini* to compile *The Prophecy of the Six Kings to Follow John*. The six kings had different spirit animals: (1) the Lamb, (2) the Dragon, (3) the Goat, (4), the Boar, (5), the Ass and (6) the Mole. T. M. Smallwood established that the Lamb was clearly modelled after the life and reign of Henry

Adam Orleton, bishop of Worcester, and Roger Northborough, bishop of Lichfield and Coventry, advanced the Plantagenet claim to the regency of France in 1329, they opened their address declaring that

> Ce fameux Prophete Merlin aux yeux duquel les plus memorables evenemens des choses humaines ont esté clairement presens, nous a distinctement marqué dans ses predictions, qu'au temps où nous sommes les Lys & les Leopards seroient unis dans un mesme champ, & que les nobles Royaumes de France & d'Angleterre n'auroient plus qu'un mesme Monarque. Ce bien-heureux jour est arrivé, Seigneurs François, que ces deux puissantes Nations seront inseparablement unies ensemble, & qu'aprés quatre ou cinq siecles les deux branches Royales qui s'estoient éloignées, se rejoindront en un mesme tronc. La tres-illustre race des Rois de France & celle des Rois d'Angleterre sont toutes deux sorties d'un même sein & d'une mesme maison.[67]

III (r. 1216–72), the Dragon after Edward I (r. 1272–1307) and the Goat accurately reflected the life of Edward II (r. 1307–27) up to 1312, which was the year of the death of Edward's favourite, Piers Gaveston, and of the birth of the future Edward III at Windsor. On these grounds Smallwood concluded that the 'Original Prose Version' of the *Prophecy* dated from about 1312. The earliest manuscripts of the 'Original Prose Version' date from about 1325. Around the time of the death of Edward II (1327), the 'Revised Prose Version' was produced. This version made the prophecy for the Goat reflect the life and deeds of Edward II up to his deposition. Smallwood notes that '[t]he account of the Boar (the successor to the Goat) is the same as that in the *"Original" Prose Version*, if slightly garbled at a few points'. See T. M. Smallwood, 'The Prophecy of the Six Kings', *Speculum* 60.3 (1985), 571–92 (esp. pp. 571–8). The prophecy of the Boar, according to the 'Original Prose Version', holds that the boar will have a sound head and the heart of a lion. He will come out of Windsor and will march all the way up to Jerusalem. Spain and Germany will tremble out of fear of him, and he will sink his teeth on the gates of Paris. He will regain all the land that his ancestors had lost. He shall bear three crowns and he will be buried in Cologne. See 'Merlin's Prophecy of the Six Kings', in Rupert Taylor, *The Political Prophecy in England* (New York, 1911), pp. 160–4 (p. 162). The prophecy of the Boar was clearly modelled after the prophecy of the Boar of Cornwall (Arthur Pendragon) and the 'second boar' (*Arthurus redivivus*?) in Geoffrey's *Prophetia Merlini*. As Smallwood points out, 'it is impossible that all of this was written after Edward III had achieved even the earliest of his successes in France' (p. 577). Poets and chroniclers active in the 1350 increasingly came to recognize Edward III as fulfilling the prophecy of the Boar. See, for example, *The Poems of Laurence Minot, 1333–1352*, ed. Richard H. Osberg, TEAMS Middle English Texts (Kalamazoo, 1997), p. 48 (6.3–8) and p. 51 (7.1–16). Minot presents Edward III as Merlin's Boar in the context of the Siege of Tournai (1340) and Crécy campaign. On this topic, see L. A. Coote, *Prophecy and Public Affairs in Later Medieval England* (York, 2000), pp. 105–7.

[67] The ambassadors' statements are preserved in François Eudes de Mezeray, *Histoire de France depuis Faramond jusqu'au regne de Louis le Juste*, 2 vols. (Paris, 1685), II, 384.

(This famous prophet Merlin, before whose eyes the most memorable events of human affairs were clearly present, has distinctly pointed out to us in his predictions that, at the time in which we live, the lilies and the leopards should be united in the same field; and that the noble kingdoms of France and England should for the future have but one monarch. This most auspicious day has come, French lords, that these two powerful nations will be inseparably united together and that after four or five centuries the two royal branches that were stretched apart, will rejoin in one single trunk. The very illustrious race of the kings of France and that of the kings of England are both offspring of a single womb and from a single house.)

When reasserting his dynastic claim to France in 1340, Edward went halfway toward fulfilling this prophecy by quartering the *fleurs-de-lis* of France with the leopards of England in the same heraldic field, the Plantagenet coat of arms. He evoked this prophecy yet again in tandem with his Round Table feast of January 1344 by releasing the leopard half-florin as England's first gold coin.[68] Eleven years later in 1355, he also released a similar gold coin, the *Léopard d'Or*, in Gascony. As the new Arthur, Edward promised order and good governance to a kingdom of France ravaged by *routiers*, even if many of these brigands had been serving in his name.

The First Treaty of London, signed by Edward III and Jean II on 8 May 1358, never took effect. The Dauphin Charles failed to produce the required ransom and sureties (hostages) by the first instalment due date of 1 November 1358. The French also did not obtain the concessions from the papacy for the English that Parliament demanded in order to ratify the treaty. Edward waited two months after the November deadline before making preparations for another French campaign. On 2 January 1359 the first order for bows and arrows was sent to the Tower of London, and the commissions of array were appointed on 12 January. This suggests to Clifford Rogers that Edward III was not eager to see the First Treaty of London fail.[69] At this juncture, Edward seems to have decided to realize his pretentions to the throne of France. As Rogers has noted, '[h]is design for the new campaign, probably from the start, involved an effort to capture the city of Reims, where he could be anointed with the holy oil of

---

[68] See C. Shenton, 'Edward III and the Symbol of the Leopard', in *Heraldry, Pageantry and Social Display in Medieval England*, ed. P. Coss and M. Keen (Woodbridge, 2002), pp. 69–81 (p.75): 'The new half-florin displayed, on one side, a crowned leopard bearing the arms of England and France round its neck, and on the other was a quatrefoil design with a leopard in each angle. So powerful was the design of the half-florin that it was given the nickname "The Leopard".'

[69] Rogers, 'Anglo-French Peace Negotiations', pp. 202–3.

St Remy and re-crowned as king of France.'[70] These developments reveal that Edward on the one hand had high hopes for the proposed peace, but on the other was prepared to prosecute his claim to France. Moreover, Edward's desire to secure the holy oil of St Remy, like his Arthurian self-representation, bespeaks a concern for establishing his legitimacy as a double monarch in symbolic terms.

The St George's Day Feast of 1358 did not result in the hoped-for resolution of the conflict between the kings and the realms of France and England, but it furnishes historians with an excellent case study in how monarchical self-fashioning and court pageantry in pre-Tudor England were not rudimentary and frivolous, but rather sophisticated social displays of existing authority and legitimacy that could be put to use as an effective diplomatic lever for securing further power and influence. The lasting effect of the round table held during the Windsor feast of 1358 seems to have been not political, but rather historiographical in nature.

The Round Table of 1358 and the conflations of the Garter and Round Table projects

Did the round table held during the Garter feast of 1358 prompt the many round table / Garter conflations that arose soon after the English order's establishment? Jonathan Boulton has observed that virtually all 'chroniclers writing after 1350 ... generally regarded the historic Order as the ultimate product of Edward's project to revive the Round Table.'[71] In light of the foregoing discussion of the Garter festival / Round Table of 1358, Boulton's cogent observation raises a central and related historiographical issue. Aside from difference in the number of members, was there ever a meaningful distinction between Edward III's proposed Order of the Round Table and actualized Order of the Garter? After all, we now know that Arthurian and Garter iconography could and did coexist. The only indicators of a change in plan, at least as far as we are aware, are the cessation of work on the *domus tabule rotunde* and the absence of explicit reference to King Arthur and his fellowship in the surviving statutes of the Garter. These circumstances suggest three possibilities. One is that the Order of the Garter was not Arthurian, formally speaking, but, from its very outset, had Arthurian overtones that may or may not have included round table events. By retaining an informal Arthurian compo-

---

[70] Rogers, 'Anglo-French Peace Negotiations', p. 203.
[71] Boulton, *Knights of the Crown*, p. 103.

nent in Garter pageants, Edward may have hoped that the Order of the Garter would be received as the fulfilment of his 1344 oath to re-establish Arthur's Round Table. A second possibility is that Edward III made a deliberate break from his earlier Arthurian plans when instituting the Order of the Garter (c. 1348–9), but later (c. 1356–8) changed his mind. If Edward initially sought to distance the Order of the Garter from the Round Table project, then perhaps there was a conscious effort on the part of the royal court to rewrite recent history: to retroactively construct or tighten the association between Edward's Garter and Arthur's Round Table. Were Edward III and the Founder Knights of the Garter already beginning to mythologize the origins of their Order in the 1350s and 1360s? A third possibility is that Edward III presided over a singular, albeit extremely memorable, Arthurian revival in 1358, and this gave rise to the conflation of the Order of the Round Table and the Order of the Garter. With these possibilities in mind, let us now consider the textual history of this conflation. Particular attention will be paid to the date of composition of each entry containing the conflation. If one or more predate 23 April 1358, we know for certain that the St George's event of that year did not influence it.

As observed by Ingledew, four notable early conflations of the Round Table and the Garter are of English provenance.[72] The first example appears in a manuscript containing a variant version of the *Continuatio Chronicarum* of Adam Murimuth (1275–1347): London, British Library, Cotton Nero D x, fols. 105r–137r. Beside its account of Edward III's January 1344 feast where the king announced his intention to re-establish the Order of the Round Table, there appears an erroneous rubric reading on folio 132a that refers to the 1358 Garter Feast: 'De solempnitate facta Wyndelsore per illustrissimum regem Edwardum, regem Angliæ et Franciæ, in die sancti Georgii martyris' (On the solemnity made at Windsor by the most illustrious King Edward, king of England and France, on the day of St George the Martyr).[73] It is out of place as no reference is made in the body of the text to St George or the feast of St George. On folio 134b, the same hand records a great storm in 1361–2.[74] Thus, this conflation of the planned Order of the Round Table and the actualized Order of the Garter appears to date from about 1361.

A second English example of conflation appears in the abstract of the *Scalacronica*, an Anglo-Norman prose chronicle (Creation to 1363) written by the Northumberland knight Sir Thomas Gray (the younger) of Heaton (d. 1369), attributed to the sixteenth-century Tudor antiquarian

---

[72] Ingledew, *Sir Gawain*, pp. 107–10.
[73] Adam Murimuth, *Continuatio Chronicarum*, p. 231.
[74] Adam Murimuth, *Continuatio Chronicarum*, p. xx.

John Leland (*c.* 1503–52).[75] The conflation occurs in the coverage of Edward III's Windsor feast of 1344. Before considering the entry itself, there are some contextual details about this knight-chronicler that warrant our attention. First, Gray seems to have had the interest and the means to learn about the noteworthy chivalric and Arthurian developments at the royal court and in the metropolis – in particular about the proclamation of the Order of the Round Table and the institution of the Garter. His interest in and opportunities for insider information about these matters makes his conflation of the Round Table and Garter all the more deserving of critical scrutiny. We know that Gray was interested in Arthur because in the first book of his *Scalacronica* he provides a lengthy account of the life and deeds of King Arthur that weaves together narrative elements from the Galfridian historiographical tradition and from the Old French verse and prose romance traditions. In this Arthurian section Gray also provides a spirited defence of the figure's historicity.[76] And throughout his *Scalacronica*, he displays great interest in feats of arms (both in war and in tournaments) and the ethics and conventions of knighthood.[77]

Let us now consider Gray's opportunities for obtaining information about the Round Table and Garter projects. We are fortunate to have a record of some of his movements and activities. This gives us at least a vague sense of his social status, political connections and geographical location at the time of the Windsor feasts of 1344 and 1358 respectively.[78] Our chronicler received a letter of protection (extending from June of 1338 until Christmas of 1339) to serve in Flanders in the retinue of William de Montague, the newly created earl of Salisbury. Earl William, it should be noted, went on to perform the office of Marshal of England at

---

[75] See 'Notable thinges translatid in to Englisch by John Leylande oute of a booke, callid Scala Chronica, the which a certein Inglisch man (taken yn werre prisoner, and brought to Edingeburgh yn Scotland) did translate owte of French ryme to Frenche prose', in *Scalacronica: By Sir Thomas Gray of Heton, Knight. A Chronicle of England and Scotland from A. D. MLXVI to A. D. MCCCLXII*, ed. Joseph Stevenson (Edinburgh, 1835), pp. 259–321. Leland's summary is important as it supplements extant passages of Gray's *Scalacronica*, including the events of 1344.

[76] See R. J. Moll, *Before Malory: Reading Arthur in Later Medieval England* (Toronto, 2003), pp. 31–63. For an analysis of Gray's defence of Arthur, see pp. 64–80.

[77] See A. King, 'A Helm with a Crest of Gold: The Order of Chivalry in Thomas Gray's *Scalacronica*', *Fourteenth Century England* 1 (2000), 21–35; A. King, 'War and Peace: The Ethics of War in Sir Thomas Gray's *Scalacronica*', in *War, Government and Aristocracy in the British Isles, c. 1150–1500*, ed. C. Given-Wilson, A. Kettle and L. Scales (Woodbridge, 2008), pp. 148–62.

[78] See Sir Thomas Gray, *Scalacronica, 1272–1363*, ed. A. King (Woodbridge, 2005), pp. xxxiii–xliv. Also see J. C. Thiolier, 'Gray, Sir Thomas (*d.* 1369)', in *The Oxford Dictionary of National Biography*, ed. Lawrence Goldman (Oxford, 2004), http://www.oxforddnb.com/view/article/11355, accessed 14 August 14 2015.

the Windsor tournament of 1344 and died a week later owing to jousting-related injuries. By 1340, Gray had returned to the Scottish border. As far as I am aware, his whereabouts during the Windsor feast of 1344 are unknown, but less than two months later (March 1344) the Crown awarded him custody of a manor 'in consideration of his good service beyond the seas as well as within'.[79] In April of 1345, Gray was made Constable of Norham; he went on to fight against the Scots at the battle of Neville's Cross (17 October 1346) and subsequently represented the interests of the Crown in a variety of Anglo-Scottish juridical and diplomatic issues. In 1355, the Scots attacked Norham and captured Gray. He did not have the funds to pay his ransom and was kept prisoner at Edinburgh Castle. While in prison, he had access to an excellent library and began his chronicle, which he divided into four books: (1) the legendary history of Britain, (2) the early Anglo-Saxon period, (3) the unification of England and (4) post-Conquest England to the present day, namely 1066–1363. Gray was freed at an undetermined date before 28 November 1356, for on that date the Crown appointed him to investigate cases of tax evasion via the smuggling of sheep into Scotland.[80] He would continue to serve the Crown on the Scottish border for the next few years. It is theoretically possible that Gray attended the 1358 feast at Windsor, but it is more likely that he remained near the border. Be that as it may, by 1358 (in contrast to 1344) he was committed to writing a chronicle of his times and undoubtedly sought to learn the particulars of the 1358 event. Gray would go on to serve in the retinue of the Black Prince during Edward III's 1359–60 French campaign. In 1367, he served as Warden of the East March, and he died in October of 1369.[81] Given that Gray only began his lengthy *Scalacronica* in 1355 and that the 1344 event, which contains the round table / Garter conflation, only appeared in the final book of the *Scalacronica*, it is quite conceivable that Gray wrote this entry after the St George's Day Feast of 1358.

Unfortunately, Gray's original entry for 1344 is lost to us. There is only one surviving manuscript of Gray's *Scalacronica*, Cambridge, Corpus Christi College 1333, and the critical portion is missing from it. As King notes, 'the narrative jumps, in mid-sentence, from 1340 at fol. 219v to 1356 on fol. 220'.[82] For a summary of the contents of the missing material, we must consult John Leland's later abstract. With respect to the 1344 Windsor event, it reads: 'King Edwarde made a great fest at Wyndesore at Christemes, wher he renewid the Round Table, and the name of

---

[79] Gray, *Scalacronica*, p. xxxvii.
[80] Gray, *Scalacronica*, p. xli.
[81] Gray, *Scalacronica*, pp. xliii–xliv.
[82] Gray, *Scalacronica*, p. liii.

Arture, and ordenid the Order of the Garter, making Sainct George the patrone thereof.'[83] Given that he began his chronicle a little over a decade after the Windsor 1344 feast, Gray's memory or the memory of his source may have been hazy. The feast did not occur at Christmas, but rather approximately one month after Christmas.

As we do not have access to Gray's original entry, we must ask if the conflation of the Garter and Round Table project was original to his *Scalacronica* or if it reflects the learning of Leland. In Leland's day, the Order of the Garter was thought to have been instituted by King Arthur.[84] We cannot answer this question definitively, but we can get a sense of Gray's handling of such occasions and Leland's faithfulness to his source by juxtaposing their respective entries on the Garter feast of 1358. Gray writes:

> La Royne Descoce et sore le dit Roy Edward Dengleter veint meisme la sesoune a Wyndesore a parler od le Roy soun freir, et de boter en parlaunce greignour tretice; et fust delee sa mere la Royn Isabelle, qe morust a Herforthe meisme la sesoun, qe ne lauoit pas vieu xxx. aunz. A quel lieu de Wyndesore, le dit Roy Edward teint sa graunt fest de joustes et reuelle le iour saint George, com acoustomez estoit, ou le Roy Johan de Fraunce estoit en le hour en prisoun, et ou le Duk Henry de Lancastre fust naufre; com iousta oue vn chiualer, vn autre a trauers ly fery de sa Launce hu coste, moult perillousement, de quoy il gary.
>
> A queux ioustes veint le Duk de Braban et de Lenburgh, qi freir estoit al Emperour Charlis de Bahayn, pur demaunder eyde encountre le Count de Flaundres, qi bon pece ly auoit guerroie pur la vile de Malyns et autres debatis entre eaux ...'[85]

(The queen of Scotland, the sister of King Edward of England, came to Windsor in the same season, to speak with her brother the king, and to put forward a longer treaty for discussion; and she was with her mother Queen Isabella, who died at Hertford in the same season, whom she had not seen for thirty years. At Windsor, King Edward held a great feast with jousts and revelry on St George's day, as was customary. King John of France was there, being prisoner at the time, and Duke Henry of Lancaster was wounded there; as he jousted with a knight, another struck across him, hitting him in the side with his lance very dangerously, but he recovered.

---

[83] 'Notable thinges', p. 300.
[84] See *Calendar of State Papers, Venetian*, ed. R. Brown et al., 38 vols. (London, 1864–1947), I (1202–1509), 281 n. 790 (1 April 1499). In response to a request by the Duke of Milan to be given the badge of the Garter, Henry VIII responds 'the Garter is the badge and first order of King Arthur, and that the knights of old who bore this badge swore to be the friends of friends and foes of foes, and the King of France being a member of the order, the Duke [of Milan] cannot enter it.'
[85] Gray, *Scalacronica*, pp. 150–1.

The duke of Brabant and Luxemburg, brother of Emperor Charles of Bohemia, came to these jousts to ask for help against the Count of Flanders, who had been at war with him for a good while over the town of Malines and other points of contention between them ...)

Leland summarizes this entry as follows:

The quene of Scotland, sister to king Edward, cam oute of Scotland to Wyndesore to speke with hym, and after was with her mother quene Isabel at Hertford, and ther dyed abowt the 30. yere of her age.

King Edward kept his great feast of Saynct George at Wydesore, and there were great justes to the which cam the duke of Braban, and the duke of Luneburge, brother to Charles king of Boheme and emperor, desiring help agayne the erle of Flaunders.[86]

Leland's entry is a faithful summary of Gray's *Scalacronica*; it does not contain any learned accretions. The only noteworthy inconsistency is Leland's incorrect statement that Joan, Queen of Scotland, died in 1358 at about thirty years of age. He seems to have mistaken 'vieu' (for 'veu', seen) for 'vecu' (lived). There do not appear to be any grounds to presume that the antiquarian consciously strayed from his source material. Gray's remark (which does not appear in Leland's abstract) that King Edward held a 'graunt fest de joustes et reuelle le iour saint George, com acoustomez estoit' is tantalizingly vague. Evidently jousts and revels were customary activities during the Garter feast of St George, but did they typically or traditionally have an Arthurian theme? Did the king, to borrow Leland's language, 'renew the Round Table and the name of Arthur' at these annual feasts? The conflation of the Garter and the Round Table in Leland's abstract appears to have been original to Gray's *Scalacronica*. The 1344 entry suggests that there was an Arthurianizing of the Garter, but the all-important question of when this occurred – whether before or after the 1358 Windsor feast – remains unclear. Yet the 1344 entry was most likely written after the 1358 Garter event.

A third conflation of the Round Table and Garter projects occurs in the prose *Commentary* of the *Prophecy of the Six Kings to Follow John* ascribed to John of Bridlington (d. 1379).[87] Twenty-nine poems, each about twenty to thirty lines in rhyming hexameter, constitute the *Prophecy*. Thirty-one manuscripts contain the *Prophecy* alone, and an

---

[86] 'Notable thinges', p. 306.
[87] See 'John of Bridlington', in *Political Poems and Songs relating to English History, composed during the period from the Accession of Edward III to that of Richard III*, ed. T. Wright, RS 14, 2 vols. (London, 1859–61), I, 123–215 (p. 123); A. G. Rigg, 'John of Bridlington's Prophecy: A New Look', Speculum 63.3 (1988), 596–613 (p. 597).

additional four feature the *Prophecy* with its *Commentary*. The *Commentary* is dedicated to Humphrey de Bohun, seventh earl of Hereford, Essex and Northampton, who succeeded to his title in 1361 and died in 1372. It contains a cryptogram, which M. R. James deciphered to read 'Ergom'.[88] 'Ergom' is thought to have been John Ergom (Erghom, Erghome, d. *c.* 1408), an Oxford-trained Austin friar of the priory at York.[89] Regardless of whether the reader accepts (primarily on the strength of the cryptogram) that John Ergom authored the commentary, A. G. Rigg has shown that 'Ergom' based his commentary on an imperfect copy of the *Prophecy*, which was lacking some verses and contained at least one textual error. This proves that the commentator was not the author of the *Prophecy* and that the *Commentary* was written after the *Prophecy*.[90] The *Commentary* makes reference to the plague of 1361 and the death of Henry, duke of Lancaster, in 1362, but it does not allude to the death of Jean II of France in 1364. It is the scholarly consensus that the *Commentary* dates from between 1362 and 1364.[91] Rigg has noted that some of the commentator's 'solutions to numerological clues run counter to a natural reading; several passages which Ergom applies to later events can with equal (often greater) probability be referred to happenings of 1348–49'.[92] After providing evidence to support his observations, Rigg concludes that *Prophecy* itself is 'a semi-satirical retrospective on the events of 1327–49, written about 1349–50 and cast in the form of a prophecy.'[93] The *Commentary* thus appears to have been written approximately thirteen years after the *Prophecy*.

With this in mind, let us now consider a passage in the *Prophecy* under the heading *Capitulum vij. docet de pace inter Anglicos et Gallicos, et de cæteris accidentibus usque ad præparationem belli de Crecy* (Chapter Seven teaches about the peace between the English and the French and the rest of the happenings up to the preparation of the battle of Crécy).

---

[88] See M. R. James, 'The Catalogue of the Library of the Augustinian Friars at York', *Fasciculus J. W. Clark dicatus* (Cambridge, 1909), pp. 2–96 (pp. 10–11).
[89] For a discussion of the life of John Erghome, see John B. Friedman, *John de Foxton's Liber Cosmographiae (1408), An Edition and Codicological Study* (Leiden, 1988), pp. xvii–xxix. Friedman contends that Erghome was the patron of the *Liber Cosmographiae*. He notes that John Erghome came from an important landowning family in the East Riding of Yorkshire, which in the fourteenth century had ties with the families of Thomas of Lancaster, Humphrey de Bohun, the Percys and the Nevilles (pp. xvii–xviii).
[90] Rigg, 'John of Bridlington's Prophecy', p. 597.
[91] Rigg, 'John of Bridlington's Prophecy', p. 597; Friedman, *John de Foxton's* Liber Cosmographiae, p. xix.
[92] Rigg, 'John of Bridlington's Prophecy', p. 597.
[93] Rigg, 'John of Bridlington's Prophecy', p. 613.

It reads: 'Tristia post fata succedent tempora grata. / Festa rotundabit ...' (After a sad turn of events, pleasing times will follow. He will make feasts round ...). [94] The commentator provides the following gloss on this passage:

> Tertio ostendit auctor actus tauri tempore pacis dum fuerat quietus a bello, dicens quod *tempora grata*, i. tempora læta, *succedent post tristia fata*, i. post istas tribulationes maris. Pro quo est notandum quod rex illo tempore posuit se ad otium et quietem, et ordinavit festum Sancti Georgii, congregans sibi bonos milites Angliæ, ut essent in illa societate propter opera sua strenua et bellicosa, sicut narratur quod rex Arthurus fecit in tempore suo, et vocavit milites illos milites de rotunda tabula; unde dicit auctor quod *festa rotundabit*, i. faciet festum ad modum rotundæ tabulæ, scilicet festum Sancti Georgii apud Wyndesore. (150)

> (Third, the author reveals acts of the bull [Edward III] in a time of peace while there had been respite from battle, saying that *tempora grata*, i.e. joyful times, *succedent post tristia fata*, i.e. after these tribulations of the sea. For which reason, it should be noted that the king put himself at leisure and peace at that time and arranged a feast of St George, gathering around himself good knights of England, so that they were in that society on account of their active and warlike deeds, just as it is told that King Arthur did in his time, and he called those knights the Knights of the Round Table; on account of this the author says that *festa rotundabit*, i.e. he will make the feast in the manner of the Round Table, namely the feast of St George at Windsor.)

The *Prophecy* itself, which was written around the time of the institution of the Garter, seems to refer to Edward III's Arthurian activities (*c.* 1344) before the Crécy campaign and does not mention St George or the Order of the Garter. The *Commentary*, on the other hand, not only conflates the Round Table with the Garter, but also states that a 'feast of St George' was held 'ad modum rotundæ tabulæ'. The basis of this claim is unclear. Was 'Ergom' speaking in general or specific terms? Given that the commentator was writing between 1362 and 1364, it is possible that the grand Arthurian Garter feast of 1358 impacted his understanding of the Windsor St George's Day celebrations.

Continental chroniclers also conflated the Round Table and Garter projects, and their writings also seem to postdate the Garter extravaganza of 1358. The first example appears in the *Vrayes Chroniques* (to 1361) of the canon of St Lambert in Liège, Jean le Bel (d. 1370).[95] According

---

[94] Rigg, 'John of Bridlington's Prophecy', p. 149.
[95] A. Gransden, *Historical Writing in England, Vol. 2: c. 1307 to the Early Sixteenth Century* (London, 1982), p. 84, and see Bryant, *True Chronicles of Jean le Bel*, p. 15.

to another fourteenth-century Liègois chronicler, Jean d'Outremeuse (d. 1400), Jean le Bel began his *Vrayes Chroniques* at the request of John of Hainault, who was the lord of Beaumont, brother of William I (d. 1356), count of Hainault, and uncle of Queen Philippa.[96] Jean le Bel submitted his narrative of events (Chapters 1–39), which extended to just after the signing of the Truce of Esplèchin (25 September 1340), to John of Hainault for inspection and correction.[97] At the close of Chapter 39, Jean le Bel seems to have paused his writing.[98] Jean le Bel, in his account of the Windsor Garter feast of 1358 (Chapter 94), declined to speak of the precise terms and conditions of the peace made between Edward III and Jean II because they were not commonly known when he was writing. On this basis, Nigel Bryant believes that Chapters 40–94 inclusive were written in 1358, after the Garter feast of that year.[99] If he is correct, then the Windsor Round Table of 1358 may have influenced Jean le Bel's account of Edward's earlier round table and Garter activities. Let us now look at those accounts.

In Chapter 64 of his *Vrayes Chroniques*, Jean le Bel provides an entry on Edward III's 1344 declaration of intent to establish an equivalent to Arthur's Order of the Round Table to increase the honour of his knights:

> Quant il fut retourné en Angleterre, de gentillesse de cœur il s'avisa qu'il feroit refaire et rediffier le chastel de Windesore, que le roy Artus avoit fait faire, et où fut establye premierement la Table Ronde à l'occasion des prœux, et tant que on ne trouvast les semblablez en quelque royaume, et luy sembloit qu'il ne les pouoit trop honnourer, tant les amoit. Si fist crier par tout son royaume feste generale et court plainiere pour ordonner celle Table Ronde, et manda par tous pays dames et damoiselles, chevaliers et escuiers, et que chascun, sans point d'excusation, y venist pour faire celle grande feste à Windesore, à Penthecouste l'an de grace mil CCC XLIIII. (II, 26–7)

> (Once he [Edward III] was back in England his noble heart inspired him not only to restore and improve the castle of Windsor, which King Arthur had built and where the Round Table was first established in honour of the worthy knights of that time, but also to create a counterpart to that Round Table for the greater honour of his own knights; for they'd served him so well and he considered them most worthy: their like were not to be found in any kingdom, and he loved them so dearly that he felt he couldn't honour

---

[96] Jean d'Outremeuse, *Ly Myreur des histors, Chronique de Jean des Preis dit d'Outremeuse*, ed. S. Bormans, 7 vols. (Brussels, 1864–87), VI, 322–3. Also see Gransden, *Historical Writing*, p. 84.
[97] Jean d'Outremeuse, *Ly Myreur des histors*, VI, 323 n. 3.
[98] Jean le Bel, *Chronique*, I, 212.
[99] Bryant, *True Chronicles of Jean le Bel*, p. 15.

them too much. So he announced a great feast and a plenary court for the founding of this Round Table, summoning ladies and damsels, knights and squires from all parts of his kingdom, insisting that no one on any account should fail to attend this great feast at Windsor, at Pentecost in the year of grace 1344. [153])

In his sixty-sixth chapter, Jean le Bel revisits this subject, and here we find the root of the conflation of the proposed Order of the Round Table and the actualized Order of the Garter:

Or vueil je retourner à parler de celle grand feste de Wyndesore, laquelle fut moult noble et bien joustée, car grande quantité y eut de dames et de damoiselles et de seigneurs chevaliers et escuiers, et fut là endroit ordonneé et conferméе une noble compaigne de chevaliers, qu'on tenoit pour vaillans hommes, et fut faitte selonc la maniere de la Table Ronde; maiz je ne sçay pas bien deviser, si m'en tairay à tant. (II, 34–5)

(Now I'll return to the great feast at Windsor. It was a magnificent affair with splendid jousting, attended by a vast host of ladies and damsels and lords and knights and squires. And it witnessed the creation and establishment of the company of knights deemed truly worthy; it was modelled upon the Round Table, but I can't describe it in detail so I'll leave it at that. [157])

This company of knights must have been the Order of the Garter, but Jean le Bel does not ever mention the Garter by name and it was not founded until 1348–9. He seems to have confused the proposed Arthurian Order of the Round Table with the actualized Order of the Garter. If Bryant's dating of the *Vrayes Chroniques* is correct, the Arthurian elements in the Garter feast of 1358 arguably led to this conflation.

Jean Froissart (1337–1410), in the first book of his prose *Chroniques* (c. 1370–1400), connects (and / or confounds) the two even more forcefully. He presents the 'chevaliers dou Bleu Gartier' (Knights of the Blue Garter) as Edward III's original idea, which arose seamlessly from the Windsor feast of 1344. Before considering Froissart's account, some biographical details demand our attention. In the prologue to the first book of his *Chroniques*, Froissart recognizes Jean le Bel's *Vrayes Chroniques* as the principal written source for his own historical writing, but he states that he augmented his work with the testimony of knights and squires and kings of arms and their marshals, all of whom he met in his travels through England and France.[100] In 1362, Froissart (born in Valen-

---

[100] Jean Froissart, *Chroniques*, ed. S. Luce, 15 vols. (Paris, 1869–1975), I, 1–2. Also see J. Taylor, *English Historical Literature in the Fourteenth Century* (Oxford, 1987), p. 163: 'So closely did Froissart adhere to his original in the first draft of the *Chroniques*, that when the solitary manuscript of le Bel's work was discovered in the nineteenth century it was at first thought to be a copy of Froissart's text.'

ciennes) left his native Hainault for England and entered the service of Edward III's queen, Philippa of Hainault. Upon his arrival in England, Froissart presented Philippa with a verse chronicle that the Black Prince's victory at Poitiers had inspired him to write. This lost verse chronicle was an antecedent to the first version of his *Chroniques*, and we do not know if it told of Edward III's round tables or the institution of the Garter. Froissart remained in Philippa's service until her death in 1369. At the English court Froissart composed poetry and songs, and he was permitted to travel widely and to interview the French captives in London.[101] Froissart's writing about the Garter was informed by Jean le Bel's *Vrayes Chroniques* and presumably also the recollections of members of the English royal court and Edward III's French captives.

It is also relevant to note that Froissart is widely thought to have composed an early version of his *Meliador* during his 'période anglaise' (1362–9), the first verse Arthurian romance known to have been composed in almost a century (since Girart de Amien's *Escanor* of c. 1280). Incidentally, if Froissart did write an early version of the *Meliador* for Philippa (the so-called A-version is thought to have been composed for the English royal court),[102] then we have firm evidence to counter

[101] See P. Ainsworth, 'Jean Froissart: Chronicler, Poet and Writer', in *The Online Froissart*, ed. P. Ainsworth and G. Croenen, v. 1.5, HRIOnline (Sheffield, 2013), first published in v. 1.0 (2010), updated for v. 1.5 (2013), http://www.hrionline.ac.uk/onlinefroissart/apparatus.jsp?type=intros&intro=f.intros.PFA-Froissart, accessed 26 October 2015. In 1365, Froissart visited Scotland; he also visited the West Country in the company of Sir Edward Despenser. He then accompanied the Black Prince to Aquitaine in 1366 and was present at the birth of the future Richard II of England at Bordeaux in 1367. In 1368, Froissart went to Italy with Edward III's son Lionel, Duke of Clarence. En route back to England he learned of Philippa's death and decided to remain in the Netherlands. See Taylor, *English Historical Literature*, p. 159. Also see Jean Froissart, *Melyador, roman en vers de la fin du XIVe siècle*, ed. N. Bragantini-Maillard, Textes littéraires français, 2 vols. (Geneva, 2012), I, 9–20, cited hereafter as *Melyador*.

[102] In 1890, Auguste Longnon discovered these fragments. They are preserved in a late fourteenth-century manuscript, Paris, Bibliothèque nationale de France, nouvelles acquisitions latines, 2374, fols. 36ra–39vb. See A. Longnon, 'Un fragment retrouvé du *Meliador* de Froissart', *Romania* 20 (1891), 403–16. For a recent edition of the A-version, see *Melyador*, II, 1313–25. For comparative analyses of the two versions that conclude in favour of the anteriority of the A-Version, see A. H. Diverres, 'The Two Versions of Froissart's *Meliador*', in *Studies in Medieval French Language and Literature presented to Brian Woledge in honour of his 80th birthday*, ed. S. B. North (Geneva, 1988), pp. 37–48 (p. 46). Also see *Melyador*, I, 63. It is unclear when Froissart first began work on *Meliador*. Longnon in the introduction of his three-volume edition suggested that Froissart began writing *Meliador*, which treats Scotland extensively, shortly after his six-month stay there in 1365 (*Méliador par Jean Froissart*, I, lxviii). A. H. Diverres examined Froissart's description of the British Isles in the romance and found that the poet made ample use of fictitious place names and seldom

Loomis' claim that there was a decline in the prestige of things Arthurian at the royal court after 1350, and the composition itself might have been part of a retroactive 'Arthurianizing' of the Order of the Garter. Only four fragments (516 lines in total) survive of the A-version, believed to be the earlier of the two. We know that the B-version was made at the request of Wenceslas of Bohemia (d. 1383); it is near complete (totalling 30,771 lines) and lacks only the ending.[103] Since we are largely dependent on the B-version for our knowledge of the romance, we do not know to what extent the A-version was tailored to Plantagenet political interests. A. H. Diverres has examined what survives of the romance for indications of Plantagenet ideology. To his surprise, Diverres did not find any signs that Froissart fashioned Arthur after Edward III, and at no point in the surviving verses of the romance 'does the king of Scotland actually pay homage to the king of Britain'.[104] The romance does, however, culminate with the marriage of Meliador, who is the son of the duke of Cornwall, and Hermondine, the daughter and heiress of the king of Scotland. This is somewhat politically suggestive. Given that 'duke of Cornwall' was one of the titles of Edward III's firstborn son and heir, Edward of Woodstock, Froissart may have been alluding to the union of the kingdoms of England and Scotland, which was one of Edward III's

---

offered realistic descriptive details or statements of relative geography. The great exception to this rule is that the division between Arthur's kingdom and Scotland perfectly corresponded to the *'de facto* border of the 1360s' between Edward III's extended kingdom of England and the slightly truncated Scotland. Since Froissart does not evince detailed, first-hand knowledge of Scotland, Diverres allows for the possibility that the poet began his Arthurian romance as early as his arrival at the English royal court in 1362. See Diverres, 'The Geography of Britain in Froissart's *Meliador'*, in *Medieval Miscellany presented to Eugène Vinaver by pupils, colleagues and friends*, ed. F. Whitehead, A. H. Diverres and F. E. Sutcliffe (Manchester, 1965), pp. 97–112 (pp. 109–10). Also see Diverres, 'The Two Versions of Froissart's *Meliador'*, p. 48. Bragantini-Maillard agrees that the romance was probably created and read at the court of Edward III and Philippa between 1362 and 1369; see *Melyador*, I.50–69 (esp. p. 69).

[103] In October of 1893, Longnon found this second, far more complete copy (*c.* 1400). This B-version survives in Paris, Bibliothèque nationale de France, français, 12557, fols. 1ra–227vb. See *Méliador par Jean Froissart, roman comprenant les poésies lyriques de Wenceslas de Bohême, duc de Luxembourg et de Brabant*, ed. A. Longnon, 3 vols. (Paris, 1895–9). The romance has recently been re-edited by N. Bragantini-Maillard; see *Melyador*. Also see Jean Froissart, *Chroniques, Livre III. Le manuscrit Saint-Vincent de Besançon, Bibliothèque municipale, ms. 865*, ed. P. F. Ainsworth, Textes littéraires français (Geneva, 2007), I, 188–9 (III, §13). The B-version contains Wenceslas' lyrical poetry.

[104] See A. H. Diverres, 'Froissart's *Meliador* and Edward III's policy towards Scotland', in *Mélanges offerts à Rita Lejeune, professeur à l'Université de Liège*, 2 vols. (Gembloux, 1969), II, 1399–1409.

political objectives.[105] *Meliador* also contains an extended sequence of adventures in Ireland that likewise would seem to have resonated with the English court.[106]

Additionally, and most importantly for our purposes, Diverres calls attention to the fact that the eponymous protagonist Meliador is known as the Blue Knight (*le chevalier de bleu armé*) and his shield is azure charged with a sunburst of pure gold (*le Bleu au Cler Soleil d'Or*).[107] Blue and gold are the colours of the Order of the Garter, and Edward III and his eventual successor, Richard II (r. 1377–99), had badges featuring a sunburst.[108] In Diverres' analysis, 'Meliador is a purely fictitious character, representing no specific historical figure, but whose actions typify those of the ideal knight. He possesses all the qualities of an idealized prince and eulogizes the sons of Edward III and Philippa of Hainault or perhaps the whole house of Plantagenet.'[109] Put another way, Meliador, the Blue Knight, could be understood to be a proto-Garter knight, an Arthurian knight who epitomizes the virtues espoused by the Knights of the Garter and their founder. *Meliador* could thus be read as a literary nexus of Arthurian and Garter imagery and as an effort to 'Arthurianize' the Order of the Garter retroactively.[110]

---

[105] Diverres, 'Froissart's *Meliador*', pp. 1403–6.

[106] See A. H. Diverres, 'The Irish Adventures in Froissart's *Meliador*', in *Mélanges de langue et de littérature du Moyen Age et de la Renaissance offerts à Jean Frappier*, 2 vols. (Geneva, 1970), I, 235–51 (esp. pp. 247 and 251).

[107] See the A-version of Froissart, *Melyador*, II, 1314 (ll. 3–7).

[108] These connections were made by Diverres, 'Froissart's *Meliador*', p. 1408. We have independent confirmation from the twelfth statute of the Order of the Garter, from the *Chronicon* (c. 1360) of Geoffrey le Baker and from the mid-fourteenth-century alliterative poem *Wynnere and Wastour* that the Garter itself as well as the formal mantle that the Founder Knights of the Garter wore during their annual St George's Day festivities were blue. See Jefferson, 'MS Arundel 48', pp. 378–9, ll. 98–104; *Chronicon Galfridi le Baker de Swynebroke*, ed. E. M. Thompson (Oxford, 1889), pp. 108–9; *Wynner and Wastour* (line 94), in *Wynnere and Wastour and The Parlement of the Thre Ages*, ed. W. Ginsberg, TEAMS Middle English Texts (Kalamazoo, 1992), p. 16.

[109] Diverres, 'Froissart's *Meliador*', p. 1406.

[110] This same principle may also hold true for Froissart's 504-line *Dit dou bleu chevalier*. In it the narrator states that when April was running its course and May was approaching (that is around the time of St George's Day), he was walking in a wood and happened to see a lovesick knight dressed all in blue singing about his fair lady. Later in the *Dit* the Blue Knight faints, and the narrator comes to his aid and attempts to advise him. The two engage in conversation. The narrator recommends to the Blue Knight the examples of Tristan, Ywain, Lancelot, Guiron le Courtois and Perceval le Gallois, who sought adventures all over and performed deeds of chivalry that honoured their ladies and enhanced their own knightly reputation. The Blue Knight laments that he cannot match them because he is imprisoned in the wood and cannot be freed. He therefore honours his lady and upholds his honour by directing all his thoughts towards her and loving her with constant fidelity. See Jean Froissart, *Le Dit dou bleu Chevalier*, in *Jean Froissart 'Dits' et 'Débats'*, ed. A. Fourrier, Textes

When Froissart learned of Philippa's death (15 August 1369), he went to Hainault and undertook to write the first (A) version of the first book of his *Chroniques* for Robert of Namur (d. 1391), lord of Beaufort-sur-Meuse and Renaix. This A-version, completed in 1373, survives in approximately forty manuscripts (including Besançon, Bibliothèque municipale, 864). Section 203 of the A-version contains Froissart's earliest surviving chronicle account of the institution of the Garter:

> En ce temps vint en propos et en voulenté au roy Edouart d'Angleterre qu'il feroit faire et reedifier le chastel de Windesore, que le roy Artus fist jadiz faire et fonder, la ou premierement fut commencee et estoree la noble Table Ronde, dont tant de bons et vaillans chevaliers et bons hommes yssirent et traveillerent en armes et en prouesces par tout le monde. Et feroit le dit roy une ordonnance de chevaliers, de lui et de ses enfans et des plus preux de sa terre, et seroient en somme XL, et les appelleroit on et nommeroit les Chevaliers du Bleu Gerretier, et la feste a tenir et a durer d'an en an, et a sollempniser a Windesore le jour Saint George. Et pour ceste feste commencier, le roy d'Angleterre assembla de tout son païs contes, barons et chevaliers et leur dist son entention et le grant desir qu'il avoit de la feste commencier et entreprendre. Si lui accorderent lieement, pour tant que ce leur sembloit une chose honnourable, et ou toute amour se nourriroit.
>
> Adoncques furent esleuz quarente chevaliers, par advis et par renommee les plus preux de tous les autres: et seelerent et sirologierent [s'obligierent?], sur foy et par serement, avecques le roy a tenir et a pousuivir la feste et les ordonnances telles que elles estoient accordees et devisees. Et fist le roy fonder et edifier une chappelle de Saint George ou dit chastel de Windesore, et y establist chanoinnes pour Dieu servir, et les arenta et prouvenda bien et largement. Et pour ce que la dite feste feust sceue et congneue en toutes marches, le roy d'Angleterre l'envoya publier et denoncier par ses heraulx en France et en Escoce, en Bourgoingne, en Haynault, en Flandres et aussi en l'empire d'Allemanie. Et donnoit a tous chevaliers et escuiers qui venir y vouloient, quinze jours de saufconduit aprés la feste. Et devoit estre a ceste feste une jouste de XL chevaliers pardedens, attendans tous autres, et de XL escuiers aussi. Et devoit seoir ceste feste le jour de la Saint George proche venant, que on compteroit l'an de Grace mil CCC XLIIII, dedens le chastel de Windesore.[111]

---

littéraires français 274 (Geneva, 1979), pp. 155–70. Also see R. T. Pickens, 'History and Narration in Froissart's "The Case of the *Bleu* chevalier"', in *Froissart Across the Genres*, ed. D. Maddox and S. Sturm-Maddox (Gainesville, 1998), pp. 119–52 (esp. pp. 136–7).

[111] 'Besançon, Bibliothèque municipale, MS 864', ed. G. Croenen, with the collaboration of P. Ainsworth and I. Villela-Petit, in *The Online Froissart*, ed. Ainsworth and Croenen, v. 1.5, fol. 105 r–v, http://www.hrionline.ac.uk/onlinefroissart, accessed 26 October 2015.

(At that time it came into the purpose and will of King Edward III of England that he would have made and rebuilt the castle of Windsor, which King Arthur had long ago made and founded. That was the place where the noble Round Table was first begun and established, from whence so many good and valiant knights and good men issued forth and performed deeds of arms and of prowess throughout the world. And the aforesaid king made an order of knights, which included himself, his children and the most worthy men of his land, and they would number forty in total and they would be called and named the Knights of the Blue Garter and the feast was to be held and continued from year to year and solemnized at Windsor on St George's Day. And in order to begin this feast, the king of England assembled from all his lands earls, barons and knights and he told them his intention and the great desire that he had for beginning and undertaking the feast. So they willingly agreed with him in as much as it seemed an honourable thing to them and something where all love would be nourished.

Then forty knights (by opinion and renown the most worthy of all) were chosen and they sealed and obligated themselves, on faith and by oath, to hold and uphold, along with the king, the feast and the ordinances just as they were arranged and devised. And the king had a chapel of St George founded and built in the aforesaid castle of Windsor, and he established canons there in order to serve God and he endowed them and provided for their needs well and generously. And because the said feast was known and recognized in all the marches, the king of England had it proclaimed and announced by his heralds in France, Scotland, Burgundy, Hainault, Flanders and also in the German empire. And he was giving to all knights and squires who wished to attend fifteen days of safe conduct after the feast. And there would be at this feast a joust of forty knights indoors, in front of all others, and also of forty squires. And this feast was to be held on the next coming St George's Day, which one would reckon the year of grace 1344, inside Windsor Castle.)

Froissart's account begins much like that of Jean le Bel. In both cases we learn that Edward III was moved to restore and rebuild Windsor and we are told that King Arthur established his knightly fellowship of the Round Table there. Jean le Bel explains that Edward wanted to create a contemporary counterpart to the Round Table in order to honour his worthy knights. Froissart does not provide an explanation for why Edward III saw fit to establish a society of knights; he notes instead that it would include the king himself and his children. Jean le Bel does not name this *noble compaigne de chevaliers* nor does he specify its number. Froissart states that it would consist of forty members and that its name was 'les Chevaliers du Bleu Gerretier' (the Knights of the Blue Garter). The poet-chronicler's inclusion of the colour of the Knights of the Garter is interesting in light of *Meliador*. It is curious, given Froissart's familiarity with the members of the English royal court in the 1360s, that he did not correct what Jean le Bel had somewhat tentatively written about the institution of Edward III's order of knighthood. Were the proposed Order of the Round Table and actualized Order of the Garter truly separate and distinct? Have modern scholars overstated the difference? If they were separate and distinct, why did Froissart continue Jean le Bel's conflation of them? Was it a deliberate choice or was he unaware of the difference?

The final version of Book I of his *Chroniques*, found in the 'Rome manuscript' (Rome, Vatican Library, Reg. Lat. 869), which Froissart began in 1399, seems to suggest that the poet-chronicler had been either innocently confused or had taken some poetic licence with history for the sake of a smooth narrative. Froissart extended section 203 in this version. To the pre-existing entry, quoted in full above, he added that Edward III, when making plans for his *ordenance dou Bleu Gertier*, also had commissioned the construction of a chapel at Windsor Castle in honour of God and St George and planned for it to have twelve canons, who would hold services there and pray for the Knights of the Order of the Garter. In the Rome version, Froissart also speaks of further great works at Windsor Castle, including 'un grant palais de salles, de cambres et de toutes ordenances' (a great *palais* of halls, chambers and all arrangements), which were built on such a grand scale that they could comfortably accommodate the king and his retinue, the queen and her retinue, and even a great assemblage of prelates, barons and knights of England.[112] He adds that all the old works were still remaining in their entirety, including the dungeon of Windsor and the halls and the great hall where King Arthur gathered his retinue of adventurous knights, ladies and maidens. Froissart proceeds to state explicitly that the work at Windsor began in 1343 and that King Edward placed in charge of the construction a clerk named William of Wykeham, who, thanks to the grace of the king, rose from obscurity into a figure of great authority in England.[113] Geoffrey le Baker, a secular clerk from Swinbrook, Oxfordshire, states in his *Chronicon* (*c.* 1360) that it was in 1350 (not 1343) that Edward III founded at Windsor Castle a chapel of twelve priests, and thanks to the survival of royal letters patent we know that Edward III in fact established St George's Chapel at Windsor on 6

---

[112] Jean Froissart, *Chroniques: dernière rédaction du premier livre, édition du manuscrit de Rome Reg. lat. 869*, ed. G. T. Diller, Textes littéraires français 194 (Geneva, 1972), p. 596.

[113] Jean Froissart, *Chroniques: dernière redaction*, p. 596.

August 1348.[114] As noted above, the Clerk of the Works responsible in 1344 for construction of the *domus tabule rotunde* was not William of Wykeham, but rather Alan of Kilham.[115] It was only on 10 July 1359 that William of Wykeham was made chief keeper and surveyor of the castles of Windsor, Leeds, Dover and an assortment of other royal manors.[116] When speaking of the work at Windsor, Froissart evidently conflated the 1344 project with William of Wykeham's work at Windsor in the late 1350s and throughout the 1360s. If Froissart was innocently confused about who headed the Windsor building project in 1344, then he may just as easily have been confused as to its nature. Froissart knew that William of Wykeham eventually became involved with the great works at Windsor, but he made the mistake of placing him in charge of it fifteen years too early. Analogously, Froissart knew that Edward's planned order of knights at Windsor turned out to be the Order of the Garter. He seems to have used this knowledge to inform his coverage of the 1344 chivalric project as well.

Conclusion

In conclusion, we know that the Order of the Garter replaced the proposed Round Table as Edward III's monarchical order of knighthood. And yet the Garter was an esoteric symbol. There does not appear to have been a single concrete and widely known mythology behind its creation. The indeterminate and unfixed origin of the Garter appears to have been a deliberate choice on Edward III's part. It enabled the Order of the Garter to be an outlet for Arthurianism. From their earliest occurrences, the Windsor Garter feasts may have involved round table events and these may have taken place at the *domus tabule rotunde*. This is uncertain, but we can point to a fusion of Arthurian and Garter elements occurring on St George's Day 1358. And at virtually the same moment (with the theoretically possible, but improbable, exceptions of Gray's *Scalacronica* and Jean le Bel's *Vrayes Chroniques*) we find historiographical conflations of the proposed Order of the Round Table and the actualized Order of

---

[114] *Chronicon Galfridi le Baker*, p. 108. See W. M. Ormrod, 'For Arthur and St George: Edward III, Windsor Castle and the Order of the Garter', in *St George's Chapel Windsor*, ed. N. Saul, pp. 13–34 (p. 21).

[115] See J. Munby, 'The Round Table Building: The Windsor Building Accounts', in ed. Munby, Barber and Brown, *Edward III's Round Table*, pp. 44–52 (p. 45).

[116] See P. Partner, 'Wykeham, William (*c.* 1324–1404)', in *The Oxford Dictionary of National Biography*, online edn, http://www.oxforddnb.com/view/article/30127, accessed 31 August 2015.

the Garter. This does not appear to be a mere coincidence. Furthermore, some time between 1362 and 1369, a span of time that coincides with the majority of known round table / Garter conflations, Jean Froissart appears to have written an early version of his verse romance *Meliador* for Edward III's consort, Queen Philippa, and the text's eponymous hero is an Arthurian and proto-Garter knight. All of the foregoing discussion points to an Arthurian mythologizing of the Order of the Garter dating from the late 1350s and 1360s. The most widely known witness to this idea appears at the end of *Sir Gawain and the Green Knight* in its sole-surviving manuscript (*c.* 1400): London, British Library, Cotton Nero A x (art. 3), fol. 128v. There we find the motto 'HONY SOYT Q MAL PENCE', which invites all spectators to read the greatest of Middle English Arthurian romances as a Garter poem.[117] The political advantage of Edward III's Arthurianism was temporary at best, but its literary legacy remains with us to this day.

---

[117] Whether *Sir Gawain and the Green Knight* was written in the third or fourth quarter of the fourteenth century is much debated; whether the motto was original to the poem or a copyist's gloss is also unclear. My analysis is not contingent on these issues. I do, however, wish to call attention to W. G. Cooke and D'A. J. D. Boulton's theory that the romance was written for Henry of Grosmont, first duke of Lancaster and founding Knight of the Garter, shortly before his death in 1361. See their '*Sir Gawain and the Green Knight*: a poem for Henry of Grosmont?', *Medium Ævum* 68 (1999), 42–54. Perhaps the alliterative poem was read to Henry as he was recovering from the lance wound he sustained at the Garter feast of 1358.

IV

'THANKED BE GOD THERE HATH BEEN BUT A FEW OF MYNE AUNCYTOURS THAT HATHE DYED IN THEIR BEDDES': BORDER STORIES AND NORTHERN ARTHURIAN ROMANCES[*][1]

Ralph Hanna

This essay attempts to situate two northern Arthurian romances, the Alliterative *Morte Arthure* and *Ywain and Gawain*, within the culture from which they emerged. This surround, of course, is typically conceived – particularly by inhabitants of southern England – as over-militarized and violent. While my opening move, signalled by my title, acknowledges such perceptions, I hope to perturb this image of the 'uncouth / violent North' somewhat, to draw attention to a more varied set of local interests. Ultimately, I will suggest that such a cultural context may help to explain some of the differences between these poems and their immediate sources. But violence first!

---

[*] I owe particular thanks to the Radcliffe Institute for Advanced Study, Harvard University, who sponsored my work during 2011–12, when I produced a first draft of this essay. Not only did the Institute provide supportive and lavish surroundings; it also sponsored a writing group, whose members mulled over the incoherencies of earlier versions and demanded clarifications. I am especially indebted to them: Laurel Bossen (Anthropology, McGill), Susanne Freidman (Geography, Dartmouth), Gal Kalinka (Computer Science, Bar-Ilan) and John Plotz (English, Brandeis). I am further grateful to my more usual readers, Thorlac Turville-Petre and Sarah Wood, for a variety of suggestions.

[1] For this citation, see Jean Froissart, *The Thirde and Fourthe Boke of Sir Iohn Froissart of the Cronycles of Englande, Fraunce, Portyngale, Scotlande, Bretayne, Flaunders, and Other Places Adioynyng*, trans. J. Bourchier, Lord Berners (London, 1525 [STC 11397]), ch. 144, fol. 159rb (the full account covers chs. 140–6, fols. 155va–162ra). This version is probably more readily available in *Early English Books Online* than is the modern edition, *The Chronicle of Froissart*, trans. Sir J. Bourchier, Lord Berners, intro. by W. P. Ker, 6 vols. (London, 1901–3), V, 221 (the full account is at chs. 136–43, V, 210–33).

My title cites James, second earl of Douglas, dying at the battle of Otterburn in 1388. Certainly, Douglas knew the rules for heroes. Blessed, as the rest of his line, with a magnificently arrogant intransigence that would befit a Roland or an Achilles, he understood that proper heroism must always be tragic. Whether it occurs willingly or wilfully, only death in extreme circumstances displays that heedless courageousness which, paradoxically, creates a hero. Indeed, James had suffered five wounds (!) in turning the course of the battle, rallying the Scots, surprised in their tents by the forces of Henry Percy ('Hotspur'), through his wild charge into the English ranks, brandishing his battle-axe: 'He went euer forwarde lyke a hardy Hector, wyllyng alone to conquere the felde and to dyscomfyte his enemys'.[2]

Equally, in his final words to John Sinclair, James Douglas required of his retainer the act that would reveal why his violent recklessness and subsequent death had been worthwhile:

> I praye you, rayse vp agayne my baner, whiche lyeth on the grounde and my squyer slayne. ... Shewe nother to frende nor foo in what case ye se me in, for if myne enemyes knewe it, they wolde reioyse; and our frendes discomforted. (fol. 159rb)

Sinclair rescues and re-erects the standard, and he also raises up his lord's family battle-cry, 'Douglas'. Although by this point Douglas has died, he nonetheless lives – he is simultaneously dead and the triumphant victor of the field. In offering his last command, 'dead as living' as Spenser has it, he has literally enacted the 'fama perennis' that the Glasgow canon Thomas de Barry, in a Latin poetic account, believed that Douglas sought and that he had achieved in the battle.[3] As Barry perceived, Douglas commanded his subordinate to perform a gesture that would adumbrate

---

[2] Froissart, ch. 143, fol. 158vb. Froissart here alludes to one of the many examples of Hector's heroism in Guido de Columnis, *Historia Destructionis Troiae*, ed. N. E. Griffin (Cambridge, MA, 1936), and a sentence from Guido's prologue is germane: 'Antiquorum scripta, fidelia conseruatricia premissorum, preterita uelud presenti representant, et viris strenuis quos longa mundi etas iam dudum per mortem absorbuit, per librorum uigiles lectiones, ac si viuerent, spiritum ymaginarie uirtutis infundunt' (The writings of the ancients, faithful preservers of past deeds, present things past as if present. For valiant men, whom the world's great age has long absorbed in death, these writings pour forth, if one reads them attentively, the very soul of their imagined prowess, as if they yet lived [3]).

[3] I cite the text from W. Bower, *Scotichronicon*, gen. ed. D. E. R. Watt, 9 vols. (Aberdeen, 1987–98), here 7.428/161–3; 438/304; and cf. further 7.426/95–105, 124–6; 432/211–14. Bower's full account appears at 7.414–43 (Book 14.50–2, the last of the three chapters given over totally to Barry's poem); cf. Barry 7.436/274–75: 'Hic victor moritur; res ardua resque stupenda; / Martyrium patitur pro libertate tuenda'.

his eternal glory in the chronicle accounts his brave deeds would inspire.[4] Even while dead he had triumphed, through bravery and grace,[5] over the wilful Fortune that rules all battles – and that had ironically deflated his proud rival Hotspur, left living yet defeated and shamed.[6]

Even in this extremity, as his allusion to his ancestry indicates, James Douglas was only doing 'what came naturally', enacting what it meant to be a Douglas. As will appear more fully below, family mythmaking was a castle industry in the north, and the oldest (late 1440s) and best of these efforts is Douglas-sponsored, Richard Holland's *Buke of the Howlat*.[7] The centre of the poem (ll. 378–546) offers a lengthy account of the deeds of the first James Douglas, companion of the Bruce, and after the king's death, custodian of his heart. James the Black sustains Bruce's heroism, even after his lord's death, by constantly placing his heart where it always was in life – slinging the encased relic into the forefront of battle. This gesture allows him an emulative one, ceaselessly renewing his own faithful heroic service, by pursuing and relieving his lord (retrieving his heart-shrine), until he too falls in the field. In its turn, his 'bearing the heart' is immortalized in the Douglases' 'bearing the heart' throughout their testy generations, as a centrepiece in their coat of arms.

The battle of Otterburn was, of course, instigated by a Scottish invasion of northern England and points to one distinctive character of the region. As far south as the North Riding, this was an area prepared for and often subjected to warfare. While there had been a border at roughly its modern line since the tenth century, it had long been nominal.[8] It had separated two peoples with comparable interests, language and custom, once inhabitants of a single Northumbrian kingdom, and cross-border relations were usually unproblematic. Indeed, perhaps counterintuitively, the greatest disparity between the peoples thus artificially divided concerned the relative wealth of the Borders, in the thirteenth century the most prosperous

---

[4] 'in cronicis', Bower, 7.428/163; 438/306.
[5] 'Deo agente', Bower, 7.432/217.
[6] Not only were the English put to flight, but Hotspur was captured, taken away to Scotland and only released on payment of ransom, the booty of war that had been Douglas' original motivation for his 'chivauchee'. More pointedly, in Froissart's account, Hotspur's pursuit of Douglas had been motivated by losing his 'penon' to his adversary in an earlier exchange at Newcastle and by Douglas' challenge for Percy to come to his tent to retrieve this standard (ch. 141, fol. 157ra–va).
[7] See *Richard Holland The Buke of the Howlat*, ed. R. Hanna, Scottish Text Society 5th series, vol. 12 (Woodbridge, 2014). For an impressive(ly horrifying) family history, see M. Brown, *The Black Douglases: War and Lordship in Late Medieval Scotland 1300–1455* (East Linton, 1998).
[8] See G. W. S. Barrow, *The Kingdom of the Scots: Government, Church and Society from the Eleventh to the Fourteenth Century*, 2nd edn (Edinburgh, 2003), pp. 112–29 and 296–311.

parts of the Scottish kingdom – and of its port, Berwick-upon-Tweed, perhaps the richest borough in contemporary Scotland.

Edward I's initiation of The Great Cause changed everything and began what has sometimes been described as 'the three hundred years' war' (1296–1603). His first invasion was devastating; in his initial campaign, he ravaged Teviotdale and the Tweed valley, burned Berwick and massacred its inhabitants. From that point until the Union of the Crowns, two nations, each of which considered itself distinct (and wronged), hostilely faced one another across a national frontier, the only truly active 'march' area in Great Britain in the later Middle Ages.[9] All accounts agree the area was marked – but both marred *and sustained* – by endemic violence.

While the disastrous results of mutual antagonism are inarguable, the three centuries of hostility were marked by many periods of international truce and a considerable amount of cross-border cooperation.[10] Moreover, one needs to distinguish 'war', conflict in an interest perceived as national, from the more neutral but every bit as destructive 'violence'. Henry Percy's and James Douglas' meeting at Otterburn provides a telling instance. The third most storied battle in the conflict after Bannockburn and Flodden, alive in ballad well into the seventeenth century, this was, from the national perspective of warfare into which the encounter became enfolded, a thorough accident that should never have occurred.[11]

Certainly, Douglas was supposed to be engaged in warfare on behalf of Scotland. He led one of a pair of troops on an expedition designed to harry and destroy in both English marches, Cumberland in the west and Northumberland in the east. The Scottish plan had been for both invading forces to avoid open combat, to retreat northward, drawing the English after them, and to engage only as a large single unit (which would, in this plan, crush the pursuing English). But James was, after all, a Douglas, violent and intransigent to the core, and he chose not to follow the order of command. He saw in the invasion a chance for revenge on a rival

---

[9] Cf. J. A. Tuck, 'The Emergence of a Northern Nobility, 1250–1400', *Northern History* 22 (1986), 1–17.

[10] See A. Goodman, 'The Anglo-Scottish Marches in the Fifteenth Century: A Frontier Society?', in *Scotland and England 1286–1815*, ed. R. A. Mason (Edinburgh, 1987), pp. 18–33, and C. J. Neville, *Violence, Custom and Law: The Anglo-Scottish Borderland in the Later Middle Ages* (Edinburgh, 1998).

[11] The ballads are those F. J. Child presented as nos. 161–2 in *The English and Scottish Popular Ballads*, 5 vols. (Boston, 1882–98). For the planned campaign, see Froissart, ch. 140, fol. 155va, and Bower, 7.414/3–7. For modern discussions, see Tuck, 'Richard II and the Border Magnates', *Northern History* 3 (1968), 27–52, at pp. 32, 36–9 and 43–5; and 'War and Society in the Medieval North', *Northern History* 21 (1985), 33–52, at p. 40; Neville, *Violence*, pp. 54 and 56–7; and for the 'war of chivalry' between leading border families of both allegiances, Neville, *Violence*, pp. 96 and 188–9.

with whose family the Douglases had been contending for the last fifteen years; in the heartland of Douglas properties, Ettrick Forest, Jedburgh had been awarded to the Percys years before (1334) but was once again a live subject of legal actions. Pillaging and burning Percy Northumberland was, for Douglas, appropriate retaliation for his losses, and whatever the national plan of war, it proved less compelling than familially motivated violence for gain.

Indeed, on both sides of the border, those most responsible for defending 'the nation's' territory were probably those most interested and engaged in encouraging violence, and not necessarily against cross-border 'national enemies'. The Percys and their great rivals, the Nevilles, monopolized the office of warden of the English east march for nearly two centuries, and holding the office was crucial to both families' power and their economic success.[12] A stable peace would have rendered their office otiose. Thus, an insistence upon manifold local violence that they lacked the resources to control was integral to convincing the distant central authorities to continue and increase support for the family office. Yet when such support was forthcoming, the Percys invested the funds in expanding their personal retinue, in essence, as Tuck wryly observes, mounting a private army from public funds. However, the retinue was largely drawn from locals, men intent on pursuing both their own cross-border agendas and local rivalries. Thus, much of the Percy effort to achieve magnatial 'good governance' was invested in the legal support of retainers engaged in personal vendettas and random violence – only renewing the cycle.

Moreover, violence was scarcely restricted to those who might be considered 'men of war', those like James Douglas, committed to an honour code. War and raiding rendered agriculture a particularly unpredictable occupation in both marches, and this was consequently a country where the main activity was stockbreeding and much of the grain was imported. Frequently, the land does not seem to have offered enough sustenance to support families, and in such circumstances the vocation 'thief' does not seem to have been an altogether dishonourable one. Kin-bands, 'the surnames', lived simply by pillage, especially theft of livestock, and, like retainers of the great, they appear not always to have been particularly scrupulous about the nationality of those whom they victimized. However, just as border conflict was profitable to lords like the Percys, the existence of two separate legal jurisdictions along the border might have encouraged 'the surnames' to pillage 'over the line', since

---

[12] The Nevilles were originally a baronial family, 'of Raby' in southern County Durham, but built up a solid block of properties across the North Riding, including such defensive seats as Middleham, and were eventually elevated to become earls of Westmorland.

bringing malefactors to justice in a 'foreign' court might have proven particularly difficult.[13]

Social history, then, posits border society as answering two differing motivations, both the pursuit of honour, certainly personalized but potentially in a national interest, and a much less focussed, and certainly non-nationalized, search for gain through violence. Each view has its advocates in accounts of Otterburn. For the connoisseur Froissart, the battle ranks among the most glorious shows of raw courage and honourable endeavour he knows:

> one of the sorest and best foughten, without cowardes or faynte hertes, for there was nother knyght nor squyer but that dyde his deuoyre and fought hande to hande. (ch. 144, fol. 159ra)[14]

In contrast, Canon Barry refers to his account as a 'metra mixta': both a lament, in part for the fallen James Douglas but primarily for an elusive cessation of violence that will not come, and a paean of national triumph. Whether or not Otterburn provided 'Gloria victorum nulla moritura per evum' (the concluding line, 7.442/344), the poem is marked by heroic horror, its dissonances echoing the fierce mutual blows of the combatants in hyper-rhymed disphonic leonine hexameters.

Of course, the great simultaneous expression of both views, national triumphalism and continuously destructive violence in a personal interest (which may also be a royal one), appears in the distinguished northern tradition of alliterative historical poetry. *The Destruction of Troy*, although perhaps composed very late indeed, probably exemplifies the situation in which these poems were composed and transmitted, customarily, it would appear, to distinctly local and familiar magnatial audiences. The author

---

[13] For the preceding discussion, see Tuck, 'Richard II', 'War and Society', and 'Northumbrian Society in the Fourteenth Century', *Northern History* 6 (1971), 22–39; C. J. Neville, 'Local Sentiment and the "National" Enemy in Northern England in the Later Middle Ages', *Journal of British Studies* 35 (1996), 419–37; J. Gray, 'Lawlessness on the Frontier: The Anglo-Scottish Borderlands in the Fourteenth to Sixteenth Century', *History and Anthropology* 12 (2001), 381–408; somewhat quirkily, R. L. Storey, 'The North of England', in *Fifteenth-Century England, 1399–1509: Studies in Politics and Society*, ed. S. B. Chrimes et al. (Manchester, 1972), pp. 129–44; and often provocative medieval views reported in A. King, 'Englishmen, Scots and Marchers: National and Local Identities in Thomas Gray's *Scalacronica*', *Northern History* 36 (2000), 217–31.

[14] Similarly, ch. 146, fol. 161va; ch. 147, fol. 162ra. Cf. Child's ballad 161A, st. 58 (and 162A, st. 47): 'Ther was no freke that ther wolde flye, / But styffely in stowre can stond, / Ychone hewyng on other whyll they myght drye, / Wyth many a bayllefull bronde'; or, more pungently, Child 162B, st. 50 (and 162A, st. 54): 'For Witherington needs must I wayle / As one in dolefull dumpes, / For when his leggs were smitten of, / He fought vpon his stumpes'.

of *Troy* identifies himself as a John Clerk of Whalley (extreme northeast Lancashire) and says that he writes for a specific and, one imagines, noble patron.[15] Certainly, the great Cistercian abbey at Whalley might have provided the text he here Englishes, the standard account, Guido delle Colonne's *Historia Troiana*. Other texts in this tradition also appear to emerge from contexts where obliging clerics might have transformed Latin historical writing, most readily available in monastic libraries, for local magnates.[16] Both manuscripts of *The Wars of Alexander*, probably the finest alliterative verse in Middle English, come from Durham; *The Siege of Jerusalem* was written in Craven, perhaps at Bolton Priory (for the house's local patrons, the Clifford barons of Skipton?).

Within this tradition, pride of place has always been accorded to the one poem not composed in the north. However, the Alliterative *Morte Arthure* today is known only in its unique circulation in the most famous northern manuscript of romance, the Yorkshire gentryman Robert Thornton's Lincoln, Cathedral Library, 91. But, although probably composed in southern Lincolnshire (Croyland would be an appropriate monastic house with which to associate the poem), Thornton's rendition is but a single example of extensive knowledge of the *Morte* recorded in other northern and Scots works.[17]

---

[15] See T. Turville-Petre, 'The Author of *The Destruction of Troy*', *Medium Ævum* 57 (1988), 264–9, esp. p. 269 n.1, and E. Wilson, 'John Clerk, Author of *The Destruction of Troy*', *Notes and Queries* 235 (1990), 391–6.

[16] Cf. R. Hanna, 'Alliterative Poetry', in *The Cambridge History of Medieval English Literature*, ed. D. Wallace (Cambridge, 1999), pp. 488–512.

[17] For the provenance of Thornton's textual sources, see the groundbreaking essay by A. McIntosh, 'The Textual Transmission of the Alliterative *Morte Arthure*', in *English and Medieval Studies Presented to J. R. R. Tolkien*, ed. N. Davis and C. L. Wrenn (London, 1962), pp. 231–40. Authorial forms in the poem would connect composition with Kesteven, one of the linguistic levels McIntosh teases out; and M. Hamel offers further evidence for an early Lincolnshire audience in 'Arthurian Romance in Fifteenth-Century Lindsey: The Books of the Lords Welles', *Modern Language Quarterly* 51 (1990), 341–61. Since Hamel's edition of the *Morte Arthure*, although excellent on the sources, refuses to undertake editorial treatment of the received text (see *Morte Arthure: A Critical Edition* [New York, 1984], pp. 21–2), I cite E. Björkman (ed.), *Morte Arthur mit Einleitung, Anmerkungen, und Glossar*, Alt- und Mittelenglische Texte 9 (Heidelberg, 1915), who did consider the text carefully, if not with much discipline; this criticism is lodged in the important and ignored essay by J. L. N. O'Loughlin, 'The Middle English Alliterative *Morte Arthure*', *Medium Ævum* 4 (1935), 153–68. See also the fine critical discussion by L. Patterson in *Negotiating the Past: The Historical Understanding of Medieval Literature* (Madison, WI, 1987), pp. 197–230, as well as the useful R. A. Shoaf, 'The Alliterative *Morte Arthure*: The Story of Britain's David', *Journal of English and Germanic Philology* 81 (1982), 204–26; J. Finlayson, 'Rhetorical "Descriptio" of Place in the Alliterative *Morte Arthure*', *Modern Philology* 61 (1963), 1–11, and 'Alliterative Narrative Poetry: The Control

Here, it is most expedient to examine the centre of the *Morte*, roughly lines 2300–3456. At this point, the poet departs from the received account (most likely Wace or a derivative) that provides most of his narrative. This innovative material immediately succeeds the poem's dead centre, if you will, the moment that should provide its triumphant ending: the death of the Roman emperor Lucius (2242–55) and the sealing of English / British national independence that has been the poem's promised narrative. Thus, this segment of the poem offers, ostensibly, a point of not just ending – throwing off Roman tyranny – but beginning anew, enunciating some vision of what a liberated England / Britain means. However, like all great alliterative poems, the *Morte* forms a 'broken-backed' narrative; thus, this centrally disposed, individualized rendition of received history, much of the narrative inspired by other works that are well-known within the alliterative tradition, ends with the poet's great set-piece of disaster, his frontloading and elaboration of Arthur's second dream.[18]

Arthur's dream might be seen as a return to a moment all medieval literary dreams essentially replay, Odysseus' encounter with the shades of the dead. In the conventional Chaucerian account, for example, dreams posit past literary achievement (the book) against a newly achieved imaginative construction, a potential guide to future composition (the poem we read). Hence, dream appears as a mode of mediating history. On the one hand, visions rely upon the past that has provided a model for advancing the narrative to this point and that at this moment must be recognized as securely past or at least material of retrospect. On the other, as dreams, by convention they include an element conceived as oracular or prophetic, inspiration for future activity.

Central to Arthur's vision is, of course, the goddess Fortune, the most prominent (and, readers are asked to believe, most active) female figure in a compulsively male poem.[19] One might expect that the vision here should offer a particularly projective view. After all, Arthur stands as the first Christian hero among Fortune's minions, the 'Nine Worthies'. Thus, he is not simply at the achieved apex of his career but occupies an important juncture between pagan past, perhaps especially its most recent avatar, Julius Caesar, representative of the now overcome Rome, and a new dispensation.

---

of the Medium', *Traditio* 44 (1988), 419–51, at p. 429; and C. Chism, *Alliterative Revivals* (Philadelphia, 2002), pp. 189–236.

[18] Most explicitly, as W. Matthews pointed out in the only full-length study of the poem, *The Tragedy of Arthur: A Study of the Alliterative 'Morte Arthure'* (Berkeley, 1960), in importing the 'fuerre de Gadres' episode from accounts of Alexander the Great.

[19] As in many depictions of territorial conquest, that activity is conceived as little short of rape, e.g. 'We sall blenke theire boste for all theire bolde profire, / Als bouxom as birde es in bede to hir lorde' (Gawain at 2857–8); cf. Hector at 3292 and 3409, and Fortune's imagined grooming behaviours with Arthur at 3351–3.

In this account, however, such an assumed predictive and prophetic value of dream, the generic presumption that visions offer materials that change / shape history anew, is frustrated. Instead, the poet offers a vision one may aptly signal by the Spenserian phrase 'eterne in mutabilitie'.[20]

There is little surprising about the poet's conception of Fortune here. Rather conventionally, she is personalized as a grand courtly lady, in essence the *donna* of amatory lyric, the figure of grand disdain and accompanying male frustration and despair, although Fortune in the *Morte* disrupts the expected temporal order of lyric. She appears as caprice itself, first leading Arthur on and then subjecting him to her disdain, at once both the Bel Accueil and Daunger of the *Roman de la rose*. The dream describes a flirtatious whimsy in which the hero is greeted as worthy of the most special attention – and then unceremoniously dumped. Like the bereft lovers who sigh out most medieval love complaints, Arthur and his fellow victims perceive the figure as inscrutably cruel, and the sacrificial blood that Odysseus had shed to receive prophecy here is only their own (cf. 3274–5).[21]

The presence of other warriors (the six already fallen and the two Christians to come), of course, implies the foolishness of Arthur, the kingly lover, in believing that there is anything personal in all this, and solidifies his sense that he is just another random victim. Arthur receives no educational aid within the vision, only the laments of those failed lovers who have preceded him, all of whom simply bewail the indifference (and worse) finally shown by the bitch-goddess. Unlike most medieval love-poets, suitably grovelling and aware of their limitation (like Troilus, all lovers lack the requisite virtue to attain what they simultaneously believe they must have), all nine Worthies believe the favours offered them only answer their innate desert.

Concomitantly, they fail to see that the withdrawal of gifts, and their subsequent fall from Fortune's wheel, may reflect failure on their own part. Indeed, accepting a place on Fortune's elevator should be understood, retrospectively, not as engaging with an alien other but as a kind of mirroring portrayal. If she is indeed a capricious tyrant, eagerly accepting her favours at least accepts this quality as one equally proper to oneself.[22]

---

[20] *The Faerie Queene*, 3.6.47/5, but cf. 7.7.59/3, 'For thy decay thou seekst by thy desire'.

[21] Indeed, 'blode' is virtually the poem's signature lexical item (occurring thirty-eight times): vital fluid (here usually visible as exsanguination, its passage from sustaining life to marking the limit of vitality), the national or familial line and an overwhelming passion not subject to restraint.

[22] Cf. J. S. Bothwell's citation of Henry of Huntingdon in *Falling from Grace: Reversal of Fortune and the English Nobility, 1075–1455* (Manchester, 2008), p. 17: 'In these times no one achieves a great name except by the greatest of crimes'. Bothwell's study, although limited in that it examines only noblemen's loss of royal favour, indicates, with spectacular exemplification, the extent to which intelligent medieval magnatial

If her ability to harm, apparently irrespective of desert, is absolute and inevitable, so is the suitor's own. If she is impermanence, her votary has already created his own cycle of impermanence, predicated upon his violence and tyranny. Arthur is no different from anyone else, as the poet's narrative elaboration shows; the central 'original' material of the *Morte*, in recycling texts historically precedent, displays them not as an alien 'source' but simply as Arthurian subject matter, the alleged English historical paradigm rendered as only miming, derivative 'rewriting'.

Thus, the fallen Worthies also fail to get the message ceaselessly announced by landscape here, the succession of circles, of which Fortune's wheel provides only the central example (3238, 3240, 3242). Rather than revealing history as one eternal 'endless round', Arthur's dream announces the paradox that change is so constant – indeed, inherent in a natural landscape of God's creation – as to form the persistent, immutable, unchanging norm. Thus, narrative history becomes, as the wheel indicates, simply a sequence of cycles – different players, same old lesson – in which the purported individuality of vision and prophetic experience becomes levelled as identical with everyone else's.[23] Although succession in time exists, change fundamentally does not, only a cycle that runs down, again and again, to exhaustion.

Arthur's dream thus undermines the expectation inherent in its form, that there is meaningful change to be created or constructed, and reveals this as, at best, myth or hope. Having endured centuries of subjection, the only conscious model for 'lordship' available to Arthur is what has just been overcome. Thus, the imaginable 'noble' act only replicates that same tyranny to which England has been subjected. This should be a particularly chastening lesson, insofar as those who initially set what seemed such hopeful patterns are the grandest of men – and also, like Arthur, not altogether the drivers of process, but blind and uncomprehending subjects to it, all of them abject failures. In this context, Arthur appears simply as the repetitive latest child of the most archaic moment to which the dream alludes, Hector's Troy. Arthur's Christian intrusion into the six existing Worthies, quite in contrast to Froissart's unironized reading of Douglas' heroism at Otterburn, signals neither restoration nor difference; Priamus'

---

life should have been bound up with constant concerns over perpetuity, retaining lordship – and perhaps an interest in mutuality and interdependency as well. For discussion of some topics offering interesting parallels to the poem, cf. pp. 34–6, 55 and 226.

[23] Cf. Chism, *Revivals*, pp. 189 ('enemies ... at once ancestors and rivals, doubles and others') and 226–7; and lines 2268–73 where conquering 'chiftaynes' and annihilated 'cheualry noble' echo one another, only differentiated by the victors' 'chalke-whitte' accoutrements receiving an exsanguinated stain in the case of the vanquished (cf. 2287).

happy conversion, for example, only demonstrates the Christian ability to assimilate that past which it overtly says it is rejecting.[24]

The projective vision that most stimulates Arthur in the poem is quite opposite to that vision of limitation provided by Fortune. From a traditional 'mountain of vision', the slopes of the Alps, he surveys the lush expanse of Italian fields stretching before him with a conqueror's gaze:

> When he was passede the heghte, than the kyng houys
> With his hole bataylle, behaldande abowte,
> Lukande one Lumbarddye, and one lowde melys:
> 'In ȝone lykand londe lorde be I thynke.' (3106–9)

Thus, at least insofar as the dream presents historical process, it implies a prophetic lesson come always too late. Arthur is offered no opportunity to learn from it, and the very process of his commitment to conquering lordship has already condemned him to failure. In this context, the best one could hope for would be 'relative longevity', a sobriety that would allow consideration of how to stave off, for so long as possible, the moment when the inevitable fall will occur.[25] But to operate in this way would imply a choice, and a choice nowhere exceptionally evident in the poem until far too late, namely struggling to bridle the imperious will, choosing, as James Douglas would think, ignobly, to die peacefully and securely in one's bed rather than in the field.

Here the issues are established, rather disingenuously, in the invocation at the poem's opening (1–25). While this is indeed a *morte*, the initial narrative summary (from line 12 on) misrepresents the subject, by promising only the jingoistic narrative, 'How they whanne wyth were wyrchippis many' (22). This description, accompanied by other misleading details – 'Kynde men and courtays and couthe of courtethewes' (21) probably is less descriptive of this work than any other in the entire realm of Arthuriana, only addresses the narrative up to the

---

[24] For other examples of British Trojanism, cf. lines 896 (Arthur's gigantic double), 1696, 2603, 2634–8 and the conclusive 4342–6; and most strikingly, the profusion of 'Worthies' material associated with Gawain's adversary Priamus at lines 2602–11 and 2634–5. The grandest term for chivalric pride in the poem, 'cirquitrie', appears only twice, of Priamus at 2616 and of Arthur at the dream's end at 3399.

[25] The prospect movingly enunciated, in opposition to Arthur, by one of the poem's cagiest inheritors, the Scots *Knightly Tale of Golagros and Gawane*, ed. R. Hanna, Scottish Text Society 5th series, vol. 7 (Woodbridge, 2008), particularly lines 1223–48. In the *Morte*, Arthur only addresses the issue in his arrogant speech to the Roman embassy; cf. 'whylls my blode regnes' (2348, 2361, with devastating pun on the usually mortal 'blode rennes'), 'whilles my tym lastes' (2351, 2364, 2419). For the first, see n. 19 above.

poem's centre. It is possible to know too much as a reader, and thereby to deaden the shock of the narrative's turn. This opening implies that it is not an absolute inevitability that this be a *morte* (or a Malorian 'whole life of Arthur') and that there might be nothing amiss in hearing a nationalistic narrative of 'awke dedys', English liberation from foreign subjection 'thorowe craftys of armes' (13, 24).

Contrasted with this misdescription of the full narrative that will ensue is the poet's invocation, which strikes a very different note, a considerably broader perspective indeed:

> Now grett glorious Godde, thurgh grace of hymseluen ...
> [W]ysse me to werpe owte som worde at this tym,
> That nothyre voyde be ne vayne, bot wyrchip till hymselvyn,
> Plesande and profitabill to the pople þat heres. (1, 9–11)

In contrast to the Arthurian 'wyrchippis' described in subsequent lines, honours associated with territorial adventurism, 'wyrchip' here is denatured of the physical. In this usage, the word represents that devout honour that one may properly confer only by acknowledging the divine graciousness that has already inspired it (divine 'worship' in the modern sense).[26] Moreover, in imagining an almost muse-like divinity, the gracious source of the uttered word, the poet suggests a writing divinely inspired and thus edifying in the manner that the famous anti-romance prologue of *Cursor Mundi* suggests romance cannot achieve ('voyde ... ne vayne' evokes, as we will see, not for the first time in the north, the strongest claims lodged against this genre, only to reject them).[27] The promised 'pleasure' of the poem might well resonate with the second half of this introduction – and certainly might answer a later language of perniciously unadulterated pleasure: '[Arthur] Reuelles with riche wynes, riotes hymselfen' (3172). In these terms, Arthur and his men, however noble their initial warfare, respond to only half the poet's prescriptions. For he encourages a second and sanctified (*Cursor*-friendly) goal to comprehension, 'profit' – not here the income from tracts of conquered real estate, but rather

> ... grace to gye and gouerne vs here
> In this wrechyd werld thorowe vertuous lywynge. (4–5)

---

[26] Similarly, 'dredde ay schame' (20) addresses an honour code like Douglas', predicated upon noble acts, and not the more resonant 'Schelde vs fro schamesdede and synfull werkes' (3), which relies both on invoking divine grace and a reverent application to God's law.

[27] For this prologue, see *Early Middle English Verse and Prose*, ed. J. A. W. Bennett and G. V. Smithers, 2nd edn (Oxford, 1968), pp. 184–9.

Both in triumph and tragedy, Arthur's efforts to convert his experience into something like the poet's prescription always prove awkwardly ineffectual, if not derisory, for example describing extirpating the giant as 'pilgrimage' or the attempt to transform Gawain's blood into Eucharistic relic (896 etc., 3989–96).

Of course, as all critics recognize, the poet most strikingly writes unbridled or imperial will into the poem's central segment. As Arthur's dream shows, the noblest warriors are always conquerors, and in their pursuit, imitating their predecessor regimes, they have unfailingly exceeded limits. Whatever their 'just cause', like Arthur's pursuit of national sovereignty, their careers have always returned to the excessive behaviours inherited from their predecessors. Thus, as part of the poem's spatialization of desire, Arthur wins what he has claimed to want at the point of Lucius' death but, unsatisfied, handles the Roman ambassadors shamefully and extends his wars into an apparently neutral country, Germany / Lorraine, an initiative marked by his imperious refusal to heed personal danger at Metz (2330–5 etc., 2420–47).[28]

Indeed, the suicidally unnecessary hyperaggressiveness marking the recycled Alexandrine 'fuerre de Gadres' episode is initially motivated by the 'foreignness' of the locale to the army. It is not their 'natural place', and they do not know how to forage constructively (2484–92). Moreover, hunting another lord's land is a fruitfully long-lived trope of usurpation in northern writings.[29] The point is summarized in Gawain's avowedly 'witless' decision not to 'getteles go home' (2727), broaching the issue of daring as folly that arises explicitly only in this portion of the narrative. At this point, Gawain has completely forgotten the foragers' plan to gain subsistence – even if 'out of place', an acknowledgement of human necessity, and has given himself over to warring triumphalism, a 'gette' of either corpses or treasures. However, to follow the logic of Arthur's dream, the proud rapacity that transgresses licit limits to human endeavour here demonstrates not simply moral failure, but moral failure as the outgrowth of notable grandeur, not sufficiently subjected to moral control. Arthur, imitating Alexander and his ilk, is the proper subject of romance *and* chronicle (3438–45), but as a faultedly grand chivalric ego

---

[28] Both of these moments are channelling the earlier (*c.* 1370s) *The Siege of Jerusalem*, ed. R. Hanna and D. Lawton, Early English Text Society 320 (Oxford, 2003), lines 357–80 and 811–20, respectively.

[29] It appears, for example, in *The Siege of Jerusalem*, *Degrevant* and, with various inflections, in the ballad accounts of Otterburn (e.g. 'The hunting of the Cheviot'); see further W. P. Marvin, 'Slaughter and Romance: Hunting Reserves in Late Medieval England', in *Medieval Crime and Social Control*, ed. B. A. Hanawalt and D. Wallace, Medieval Cultures 16 (Minneapolis, 1999), 224–52.

who allows himself and his troops to rampage unchecked, ultimately to his own destruction.

Poems like the Alliterative *Morte* may stimulate feelings of melancholic grandeur, but the self-representations in northern family chronicles tell a rather different story. The complex admiration and alienation that Arthur might here evoke appear subject to fission, into self-aggrandizing tales of family conquest (like Holland's recapitulation of constantly growing Douglas estates) or of tragedy encountered in honourable national service. One can exemplify these alternate accounts through two sixteenth-century family verse histories, that of the Stanley earls of Derby and the voluminous series of accounts associated with the Percy earls of Northumberland.

'The Antiquity of the Family of the Stanleys', tentatively ascribed to a family member, Thomas Stanley, bishop of Sodor and Man (*c.* 1560), is a particularly testosterone-driven narrative. This family's eventual national prominence, as earls of Derby, depended almost solely upon their military service, first as Cheshire leaders in Ireland. As a reward for their politically belated charge into Richard III's flank at Bosworth Field in 1485, they were elevated to the peerage; in literature, they are perhaps best known for the late accounts of their Cheshire troops destroying James IV and the flower of Scottish chivalry at Flodden in 1513.[30]

---

[30] For the most extensive family history, see B. Coward, *The Stanleys, Lords Stanley, and Earls of Derby, 1385–1672: The Origins, Wealth, and Power of a Landowning Family*, Chetham Society 3rd ser. 30 (Manchester, 1983); M. J. Bennett, *Community, Class and Careerism: Cheshire and Lancashire Society in the Age of Sir Gawain and the Green Knight*, Cambridge Studies in Medieval Life and Thought 3rd ser. 18 (Cambridge, 1983), offers an extensive discussion of the family's regional lordship. I cite the poem doubly, both from *The Palatine Anthology: A Collection of Ancient Poems and Ballads Relating to Lancashire and Cheshire*, ed. J. O. Halliwell (London, 1850), pp. 208–71, and from Oxford, Bodleian Library, Rawlinson poet. 143, fols. 13r–26v. 'The Antiquity' includes a passage in praise of Cheshire / Lancashire archery, instrumental in the victory at Flodden (edn 240–2, MS fols. 19v–20r); for this battle and its poetic representations, see *Scotish Feilde and Flodden Feilde: Two Flodden Poems*, ed. I. F. Baird, Garland Medieval Texts 4 (New York, 1982), and the discussions in D. A. Lawton, 'Scottish Field': Alliterative Verse and Stanley Encomium in the Percy Folio', *Leeds Studies in English* NS 10 (1978), 42–57; J. Scattergood, 'A Defining Moment: The Battle of Flodden and English Poetry', in *Vernacular Literature and Current Affairs in the Early Sixteenth Century: France, England, and Scotland*, ed. J. and R. Britnell, Studies in European Cultural Transition 6 (Aldershot, 2000), 62–79; and R. W. Bartlett, Jr, *Against All England: Regional Identity and Cheshire Writing, 1195–1656* (Notre Dame, IN, 2009), pp. 171–95. In spite of Bennett's enthusiasm, I doubt very much whether the Stanley family (or indeed, Cheshire) has any connection with Sir Gawain and the Green Knight, but see E. Wilson, 'Sir Gawain and the Green Knight and the Stanley Family of Stanley, Storeton and Hooton', *Review of English Studies* NS 30 (1979), 308–16.

'The Antiquity' strikes its characteristically aggressive note early. In discussing the man who brought the family to regional prominence and power, John Stanley of Lathom (South Lancashire), who died in 1414, the poet offers a lengthy encomium to his chivalry:

> [He] wan honor in each place wheare he did come,
> Not setting in house with pen, incke, and paper,
> But in camp advaunsed through stout adventure.
> I do speake nor meane anie to despice
> That be enhaunsed by penn or marchandise,
> For both most be hadd and both necessarie,
> And both worthie praise, thoughe the seates do varye.
> But to saie the truth, that man ought to be most praysed
> That by hardy actes to honour is raised,
> For of those be made bookes in prose and in ryme –
> Of others not – and serues for the tyme.
> Thought of them have diuers comen full valliaunt,
> Yeat they may not their originall advaunte,
> Nor so largely set furth theire renowne so farre
> As those whose advauncement have comen by war.
>   (edn 213–14, MS fol. 14r).[31]

The Stanley poet juxtaposes indoor acts of peaceful acquisition, sedentary pursuits, with the greater activity of the camp and that war that brings honour. But this, of course, reflects a deeply garbled claim; the Stanleys pursued honour, not simply abstractly, but because it brought them gain, lands and lordship – ultimately a splendid house at Lathom. Only with difficulty can one see this acquisitiveness as incomparable to mercantile winnings. Moreover, the discussion is fractured by the very doubleness inherent in the word 'account'. Keeping paper accounts may be an activity associable with careful and less than memorable mercantile activity but, equally, the Stanleys can only be raised from obscurity and their nobility enhanced through a documentary account. Their honour, not to mention their origin, endures only as verbal *fama*.

This particular variety of verbal aggression draws attention to problems the Stanleys as a line faced which the poem acknowledges, even as it glosses over certain difficulties of family history that must necessarily be occluded. First, Stanley 'originall[s]' are not only less than 'advaunt[abl]e', but particularly obscure; the family seems to have emerged from rather anonymous

---

[31] Scarcely isolated in the poem, cf. also edn 224 (MS fol. 16r); edn 246 (MS fol. 21r) disparagingly contrasts this chronicle of 'noble acts' with the 'trifles' heralded in mercantile London examples and includes a precise satiric citation of the 1486 entry from one such chronicle.

gentry stock in either Audelay or Stanley, villages in the North Staffordshire moors. Moreover, the outstanding founders of the line were not its leaders, but younger sons forced to make their own way in the world, almost necessarily by derring-do. In this circumstance, outstanding feats allow the deserving youth to 'marry up' into higher social ranks, ones more congruous with his recognized desert, although not his birth. The great John Stanley was such a parvenu, who ultimately achieved his fortune through a rich, and bitterly resisted marriage, to Isabel, heiress of Lathom (edn 219–20, MS fol. 15r–v). Through this union, the Stanleys achieved not only wealth and increased influence and power, but the eagle and child blazon that displayed to all their identity (this was originally the badge of Oskell Lathom, as the poem recounts, the child found in an eagle's nest who preserved the Lathom line), as did Douglas' heart.

But being a younger son was not the only embarrassment John Stanley faced. His immediate forebears, the Stanleys of Storeton (Cheshire), appear to have been a particularly unpleasant sort. Minor servants of the Black Prince, their office throughout the fourteenth century was as hereditary foresters of the Wirral. They appear to have pursued their duties, mainly exacting fines from neighbouring farmers for alleged violations of forest law, with zest; since in the fourteenth century forest law was no longer supposed to be legally enforceable in Cheshire, the family basically lived through extortion, encouraged by the profiteering Prince. As a result, the Stanleys were vigorously opposed by their neighbours, and at one point in the 1350s their activities provoked a popular rebellion that required an invasion of retinues from outside the county (John of Gaunt's, for example) to be quashed.[32]

These perhaps unfortunate historical resistances mark 'The Antiquity' in two ways. First, in the poem the family's pre-fifteenth-century history ignores anything documentary and instead substitutes a heavy tincture of romance motif. John Stanley's early career, highlighted by a brief fling with a Byzantine princess, has been derived from either *Guy of Warwick* or *Bevis of Hamptoun*. Similarly, portions of the episodes concerning Lathom contain reminiscences of *Eglamour* (a child abducted by a griffin) and *Degrevant* (Isabel Lathom's failure to obey family counsel and her determination to oppose her father). Secondly, although 'The Antiquity' remains rather monotonally militaristic throughout, one of its

---

[32] There is a considerable literature on the Wirral 'forest' (that wasn't), an episode that lies behind such in-jokes as *Gawain and the Green Knight* 699–702 and *Winner and Waster* 313–18. See H. J. Hewitt, *Mediaeval Cheshire: An Economic and Social History of Cheshire in the Reign of the Three Edwards*, Chetham Society NS 88 (1929), 8–18; B. M. C. Husain, *Cheshire Under the Norman Earls 1066–1237*, A History of Cheshire 4 (Chester, 1973), 54–74; and R. A. Stewart-Brown, 'The Disafforestation of Wirral', *Transactions of the Historical Society of Lancashire and Cheshire* 59 (1907), 165–80.

few bows to anything that reveals Stanleys as having cultural interests is telling (notably edn 265–9, MS fols. 25v–26r). This material, much of it concerned with the remodelling of Lathom into a splendid house, as well as other building projects of the first earl of Derby, insists upon the earl's role as 'good neighbour'.[33] While his antecedents may have engaged in predatory local behaviours, the family activities reportable as history fill a guilty silence elsewhere in the account.

However, such embarrassments scarcely typify the narrative of 'The Antiquity'. By and large, the poem heralds the Stanleys as a sequence of men who, through their valour (widely displayed, if not, before the poem's circulation, widely acknowledged) were the equals – and at Bosworth, the creators – of kings. This role is, of course, only the Stanleys' due, since from 1406, long before kings chose to elevate them to the peerage, they had themselves been royalty, the kings of Man.[34] This note of royal recognition is first struck in the account of Thomas Stanley, the first earl. Attainted at a parliament in Coventry, he is forced to appeal to the queen, Margaret of Anjou, kneeling to her; but in a later episode, when he triumphs in a Smithfield tournament, Margaret descends from her seat to honour his bravery.[35] Roles are reversed, and the fitness of a

---

[33] The only analogue in the poem concerns Edward, Lord Monteagle's abilities on the recorder (edn 252–4, MS fol. 21r–v). As typically in the poem, this cultural skill is converted into romance allusion (the second coming of Tristram, the founder of the music of the hunt) and most flamboyantly expressed in a contest against royalty. At Henry VII's command, Edward outperforms the musicians of the visiting 'king of Castile'. This dates the occasion to early 1506, when Philip, Archduke of Burgundy, and master of perhaps the grandest contemporary court, was shipwrecked in England while voyaging to claim his wife Juana's rights to the throne of Castile.

[34] Thomas' brother William found Richard's crown on the field at Bosworth; accounts vary as to whether he actually crowned Henry Tudor, or merely presented it to Henry with the unfortunate witticism that having won it, he should crown himself (the latter is the poem's version [edn 250, MS fol. 22r], with only a passing allusion to Henry's alleged revenge for this quip: he executed William for alleged participation in the Perkin Warbeck revolt of 1495). At least one point worth further consideration is the Stanleys' northwestern Vikingism: the progenitor Oskell Lathom bears a pagan name (Os-kettel); the Wirral, where early Stanleys held sway, has the largest concentration of Scandinavian placenames in Cheshire (see P. Cavill et al., *Wirral and its Viking Heritage*, English Place-Name Society Popular Series 2 [Nottingham, 2002]); and the Isle of Man historically was an independent Norse kingdom.

[35] I have not found evidence for the Smithfield tournament (implicitly datable 1459–61), but Stanley involvement in Coventry attainders is real enough. At the Coventry parliament, *William* Stanley was among a large group of Yorkists accused of 'traiterous reryng of werre' against Henry VI and was further accused, individually, of not rendering aid to the king when summoned; on both occasions, the king accepted the parliamentary petition, but retained his right to extend mercy and grace. In the context, Henry VI being *non compos mentis*, that 'grace' should have been extended by

youthful upstart (another generation in conflict over the audacious choice of a bride of higher status) is acknowledged by royalty.

But perhaps a more substantial centre of Thomas' career (and of the poem) is ongoing conflict with a figure widely recognized as the premier captain of the north, Richard, earl of Gloucester, later Richard III. The pair engage in a war of retinues, in which Stanley puts Richard's troop to flight in a battle at the Ribble Bridge in Preston and captures his banner, to be hung in triumph in a local Lancashire church at Wigan. More seriously, Richard deserts the pair's mutual expedition to capture Berwick in 1482:

> With shame is he gonne, returned not againe;
> He never bod field ne fray, but when he was slayne.
> (edn 239, MS fol. 19r)

The triumph – which finally rendered this important border borough irrefutably English, not Scottish – is, in the family's account, entirely due to Stanley tenacity, and Cheshire archery.[36] Thomas' rebuilding of Lathom provokes yet more emulation of kingship. The earl entertains Henry VII there over eight days, displaying the grandest service any subject ever showed a prince; indeed, the poet avers, the king was so impressed that he constructed his new palace at Richmond on the model of Lathom (edn 265–7, MS fol. 25v). Simultaneously, the family does not just provide a model for and take an aggressive stand against English kings. Thomas defended his rights in Man against possible encroachments by James III of Scotland, and his younger son Edward was ennobled by Henry VIII as Lord Monteagle (a title reflecting the family arms) for his heroic actions against James IV at Flodden.

The lack of recognition that impels the Stanley 'Antiquity' could scarcely be associated with the motivations underlying similar materials concerning the Percy earls of Northumberland. After all, Rose's recent popular history of the line calls them 'Kings in the North', a sobriquet my earlier discussion of border conditions would certainly justify. The family was heralded in a succession of texts, extending over several centuries.[37] The fullest of these, from the 1510s, was composed by the fifth earl's

---

Queen Margaret. See *Rotuli Parliamentorum ut et Petitiones et Placita in Parliamento, tempore Edwardi R. I.*, 6 vols. (London, 1767–77), V, 349–50 and 369.

[36] This claim is nonhistorical, since Richard did capture Berwick (which had changed 'nations' thirteen times since 1147); for a moment certainly central to the pair's animosity, and narrated in the poem (edn 248–9, MS fol. 21v), see the more famous account by St Thomas More, *History of King Richard III*, ed. R. S. Sylvester, The Yale Edition of The Complete Works of St. Thomas More, 15 vols. (New Haven, 1963), II, 48–9.

[37] See A. Rose, *Kings in the North: The House of Percy in British History* (London, 2002). For the series of accounts, see M. Holford, 'Family, Lineage, and Society: Medieval Pedigrees of the Percy Family', *Nottingham Medieval Studies* 52 (2008),

secretary, William Peeris; it appears in London, British Library, Royal 18 D ii. Perhaps surprisingly, this poem opens in a mode that might well remind one of Stanley self-assertion:

> Cronykillis and annuall bookis of kinges,
> Of auncient lordes and estates riall
> Declarithe the discent, with many notable thingis,
> Their fatall endes and theire actes marshall.
> Yet a trew discent and lynage speciall
> In dyuers placis consulede in the booke,
> It is harde to fynde, bot yf a man longe looke.
>
> Wherfore I haue concludid rudely, as I can,
> In a perpetuall memory, for a president,
> Of the noble Percy blode, mayntener of many a man
> Her to entitle of auncient proffe euydent.
> So liberall a lynage, a stock so reuerent,
> So prepotent a progeny, of noble blode descendid,
> Ought to be regestered, reme[m]brede, and penyde.
> (edn 9–10, MS fol. 186r)[38]

Peeris acknowledges the well-chronicled status of kings – their widely known descent, military acts and demises. But 'lynage[s] speciall' merit a comparable treatment, a palpably 'trew' account, derived from 'auncient proffe euydent'. Hence, somewhat disingenuously, since he is here recycling an earlier, shorter version of the text in Alnwick Castle 79, Peeris offers his version as an imitable 'president' for analogous accounts which are currently (he claims) difficult to obtain. His precedent forms 'a perpetuall memory' analogous to that already available for kings, and his poem indeed fulfils the promised combination of 'auncient proffe' and 'memorial' – the Percy muniments and funeral monuments to which he makes regular reference throughout.[39]

The analogy between the Percy family and English kings forms an active part of the reading experience of Percy family history. Alnwick Castle 79 is not a codex, but a roll, and one of a sort widely dissemi-

---

165–90; he fails to emphasize adequately the manner in which retention of earlier materials in later renditions might qualify or change their meaning.

[38] The printed edition of Peeris' poem, 'The discent of the Lord Percies', ed. J. B[elsey], in *Reprints of Rare Tracts and Imprints of Antient Manuscripts &c., Chiefly illustrative of the History of the Northern Counties Volume I: Biographical* (Newcastle, 1845), pp. 7–43, is drawn from a damaged copy, Oxford, Bodleian Library, Dodsworth 50, and lacks nineteen stanzas present in the Royal manuscript (fols. 189v ff.) following edn p. 24.

[39] Cf. Alexandra Gillespie's comments, '"These proverbs yet do last": Lydgate, the Fifth Earl of Northumberland, and Tudor Miscellanies from Print to Manuscript', *Yearbook of English Studies* 33 (2003), 215–32, at p. 230.

nated *c.* 1450–90. At the centre of its joined members, the roll provides a fairly standard example of a brief chronicle of the kings of England, and this is surrounded – as both the Stanley 'Antiquity' and Peeris' opening would lead one to expect – with various Percy materials: images of the developing family arms in one margin, the verse chronicle in another.[40] These works of Percy eulogy and memorial are deliberately cloned from the conventions of the royal chronicles whose textual space they share. In Peeris' poem, which records a long succession of Henrys and Thomases, these figures are numbered, just as are English monarchs. Similarly, marriages are duly chronicled, in the Percy poems with attention to the resulting changes in the family arms, analogous to the frequent presentation in kings' rolls of the developing royal arms.[41] Again, kings of England rolls routinely identify burial places, although less intently than does Peeris, who emphasizes the shifting sites of the family pantheon, places of ancestral memory.

A second example of similar materials, in this case including an English prose Percy history, will severely qualify this apparent view of a family presenting itself, as do the Stanleys, in contestation with royalty. Oxford, Bodleian Library, Bodley Rolls 5 is a general historical roll and presents not simply kings of England down to Richard III, but also Roman and Trojan history, as well as a Percy genealogy, all in a single hand. However, the content of the Percy narrative – just as that of Peeris' poem – would rebuff any simple claim of royal emulation or to a lineage equal to that of kings. The Percys were early Norman incomers, and their first seat, always the centre of their estates, was at Topcliffe-on-Swale in the Vale of York; thus, the first Percy entry, adjoining the account of 'William Bastard, duke of Normandy' in the chronicle of kings, tells that

> After þe pompe and pride of this world, Sir William Percy was nobly borne, and as old men said, he was gretly belouyd of kyng William Conquerrour, for he gave hym þe most part of þe prouynce of Yorkshire. And he gate hym grete honour, bothe by his birthe and also by succession of possession, and there was in hym grete plentuosnes and largenes, for he endowed many placez of þe chirche and religion and gave to Godes seruantes many grete possessions and giftes. Among whiche he first gave to seint Iohn of Beuerley 8.[?] knyghtes feez [with three further grants]. ... After þat,

---

[40] For an illustration of such materials outlining English kings, see *The Scroll Considerans (Magdalen MS 248) Giving the Descent from Adam to Henry VI*, ed. J. E. T. Brown and G. L. Harriss, Magdalen College Occasional Paper 5 (Oxford, 1999).

[41] The Alnwick version, 'A Verse Chronicle of the House of Percy', ed. A. S. G. Edwards, *Studies in Philology* 105 (2008), 226–44, includes materials (lines 43–63) not taken up by Peeris, describing both the derivation of the Percy name and of its great badge, the crescent moon, from a crusading adventure in Persia.

to seint Hylde, v. knyghtes feez. And he gave to Raynfride, somtyme a knyght þat afore was his felowe, and then was a monk in þe abbey of Euesham, þe old abbey of Whithye and made hym þe first priour there. And þe seid Raynfrid belded agayn þat old abbey þat afore was destroyed with Danes, and þis William Percy gave hym all Whitby and Prestby, and also þe chirche of oure lady of the same town and þe haven of þe see in þe same with all þe appurtenances ...

Rather strikingly, there is not a word about William Percy's conquering valour here. Nor does the chronicler notice that establishing Norman 'succession of possession' in Yorkshire would have involved William in some severe acts of 'pacification', participation in the Conqueror's scorch and burn 'Harrowing of the North' (1070). Indeed, William's interest in 'possession' seems scarcely even a strong one; although one is to imagine him a conqueror, he is more strikingly someone who gains assets only to redistribute them with extravagant largesse – rather than strenuous warrior, pious patron of multiple religious foundations.[42]

The most extensive of these endowments, Whitby, subject of half the account, is particularly interesting. This discussion allows the family to be presented as completely 'nativized', in a constructive engagement with the Anglo-Saxon past (rather than the Conqueror's armed extirpation of it). William Percy's endowing and encouraging the refoundation of Whitby explicitly, in its reference to St Hild, the great abbess who convened the seminal council there, allows his line to assume a central position within Bedan history. Moreover, this refoundation expunges further violence inherent in the Percy past; Peeris explains that the Percys had come to Normandy as companions of its Viking conqueror (and first duke) Rollo (edn 11–12, MS fol. 186v). If the glorious old Whitby of Hild had been destroyed by the 'Danes', William is a munificent 'Danish' descendant who will arrange for its restoration to greater glory – and will use the site as one of family memory, a place for its dead to rest, Peeris' poem in monumental stone. Typical of all the Percy accounts, undescribed acts of conquest are transformed into contributions to reverent civil pursuits.[43]

---

[42] Cf. the further comment on William's activities: 'So not onely by marshiall actis flowrde the Percy name, / But also þe blode of them wer faders of Cristis chirche, encresinge a vertuus fame' (edn 17, MS fol. 187v).

[43] Similarly, Peeris presents his poem as that modest largesse of which he is capable; he describes his praise as the widow's mite of Luke 21. 1–4 (edn 10, MS fol. 186r). For the most impressive surviving Percy monuments, in Beverley Minster, see Nicholas Dawson, 'The Percy Tomb Workshop', in *Medieval Art and Architecture in the East Riding of Yorkshire*, ed. Christopher Wilson, British Archaeological Association Conference Transactions 9 (London, 1989 for 1983), 121–32, and 'The Medieval Monuments', in *Beverley Minster: An Illustrated History*, ed. R. Horrox (Beverley, 2000), pp. 131–5.

One might recall that even in his most aggressive moment, the opening of the poem, which I have cited above, Peeris' praise for the family insists on such matters as the size of the retinue it can support, its general largesse and the nobility of the line.

Although, as I have indicated, this was a family whose prominence in the later Middle Ages was largely dependent upon its skills at war, in general the poem suppresses such an emphasis. Instead, it persistently returns to peaceful and pious benefaction, materials recorded in muniments, not chivalric histories. Rather than conquerors in their own right, the family are the loyal companions and servants of those who conquer and rule. Reading Peeris' account, one would believe that the family had produced but a single heroic character, Henry the eighth earl of Northumberland, or Henry 'Hotspur'; although brief references to other triumphs occur, for example, Henry Percy the fifth at Neville's Cross (1346; edn 27, MS fol. 191v), the poem largely records marriages, offspring and continuing pieties.

The account of Hotspur – his nickname bestowed 'For his sharpe quycnes and spedenes at nede' (edn 35, MS fol. 193r) – raises the other main focus of Peeris' account. As one might expect, Otterburn finds no place here, but Percy's revenge triumph over a later Douglas at Hambildon in 1402 does. However, Peeris recapitulates the most striking event in Hotspur's career, the 1403 rebellion that led to his death in the field at Shrewsbury, in a manner that is utterly staggering. Rather than a power- and revenge-seeking rebel in arms against an ungrateful king who had not fulfilled promises to the family, both Hotspur and his father, dead in a further battle in 1408, were, in this representation, committed loyalists:

> The vijth. Henry had grete trobill in defendinge the right
> Of his suffereyne lord, kinge Richarde þe ij^d., to whom hee was a trew knyght.
> And in his quarell at last one Bramham More for his trouth slayn was he
> By the commaundement of Henry þe iiijth., callyd Henry Derby. ...
> [Hotspur's] entent was onely his prince owte of Pomfret from captyvyte to delyver
> and brynge.
> Of the saide Henris innocentis dethe was grete rewthe and pite;
> A more noble captayne non myght be.
> (edn 33, 35; MS fols. 192v–193r)[44]

Here Henry IV, on whom Peeris cannot bestow an unqualified royal title, appears as a perjurer and usurper; the Percys (historically his allies in the

---

[44] Cf. J. Nuttall, '*Vostre humble Matatyas*: Culture, Politics and the Percys', in *The Fifteenth Century V: Of Mice and Men: Image, Belief and Regulation in Late Medieval England*, ed. L. Clark (Woodbridge, 2005), pp. 69–83, at p. 81.

1399 deposition, not a fact bruited here) were constant in their support of the true king, Richard II. Percy encomium never expresses adversarial relations with royalty, as does that of the Stanleys; rather, the family account is assimilated to that of kings to indicate the mutually supportive roles of both parties, lords and servants, 'the Percis ... had in honoure for theire fydelyte' (edn 30, MS fol. 192r). Persistent episodes through Peeris' chronicle refer to comparable family difficulties and disasters produced by this good service to monarchy: Henry the third as faithful loyalist during the Barons' Wars with Henry III (MS fol. 191r), or three separate deaths as Lancastrian loyalists during the Wars of the Roses (edn 37, 39; MS fol. 193v). But the ultimate example of loyal service – here unrecompensed, to the virtual demise of family influence under Henry VII and Henry VIII – is that of Henry the eleventh. He was slain by a riot of his own 'commons', his retinue having treasonously fled, while attempting to collect the king's taxes in Thirsk (1489). Yet like the remainder of his line, he leaves both true deeds and a lasting memorial for family devotion, in Beverley Minster (edn 41, MS fol. 194r–v).

In its relative sophistication and abundance of carefully researched detail, Peeris' poem bespeaks a cultivation the Stanleys do not seem to have matched. The account implies that having a soft bed to die in, pursuing stable relations with the ruling monarch, patronage of religious houses and a retinue (rather than military glory) might truly characterize the noble life. Whilst this contrast is exaggerated (less than three decades after 'The Antiquity' was composed, the Stanleys patronized in their household acting troupe one William Shakespeare),[45] Peeris' account of the Percys strikes notes far more typical of northern rhyming romance than does the Stanley poem. Typically, these narratives do not follow traditional 'insular' patterns, devoted to the usurpation of the hero's patrimony, his exile and his triumphant, bloody return and resumption of right. In contrast, recent criticism of *Degrevant*, for example, has drawn attention to the poem's investment in domesticity and household issues, within which violence occurs only as a necessary means of self-preservation. Similarly, although littered with battles, the brilliant northern *Ipomadon* offers these in the service of the comic effects intendant upon the emotional responses of its central couple. The poem focusses upon the relations between two ingénues so capriciously engaged in hiding their motivations and identities as to derail the operatic love plot both would really prefer to pursue.[46]

---

[45] See E. A. J. Honigmann, *Shakespeare: The Lost Years* (Manchester, 1985).
[46] On *Degrevant*, see W. A. Davenport, '*Sir Degrevant* and Composite Romance', in *Medieval Insular Romance: Translation and Innovation*, ed. J. Weiss et al. (Cambridge, 2000), pp. 111–31; A. Diamond, '*Sir Degrevant*: What Lovers Want', in *Pulp Fictions of Medieval England: Essays in Popular Romance*, ed. N. McDonald (Manchester, 2004),

The most extraordinary of these efforts (and the oldest, conventionally dated c. 1325–50) is *Ywain and Gawain*, the unique English adaptation of the most sophisticated continental *romancier*, Chrétien de Troyes. The poem appears in a book always deemed central to northern literary aspirations, London, British Library, Cotton Galba E ix, which I have suggested elsewhere should be associated with Ripon and one of two prominent local families, either the Markenfields or the Piggotts.[47] These were people deemed important enough to be summoned as witnesses in the famous Scrope-Grosvenor case in the Court of Chivalry (1385–90). Both families remained actively engaged leaders in local affairs into the sixteenth century, when they raised the locals to join the Pilgrimage of Grace, and the Markenfields were destroyed for their efforts, along with the Nortons, in fomenting the ill-fated Northern Rising of 1569.[48]

Like many Middle English romances derived from French sources, *Ywain* presents a radically stripped and abbreviated version of Chrétien's *Yvain*. The English adapter has removed Chrétien's abundant commentary on the action in favour of an accurate emphasis upon the (customarily) involved plot. However, this emphasis manages in its own way to highlight constructively, as Chrétien's digressive intrusions often do not, narrative motif and to concentrate readerly attention. *Ywain and Gawain* demands strenuous reading, along the lines suggested in Chrétien's much discussed prologue to *La Charette*; narrative matter, in his argument, requires reading as symbolic sense, an unstated and innate *sen* ('significance') lurking within.[49] Like the other

---

pp. 82–101; and S. L. Forste-Grupp, '"For-thi a lettre has he dyght": Paradigms for Fifteenth-Century Literacy in *Sir Degrevant*', *Studies in Philology* 101 (2004), 113–35. On *Ipomadon*, see J. Sánchez-Martí, 'The Scribe as Entrepreneur in Chetham's Library MS 8009', *Bulletin of the John Rylands University Library* 85 (2003), 13–22 (supplementing R. Purdie's account of the manuscript in her edition, *Ipomadon*, Early English Text Society 316 [Oxford, 2007]); R. Field, '*Ipomedon* to *Ipomedon A*: Two Views of Courtliness', in *The Medieval Translator: The Theory and Practice of Translation in the Middle Ages*, ed. R. Ellis et al. (Cambridge, 1989), pp. 135–41; and C. Meale, 'The Middle English Romance of *Ipomedon*: A Late Medieval "Mirror" for Princes and Merchants', *Reading Medieval Studies* 10 (1984), 136–91.

[47] R. Hanna, 'Some North Yorkshire Scribes and Their Context', in *Medieval Texts in Context*, ed. G. D. Caie and D. Renevey (London, 2008), pp. 167–91, at pp. 173–5 and 181–4.

[48] On these later activities, see R. W. Hoyle, *The Pilgrimage of Grace and the Politics of the 1530s* (Oxford, 2001), and K. J. Kesselring, *The Northern Rising of 1569: Faith, Politics, and Protest in Elizabethan England* (Basingstoke, 2007). Wordsworth's 'White Doe of Rylstone' offers a tragic version of the Crown's destruction of the Nortons in the wake of the rebellion.

[49] Chrétien's poem has a deserved status as the epitome of the genre, based on Erich Auerbach's reading in chapter 6 of *Mimesis: The Representation of Reality in Western Literature*, trans. W. R. Trask (Princeton, 1953); and there are fine comments by R. W.

examples I have mentioned, the poem offers a protracted meditation on the failure of mere martial prowess to offer meaningful achievement and on its destructive effects upon differently conceived models of noble activity.

Here I concentrate upon the second movement of the romance, which begins with Ywain's shaming after he has violated his pledge to Alaudine, his wife. Having scarcely set up shop as defender of her fountain, defeated Kay and hosted a feast with the Arthurian court, Ywain is convinced by Gawain's applause of tourneying (rather than allegedly indolent rest with his wife at home) to abandon the locale. His embarrassed proposition to Alaudine forecasts his difficulties:

> '… My leman swete,
> My life, my hele and al my hert,
> My joy, my comfort and my quert,
> A thing prai I þe unto
> For þine honore and myne also.' (1486–90)

The appeal splits in the middle. Ywain invokes amatory language strictly as *captatio benevolentiae*, a rhetorical appeal that will smooth Alaudine's consent to his project; as the narrator says early on, 'trowth and luf es al bylaft' (35), and apparent amatory frankness here is only verbal, not from the heart. At his core, Ywain is committed to the 'honore' that he argumentatively first (mis)ascribes to his wife, not to himself. Her honour, it would appear from the poem, depends only upon having a resident fountain-guardian, not a rambling husband, whereas he is the party committed to pursuing an allegedly virtuous career through tournament-hopping with his male comrades. As Colgrevance has commented, echoing the earlier passage on 'trowth' (33–40):

> 'Bot word fares als dose þe wind,
> Bot if men it in hert bynd;
> And, wordes woso trewly tase,
> By þe eres into þe hert it gase,
> And in þe hert þare es þe horde
> And knawing of ilk mans worde.' (143–8)

Hanning, *The Individual in Twelfth-Century Romance* (New Haven, 1977), pp. 151–4, 167–8 and 224–8. Finlayson, '*Ywain and Gawain* and the Meaning of Adventure', *Anglia* 87 (1969), 312–37, provides a provocative reading of the Middle English, and I have previously written about Yvain's lion and the abiding influence of that episode in my *London Literature 1300–1380*, Cambridge Studies in Medieval Literature 57 (Cambridge, 2005), 109–15.

Ywayne instantiates what the poem presents as a 'modern' indifference to the love-pledge, and his overstaying the time of absence he has agreed with Alaudine demonstrates both his insincerity and the false prioritization of concerns apparent in the speech I cite. Yet simultaneously he does love, to the degree that his shallowness allows, and his career in the romance is to discover this truth, most particularly Alaudine's centrality to the 'quert' of his 'heart-hoard', and the responsibilities such a discovery should mandate.[50]

Thus, when Alaudine's handmaid Lunet appears at the Arthurian court to brand the dilatory Ywayne 'Traytur untrew and trowthles' (1626) and to retrieve Alaudine's ring, he is utterly stripped. Rather than acquiring honour, his undue absorption in self-gratifying prowess leaves him publicly shamed, even more bereft than the subchivalric Kay, whom he embarrassed in the field. Rather than heroic paragon, in his humiliated flight from human scrutiny, Ywayne morphs into the savage wild man and tamer of beasts who appeared as a prequel to his first adventure. Of course, along with this decivilizing transformation, he forfeits any social identity. 'Honore', which he has single-mindedly pursued, contributes to having a socially prominent name, but Ywayne has lost his and now becomes known only by the anonymizing cognomen 'knight with the lion'. Savage, incivil, outcast, rather than confirming honourable identity, he has thoroughly lost it.

The second half of the poem is marked by considerably more scenes of combat than the first, but this overt narrative line is misleading. After all, the central charge against Ywayne involves his crippling undue commitment to prowess. Thus, at issue in the second half of the poem is not military action *per se*, but some quality associated with the expression of prowess. As I have noted, Chrétien demands of his reader an attention not to narrative 'matter', but to an underlying 'sense'. Here two details in the poem are significant: the box of ointment, exhausted and then discarded by the over-industrious pseudo-Lunet who uses it to revive Ywayne (1779–84, 1833–60), and the lion's tail, inadvertently docked in the process by which Ywayne rescues the beast from the dragon (1995–8). In both examples, although actions avail and achieve their ends, they are rendered incomplete by the very single-minded energy with which they have been pursued. They inscribe within themselves an irredeemable loss that has resulted from unmoderated enthusiasm. And at the end of Ywayne's exilic sojourn, even within the triumph of matching Gawain and retrieving the name Ywayne, he is still unfulfilled

---

[50] Contrast Alaudine's loving commitment to Ywain's health in her gift of the magic ring, a doubling of their marriage ceremony (and a magic that she says will work only if he recalls his commitment to her), at lines 1535–45.

and unable to take on a public social role. The only role that will actually recreate Ywayne is to restore the bond he has broken, to be Ywayne *with Alaudine*.

Here I would direct attention to two features associated with the narrative of Ywayne's exile.[51] First of all, in the absence of any identity as 'Ywayne', these adventures are cast as multiple acts of surrogacy, the characters performing in roles that properly belong to others. Most trenchantly, on three occasions (including the climactic battle, where they must combat one another incognito), Ywayne performs as a stand-in for the absent Gawain, the tempter who has created the conditions underlying his exile from Alaudine. One sees the adventures, then, as performing an act Gawain cannot, and thus as implicitly redressing Ywayne's earlier effort to make himself that character's double / companion, heedless and cynical.[52]

Second, without exception, all Ywayne's exploits are undertaken on behalf of victimized women, sparing them atrocities. Perhaps the most overt example involves defending the maiden from the giant. In this episode, all involved perceive her chastity as more valuable than the lives of her four knightly brothers whom the giant offers in exchange for her. Ywayne is, as it were, haunted by persistent images of Alaudine, the woman he has wronged. As leaving an apparently triumphant position in the Arthurian court to return to the fountain near the narrative's end implies, Ywayne has been guided through all his later adventures by unaccommodated love with no appropriate willing object. Not only is he alienated from Alaudine, but he is, as a result, self-alienated as well (e.g. 'myne owin bane' [1644]; cf. 2094–6, 2116–24). Failing to fulfil one's pledge, breaking 'troth', only signals a deeper failure of integrity, of truth to self, as symbolized by the organized and unified pentangle, 'a bytoknyng of trawþe', in *Sir Gawain and the Green Knight*.

---

[51] A more complete account, relevant to my conclusion, would also develop Finlayson's important discussion of Ywain as knight of justice ('Meaning of Adventure', pp. 322, 332), to which discussion of the figure's developing piety (e.g. at 2513–22) should be added.

[52] Gawain is absent on the adventure Chrétien describes in *La Charrete*, where his participation is scarcely to his credit, and in the climactic combat here his anonymity seems designed to obscure his cynical defence of a woman whose cause he knows to be wrong. Chrétien's cheeky self-reference might remind one of his earlier romance *Erec et Enide*, mirror to *Yvain* in its transposed narrative situation (does love-slavery sap prowess?). Clearly, the French poet is engaged in posing recreational narrative conundrums, not in constructing some 'code of chivalry' (*Erec* essentially rewrites Virgil's *Æneid* in providing a narrative in which the hero does not dump his Dido, but assimilates her to his *fatum*).

More important than acts of surrogacy, however, is the poet's manipulation of the narrative line here, a deliberated 'infolding' of Ywayne's adventures into a form of simultaneity. The poem displays an absolutely central interest in 'narrative time', and Ywayne's failures are all cast within a temporal framework. The first adventure that won Alaudine is characterized by its undue precipitateness (cf. 'He wroght ful mekyl ogayn resowne', 904),[53] and, of course, the mark of Ywayne's failure concerns his erratic time sense, here not too fast but too slow, lingering with his mates past the date he had promised to return to Alaudine. This broken promise demonstrates his human failure, that something else could be more important than the lady he (says he) loves.

The narrative ordering of this portion of *Ywain and Gawain* repeatedly forces Ywayne to master time, to discipline and subject his prowess to the clock. In the first pair of episodes, for example, he is forced to confront the giant in the early morning so that he can gallop back to rescue Lunet at midday, and references to these strict time-constraints appear frequently, only apparently as empty devices to ratchet up narrative suspense.[54] Ywayne is confronted with the need to simultaneously manage conflicting dual responsibilities. He must fulfil commitments he has made – in this case, not ones directly representative of his own desire, but fortuitous obligations. Precisely because these represent bonds undertaken for reasons other than self-satisfaction (in this narrative situation, impossible), fulfilling promises in complicated narrative circumstances augurs Ywayne's growing capacity for self-control and self-definition. Through his successes in these difficultly balanced situations, Ywayne demonstrates that he has learned to manage time, which is also to manage human commitment, in a way absent from his earlier career. He may thus be perceived as restored, as a potentially fit husband, not simply errant (and erring) knight.

But this achievement represents something in excess of domestic triumph and happy castle life with Alaudine (and nobody troubling her fountain, since it now has a famous named guardian). Even if construed as a bare narrative metaphor for representing 'trowth', this theme focusses both the poem and Ywayne within the most mundane of commodities, time. Indeed, in historical terms, knightly performance becomes measured in terms strenuously bourgeois and associated with industrial workspace.[55] *Ywain and Gawain* reminds one not

---

[53] This is the subject of Hanning's important intervention, *The Individual in Twelfth-Century Romance*, and Finlayson offers useful analysis as well ('Meaning of Adventure', p. 322).
[54] See lines 2304–8, 2331–8, 3390, 3407–8, 3425–34 and 3449–50.
[55] Cf. J. LeGoff, *Time, Work and Culture in the Middle Ages*, trans. Arthur Goldhammer (Chicago, 1980), pp. 29–52.

of the battlefield, but quieter domestic duties, to which prowess is subordinate. Integrity in the poem may be presented as time-driven, but the technique equally points beyond familiar chivalric solutions toward that punctiliousness one might associate with the multitasking inherent in maintaining a household.

Given this contextualization, one can offer at least one reason for selecting this particular piece of Chrétien for an English rendition – and for the English transmission that preserves this fine poem. The craftsmen responsible for producing London, British Library, Cotton Galba E ix with the unique copy of *Ywain and Gawain* also knew *Cursor Mundi* and reproduced pieces associated with that poem in this manuscript as well (fols. 67–75). As I have already mentioned, the prologue to *Cursor* offers a theoretical justification for the outpouring of Yorkshire vernacular instruction in verse, and it does so as an answer to the 'vanity', frivolousness, impermanence and sheer time-wasting it associates with verse 'romance'.[56]

Thus, at least one way of reading Ywayne's career, as well as those of Degrevant and Ipomadon, is as a local response to the totalizing claims of religious writing like *Cursor*. *Yvain and Gawain* meticulously answers the charges lodged against 'romance' in that poem. Its original was continental French and its subject romance on an Arthurian topic, particular bugbears in the programme of linguistic nationalism proclaimed in *Cursor*. Equally, the poem avoids, as Finlayson's account insists, the outstanding moral defect of French romance, as identified in *Cursor*, its interest in 'luue paramurs' (51–68), for which the poem substitutes an unproblematic marital affection. Most importantly, the poem addresses head-on *Cursor*'s great charge against 'romance', the earlier poem's claim that such poems are only vacuous sequences of wasted moments. Chrétien's narrative interests would appear here to have resonated with local literary ones, and his poem constructively answers *Cursor* by insisting upon working in time / guarding time. This constructs a spiritual value, 'trowth', equally as important as that knowledge of biblical history with which *Cursor* would replace romance. Dedication to the personal bond – castle, wife, council, retinue – appears as a worthwhile use of time, neither vain nor superfluous. Not only does such dedication prioritize actions decidedly non-aggressive and (given the quality of this poem) invested with high cultural status, but ones potentially capable of answering the

---

[56] See my discussion in *London Literature*, pp. 149–51, and M. Furrow, *Expectations of Romance: The Reception of a Genre in Medieval England* (Cambridge, 2009), pp. 22–31, etc.

claims of accounting for one's time at the Last Judgement that loom so large in instructional accounts.[57]

---

[57] Cf. such standard injunctions as Luke 16. 2 ('Redde rationem') and Matt. 12. 36, subject of an enormous discussion in another Galba E ix text, *The Prick of Conscience*, at lines 5644–724. As I have noted elsewhere, another Yorkshire poem, *Speculum Vitae*, seems more obsessed with lost time (more than a dozen separate discussions), than any other text I know.

V

T. H. WHITE'S REPRESENTATION OF MALORY'S CAMELOT

Louis J. Boyle

Generations of readers have been introduced to the work of Sir Thomas Malory through T. H. White's *The Once and Future King*. White's Arthurian epic unreservedly praises Malory's art and has been called a 'homage to Malory'.[1] The novel refers to Malory by name several times, frequently in reverential, if not laudatory, terms: 'if you want to read about the beginning of the Quest for the Grail, about the wonders of Galahad's arrival ... you must seek them in Malory ... that way of telling the story can only be done once' (p. 459).[2] Elsewhere, the text again defers to Malory, and even offers a defence of a potential criticism: 'if people want to read about the Corbin tournament, Malory has it ... he was a passionate follower of tournaments ... the only things which are apt to be dull in Malory are the detailed score-sheets [of the tournaments] ... and even they are not dull for anybody who knows the form of the various smaller knights' (pp. 489–90). In personal correspondence, White's admiration for Malory's literary technique is ebullient; for example, in a letter to L. J. Potts, he writes 'Guenever is one of the realest *women* in literature ... read her intense scene with Elaine, just after they have driven Lancelot mad ... it is a great piece of feeling and dignity to both sides ... what a wonderful man Malory was, to do the Dostoievsky [*sic*] in four or five sentences, instead of taking a hundred thousand words for it.'[3] In another letter to David Garnett, White characterizes his own intent rather modestly: 'I never pretended to be more

---

[1] C. Hardyment, *Malory: The Life and Times of Arthur's Chronicler* (London, 2005), p. 10.
[2] This and all subsequent references to *The Once and Future King* are taken from the Putnam edition (New York, 1958).
[3] White's emphasis. F. Gallix (ed.), *Letters to a Friend: The Correspondence between T. H. White and L. J. Potts* (New York, 1982), p. 115.

than a footnote to Mallory [*sic*].'[4] Other statements by White express the same degree of self-modesty and reverence for Malory: in her study of his novel, Elisabeth Brewer notes that in White's journal he mentions that he intended to write an introduction to his book to the effect that 'these books are only a marginal embroidery upon the immortal work of Sir Thomas Malory'.[5] The introduction was apparently never published.[6]

White's novel probes Malory's text to a sophisticated level of depth. The characterizations of Gawaine, Lancelot and Guenevere, for example, emphasize nuances found in Malory, but to a greater degree, as Brewer notes:

> [White] defines Gawaine as passionate, Lancelot as muddled, Guenevere as domineering, and Arthur as kind … [and] in attributing to each major character a leading trait he may seem to oversimplify, but in fact the definition of their leading characteristics allows him also to individualize them and to reveal for the reader the 'real people' within the types that he found them to be, as he himself rediscovered in *Le Morte Darthur*.[7]

Similarly, White embellishes other aspects of the medieval world through explanations and contemporary allusions. For example, early in the novel, when Sir Ector and Sir Grummore are discussing Kay's and Wart's education, White adds: 'it was not really Eton that [Sir Ector] mentioned, for the College of Blessed Mary was not founded until 1440, but it was a place of the same sort' (p. 4). Using contemporary allusions was one way White attempted to make Malory's text more accessible to the twentieth-century reader. His view was that he was producing a 'preface to Malory'.[8]

In this essay, I wish to explore White's treatment of Malory's Camelot. I hope to show that, in a similar way, White has drawn a Camelot that does not contradict Malory's, but in fact explores the gaps Malory himself shows us in the fabric of the iconic locale. 'Camelot' is, of course, one of the best-known linguistic signifiers in all of Arthuriana. It is a place, and it is an idea: 'perhaps the most significant fact is that Camelot is a personal capital, not a national or permanent one … it is Arthur's own center … no previous overlord is mentioned, and his successor, Constantine, does not take it over'.[9] That Camelot will collapse is a given before one reads a

---

[4] D. Garnett (ed.), *The White Garnett Letters* (New York, 1968), p. 91.
[5] E. Brewer, *T. H. White's The Once and Future King*, Arthurian Studies 30 (Cambridge, 1993), p. 207.
[6] Brewer, *Once and Future King*, p. 207.
[7] Brewer, *Once and Future King*, p. 208.
[8] White's phrase for his project as stated in a letter he wrote to Potts; Gallix, *Letters to a Friend*, p. 86.
[9] N. Lacy and G. Ashe (eds.), *The Arthurian Handbook*, 2nd edn (New York, 1997), p. 293.

first page of Malory, and much scholarship has been devoted to the forces that cause its demise. In a similar sense, White's approach to Camelot lays bare disruptive forces that are nuanced in Malory. Just as White attempts to present 'real' characters with a greater degree of definition and realization, so too does he present us with a Camelot from the inside. White shows us a Camelot that is Arthur's centre, but he also reminds us that this centrality includes internal disruption and instability, and as such it is also Arthur's ground zero. In White's text, 'Camelot' is an unstable signifier, just as Arthur's reign is fraught with instability.

I will begin with a brief overview of facets of Malory's Camelot that White seems to have made more visible. Malory shows us a Camelot from the outside; though internal tension exists in Arthur's home, Malory more often uses the linguistic signifier 'Camelot' in scenes where the focus is on Camelot as a fixed centre, as an exterior point which serves as a benchmark for all that is best in Arthur's kingdom. I hope to show that in Malory's text the name 'Camelot' actually fades, just as its greatness fades; in the final books the locale is referred to exclusively as Winchester. This is best seen in Malory's Book XVIII ('Lancelot and Guenevere'), where we most clearly see how specific internal pressures, especially gossip and hearsay, disrupt Arthur's centre from the inside. I will then move to a consideration of how White's Camelot enhances and embellishes Malory's by continuing to use the signifier 'Camelot' as a way of reminding readers of what is really going on within the walls. Camelot, as a true locus of Arthur's identity, has its own internal tensions. White's Camelot reminds us that the iconic signifier is not truly a home in the way Arthur's childhood had exposed him to one, and that one of the most destructive and toxic forces at work is gossip. White's emphasis on gossip is an amplification of Malory's attention to the issue, and thus White's approach to Camelot focuses readers' attentions on the subtle yet powerful everyday tensions and competing self-interests at work within Camelot.

Caxton's Malory will be used for this essay;[10] the Vinaver / Winchester manuscript did not appear in print until after White had completed the first versions of his Arthurian story. In fact, when Potts informed White that a new version of Malory was being published, his response was less than enthusiastic: 'I don't think it's much good my worrying more about Malory's sources or manuscripts ... I've done too much of it already for a "creative artist" ... I knew quite a lot about his habit of tacking sources together without caring whether they fitted ... and I'd rather not know any more, or I shall become a "critic" instead of a "creative artist".'[11] Kurth Sprague has

---

[10] This and all subsequent references to Malory are to *Caxton's Malory: Le Morte Darthur*, ed. J. Spisak and W. Matthews, (Berkeley, 1983), cited by book, chapter and page.
[11] Gallix, *Letters to a Friend*, p. 201.

noted that of the four copies of Malory listed among the books taken from White's home in Alderney after his death in 1964, the pages of the Vinaver edition are uncut, and although 'the Dent Everyman edition has notes scattered throughout it ... it is the Strachey edition that is most profusely annotated, and it is this copy that I suppose White to have relied on most.'[12]

As mentioned, 'Camelot' is one of the best-known linguistic signifiers in all of Arthuriana.[13] While all of Malory's castles 'serve as focal points for Malory's characters', of the over forty castles named in Malory none can approach Camelot's iconic status.[14] Malory refers to Camelot by name sixty-eight times in his text with two variant spellings.[15] We are given very little explicit description of Camelot; it is referred to as a 'Castel' (II, 1.62) and as a 'cyte' (XX, 19.78). It has a 'ryuer' (X, 2.295), which Malory calls the 'Temse' (XVIII, 19.530 and XVIII, 20.530), it has a 'medowe' (XIII, 6.431) and a 'strete' (XIII, 8.434). When Gawaine and his brothers are plotting to kill Lamorak, they send for their mother, who is 'fast by a castel besyde Camelot' (X, 24.319), so there are evidently other castles in the vicinity.[16]

Malory makes clear that Camelot is a centre; it is a fixed locus that represents the greatness of Arthur's reign as a whole. He does this in

---

[12] K. Sprague, 'The Troubled Heart of T. H. White: Women and *The Once and Future King*', *Arthuriana* 16.3 (2006), 13–189 (pp. 48–9). Sprague notes that the four editions are the Dent edition, published in London in 1935; *Arthur Pendragon* (New York, 1943); the first edition of Vinaver's *Works* (Oxford, 1947), with pages uncut; and Sir Edward Strachey (ed.), *Le Morte D'Arthur* (London, 1899).

[13] For the purposes of this essay, I will focus only on those lines where Camelot is mentioned by name. There are scenes that can be assumed to occur at Camelot, of course, but if Camelot is not explicitly named this issue can become a more complex matter. For example, in the opening of XX, 1, when Gawaine confronts Mordred and Aggravayne as they are attempting to openly accuse Guenevere and Lancelot of having an affair, we are only told that it occurs 'in Kynge Arthurs chamber'. While it may very well be that this occurs at Camelot, nevertheless it is also true that a king's chamber is wherever the king is. Similarly, there are passages when Malory only refers to Arthur's court, without naming a specific castle or location. As a king's chamber and a king's court exist wherever the king is, and Malory's Arthur is, to use S. E. Holbrook's phrase, 'a peripatetic monarch', I am only focussing on scenes in which the linguistic signifier 'Camelot' actually appears in the text. See S. E. Holbrook, 'Malory's Identification of Camelot as Winchester', in *Studies in Malory*, ed. J. W. Spisak (Kalamazoo, 1985), pp. 13–27 (p. 13). I will discuss Malory's equating Camelot with Winchester as a final consideration below.

[14] For both the quote and point made, see B. Gaines, 'Malory's Castles in Text and Illustration', in *The Medieval Castle: Romance and Reality*, ed. K. Reyerson and F. Powe (Dubuque, IO, 1984), pp. 215–28 (p. 215).

[15] T. Kato (ed.), *A Concordance to the Works of Sir Thomas Malory* (Tokyo, 1974), s.v. *Camelot, Camelott*.

[16] Vinaver's glossary defines 'besyde' as 'near'; *The Works of Sir Thomas Malory*, ed. E. Vinaver, rev. P. J. C. Field, 3rd edn, 3 vols. (Oxford, 1990), III, 1709.

a variety of ways: for example, in the overwhelmingly high percentage of times he includes directional words, often functioning as prepositions when Camelot is mentioned in a sentence. For example, of the sixty-eight times he mentions Camelot by name, over half (thirty-seven references) refer to characters going 'to', 'unto' or 'towarde' Camelot. That is, over half the times the locale is referenced, it is an intended destination or endpoint, and as such represents both a literal and figurative culmination of effort. It is an achievement, and many wish to get to Camelot. Indeed, the first time Malory mentions Camelot it is as Arthur's first gathering place: in response to an incursion by King Ryons from North Wales, Arthur issues an order 'that all the lords, knyghtes, and gentylmen of armes shold drawe vnto a castel called Camelot in tho dayes' (II, 1.62), despite the fact that Arthur himself is in London when he issues these orders. Camelot is also the final gathering place for his fellowship at its greatest. At the beginning of the Grail quest, when Arthur recognizes that many of his knights will not return, he orders them to appear together at Camelot one last time:

> Now, sayd the kyng, I am sure at this quest of the Sancgreal shalle all ye of the Table Round departe, and neuer shalle I see you ageyne hole togyders. Therefor I wille see yow alle hole togyders in the medowe of Camelot to iuste and to torneye, that after your dethe men maye speke of hit, that suche good knyghtes were holy togyders suche as day. (XIII, 6.431)

Camelot represents wholeness for Arthur; he desires to see his knights 'as a whole' and 'together' one more time, and the obvious place for that to occur is Camelot. In the Winchester manuscript the king adds an additional emphasis by repeating 'hole togydirs' at the end of his statement: 'that aftir youre dethe men may speke of hit that such good knyghtes were here, such a daye, hole togydirs'.[17] While White would not have seen these lines since he apparently did not read the Vinaver edition, it is nevertheless relevant that Malory's Arthur wanted the image of the knights 'all whole together' at Camelot to be an iconic one for future generations.

Contrarily, only eight out of the sixty-eight times Camelot is mentioned in the text are characters coming 'from' Camelot; in a general sense, when Malory mentions Camelot by name it would seem overall that more often the desire to be a part of Camelot is far stronger than the desire to leave. 'Camelot' is also, of course, a linguistic sign signifying status; approximately twenty times persons, objects and locales are 'at,' 'besyde,' 'in,' 'by' or 'of' Camelot. While this is a somewhat broad quantitative consid-

---

[17] *Works*, ed. Vinaver, II, 864.

eration, it is nevertheless true that in an overwhelmingly high percentage of cases when Camelot is mentioned in Malory, it serves as an anchor of sorts; it acts as a directional marker, a fixed point by which one navigates or an identifier that grounds the identity of a person or object. In this sense, all is measured against, by or through Camelot. Camelot as identifier represents the pinnacle of status.

When Camelot is named in Malory's text, it is always as a single entity. That is, there are references to the 'medow', 'cite' or other general physical features, but other than these details 'Camelot' as a linguistic signifier is a unified whole. It is always *the* Camelot. While Malory's first mention of it reminds the reader that 'in tho dayes' it was called Camelot, there is nevertheless an assumption that readers know what Camelot is and what it stands for. Certainly outsiders know; as Elizabeth Archibald has noted,[18] in Book III King Pellinore overhears an unnamed spy speaking of Arthur's court, which has 'such a felyship that they may never be broken, and well-nyghe all the world holdith with Arthure, for there ys the floure of chevalry' (III, 14.91), and Emperor Lucius' envoys return to Rome and tell the emperor that they saw 'the noblest felauship of other prynces, lords and kyghtes that ben in the world' (V, 2.123).[19] Archibald has pointed out in her landmark study of fellowship in Malory that these passages differ from their sources with reference to the inclusion of 'fellowship' and related ideas, but my point here is that these are views of Arthur's greatness from the outside, through the eyes of outsiders. The same is true of how Malory presents Camelot: when the term is used in his text, as figures travel 'unto' it, 'away' from it or are 'of' it, as a signifier it is always viewed from the exterior perspective. This is not to say that there is no activity going on within Camelot. On the contrary, as a centre point for Arthur it must be a busy, active community. However, Malory assumes his contemporary fifteenth-century readers know this, as he never specifically mentions Camelot by name when presenting an interior scene. This is the kind of gap White recognized in Malory's text and which he chose to fill in for his readers: as I hope to show below, White does refer to Camelot by name when he presents everyday scenes. He shows what goes on inside the walls and reminds the readers what is contained within the iconic exterior. This approach is consistent with more recent medieval scholarship. For example, Abigail Wheatley has

---

[18] E. Archibald, 'Malory's Ideal of Fellowship', *Review of English Studies* n.s. 43 (1992), 311–28 (pp. 317–18).

[19] Caxton's text differs from the Winchester manuscript in this passage: the Winchester manuscript states 'we sawe on Newerys Day at his Rounde Table nine kyngis, and the fairest felyship of knyghtes ar with hym that durys on lyve' (*Works*, ed. Vinaver, II, 192).

argued for a re-evaluation of the castle as a more holistic image when presented in medieval texts: 'more and more studies in recent years have moved towards viewing the castle as an ideological architecture'.[20] Wheatley suggests that the medieval castle was more 'communal', rather than a 'private, feudal fortress'.[21] In fact, the castle with its city could suggest 'both harmony and conflict in medieval literature as in medieval life ... for both, the urban ideal was harmony and cohesion, but for both the reality might fall far short of this'.[22] In his own way, White recognized that one aspect of Malory to explore further was tension between 'the harmony of the ideal city and the social and political tensions of everyday urban experience' at Camelot.[23] Malory assumes his audience knows what is really going on inside Camelot; White shows us.

Malory's readers are well aware that he equates Camelot with Winchester, and this connection offers another pathway into White's reading of Malory's Camelot. Sue Ellen Holbrook has argued that Malory equates Camelot with Winchester because of Malory's knowledge of the Round Table at Winchester, and also because of his familiarity with John Harding's *Chronicle*, which connects the knight who achieved the Holy Grail and the table at Winchester.[24] In their discussion of Arthurian geography, Robert Allen Rouse and Cory James Rushton have examined the prevailing theory that the table was constructed on the orders of Edward I for an Arthurian-themed tournament he held at Winchester in 1290; their essay offers an interesting account of Edward's possible motivations for choosing that site in that he may have read an account of Arthur's holding a tournament at Winchester in the French Vulgate *La Mort le roi Artu*.[25] However, a consideration of when Malory refers to both Camelot and Winchester in his text suggests a pattern. While he does mention both in the same sentence on several occasions, such as in Book II when Balyn's sword, embedded in a marble stone, makes its way 'doune the streme to the Cyte of Camelot, that is in Englysshe Wynchester' (II, 19.78), it is also true that as Arthur's fellowship deteriorates, Malory tends to refer to the location only as Winchester and refrains from referring to it as Camelot. That is, early in Malory's text, as Arthur's reign is approaching its zenith, Malory tends to use the signifier 'Camelot' relatively frequently,

---

[20] A. Wheatley, *The Idea of the Castle in Medieval England* (York, 2004), p. 14.
[21] Wheatley, *Castle*, p. 39.
[22] Wheatley, *Castle*, p. 52.
[23] Wheatley, *Castle*, p. 146.
[24] Holbrook, 'Malory's Identification of Camelot as Winchester', pp. 13–27.
[25] R. A. Rouse and C. J. Rushton, 'Arthurian Geography', in *The Cambridge Companion to Arthurian Legend*, ed. E. Archibald and A. Putter (Cambridge, 2009), pp. 218–34 (see especially pp. 220–2).

but later abandons that signifier when referring to the locale in favour of its other name. In this sense Book XVIII is significant, as it is here where Malory's final mentions of Camelot occur. In the entire book he uses the signifier just three times, and these are the last three times the name is mentioned. However, in this book and thereafter he refers to Winchester a total of sixteen times. Thus, as Arthur's reign disintegrates, Camelot fades as a descriptor of the locale. The historical ideal that is Camelot, the centre of all Arthur represents, and the glory suggested by phrases like 'in tho dayes', fade, and it becomes 'Winchester' exclusively. The nostalgic voice and the looking backwards to a better time become the 'nowadays' Malory so disparagingly refers to in his famous passage about love:

> But nowadays men can not loue seuen nyghte, but they must haue alle their desyres, that loue may not endure by reason ... Ryghte soo fareth loue nowadayes: sone hote, soone cold. This is noo stabylyte. But the old loue was not so: men ans eymmen coude loue togyders seuen yeres and no lycours lustes were bitwene them; and thenne was loue trouthe and feythfulnes. Andloo in lyke wyse was vsed loue in Kynge Arthurs dayes. (XVII, 25.537)[26]

This passage occurs at the end of Book XVIII; the last reference to Camelot by name has already occurred, in XVIII, 13.[27] Future references to the locale by name will only use the linguistic signifier 'Winchester'. The instability of 'nowadays' is reflected in the fact that the historical glory that had been Camelot is now the very contemporary Winchester.

Book XVIII, the book that sees the last allusions to Camelot and the increased references to Winchester, is significant in another sense, as it emphasizes gossip as a significant factor in the development of events. Paul Strohm has noted that 'the very word is a medieval English invention ... "gossip" is a contraction of "god-sib" or "good friend," with whom one shared private information or news'.[28] Malory never uses the word 'gossip', but there is an emphasis on hearsay in his text nonetheless.[29] Book XVIII

---

[26] In the Winchester version the phrasing does vary, as with the 'fellowship' passage cited above, but the sense of 'nowadays' contrasted with 'the days of King Arthur' is still present.

[27] The last mention of 'Camelot' is XVIII, 13.521, when Gawaine goes looking for Lancelot: 'Ryght soo Syre Gawayne took a squyer with hym vpon hakneis and rode al aboute Camelot within vi or Seuen myle, but soo he came ageyne and coude here no word of hym.'

[28] P. Strohm, *Chaucer's Tale* (New York, 2014), p. 76.

[29] Malory often uses the term 'noyse' or 'noysed' to connote gossip and hearsay, and examples can be found throughout his text. For example, after Bors has returned to Camelot from Pelles' castle, he tells Lancelot about his adventures, and 'soo the noyse sprange in Arthurs courte that Launcelot had geten a childe vpon Elayne' (XI, 6.405). This news angers Guenevere, but she 'helde Launcelot excused' after he tells her that

is also the one that shows us Lancelot resuming his affair with Guenevere despite having promised during the Grail quest that he would end it. Prior to this scene, readers have seen a catalogue of events connecting Camelot to proper knightly conduct and to the chivalric community. Camelot has been shown to be *the* gathering place of the greatest knights; as noted above, it is Arthur's choice for the first gathering of his knights (II, 1.62), it is where Arthur and Guenevere are married (III, 5.83), it is the place where knights have been reporting their adventures to Arthur, and it has also been a site of feasts and celebrations. Defeated knights and knights who have broken the chivalric code have been sent there to face Arthur and Guenevere, so it has also been portrayed as a place of just punishment. However, Book XVIII sees the beginnings of a permanent shift regarding the thematic lines associated with Camelot. This section opens happily; the knights that are left after the Grail quest return to 'grete ioye' in Arthur's court (XVIII, 1.506). There is no specific mention at this point that Arthur is at Camelot, but nevertheless the celebratory atmosphere is clear. However, very soon Lancelot 'beganne to resorte vnto Quene Gueneuer ageyne and forgat the promise and the perfection that he made in the quest' (XVIII, 1.506). Just a few lines later, after Lancelot has been granting requests from ladies and damsels to be their champion, he attempts to limit his contact with Guenevere: 'and euer as moche as he myghte withdrewe hym from the companye and felaushyp of Quene Gueneuer, *for to eschewe the sklaunder and noyse,* wherefore the queen waxed wroth with Sir Launcelot' (XVIII, 1.506, my emphasis). An angry Guenevere summons him to her chamber, and during their conversation Lancelot says '"wete ye wel that there be many men speken of our loue in this courte ... the boldenes of you and me wille brynge vs to grete shame and sklaunder"' (XVIII, 1.507). These passages emphasize from the outset that gossip and hearsay constitute a primary motivating factor for the actions of Lancelot, and clearly have pervaded Camelot.

Soon after this conversation Guenevere expels Lancelot from the court and holds the feast during which Sir Patryse is poisoned; the knights present at the feast blame Guenevere, although the actual culprit is Sir Pyonel (XVIII, 3.508). What is interesting here for the purposes of this essay is that when Bors agrees to fight for Guenevere, on the day of the scheduled battle 'the kynge and the queen and all maner of knyghtes that were there at that tyme drewe them vnto the medowe

> he was tricked into sleeping with Elaine. Thus, by Book XVIII we have seen other examples of hearsay at work in Camelot. However, I have focused on Book XVIII for the purposes of this essay as it is the point where 'Camelot' disappears from the text, and as such seems to suggest a culmination of sorts regarding the destructive power of hearsay and / or gossip.

bysyde Wynchester where the bataylle shold be' (XVIII, 6.512). This is the first time Malory refers to Winchester exclusively, and he does so at a moment when division and hearsay are central to the storyline. At this point, Camelot has not yet been mentioned at all in Book XVIII. Indeed, it is not named until the beginning of the 'Fair Maid of Astolat' section, when Arthur 'let crye a grete iustes and a turnement that shold be at that daye [Lady Daye Assumpcyon] att Camelot, that is Wynchester' (XVIII, 8.515). What is significant at this latter point in the story is that this occurs just after Nineve / Nymue has arrived at court to explain the truth about the poisoning of Patryse and has cleared Guenevere's name. Thus it would seem that when there is an atmosphere of treachery and sordid hearsay, Malory chooses to use the linguistic signifier 'Winchester', whereas when reputations have been exonerated and there is no tarnish, it is 'Camelot'.

Immediately after this scene when the joust is announced, however, and when Arthur is departing, he wants Guenevere to accompany him:

> but at that tyme she wold not, she said, for she was seke and myghte not ryde at that tyme. That me repenteth, sayd the kynge, for this seuen yere ye sawe not suche a noble felaushyp togyders, excepte at Wytsontyde whan Galahad departed from the courte. Truly, sayde the queen to the kynge, ye muste holde me excused; I maye not be there, and that me repenteth. *And many demed the queen wold not be there because of Sir Launcelot du Lake, for Sire Launcelot wold not ryde with the kynge*. ... Wherefor the kynge was heuy and passynge wrothe, and soo he departed toward Wynchester with his felaushyp. (XVIII, 8.5150, my emphasis)

Despite the king's strong desire for Guenevere to accompany him she refuses, and the gossip among the court is that her refusal is because of Lancelot. An angry Arthur departs alone, but to 'Winchester', not to 'Camelot'. When division is present, in this case between Arthur and Guenevere, and also between Arthur and Lancelot, we are back in 'Winchester' again, not in 'Camelot'. Later episodes refer only to Winchester, and also involve hearsay and division. When Guenevere hears from Gawaine that Lancelot has worn Elaine's red sleeve, she tells Bors "'sholde I not calle hym a traytoure when he bare the reed slue vpon his hede at Wynchester at the grete iustes?'" (XVIII, 15.523). A few lines later 'Elayne cam to Wynchester', but this is just after Bors, in a conversation with Guenevere, has alluded to what Gawaine has been saying: "'Madame ... I maye not warne Syre Gawayne to say what it pleasyd hym'". He also says to Guenevere "'and therefor, madame ... ye may saye what ye wylle, but wete ye wel, I wille haste me to seke [Lancelot] and fynde hym wheresomeuer he be, and God sende me good tydinges of hym'" (XVIII, 15.524). Bors turns the focus onto what others are saying, and thus Elaine arrives at a place where hearsay has been rampant. This place is no longer 'Camelot'. Bors concludes his talk with Guenevere referring to God sending 'good tidings'; in a court with pervasive gossip, Bors desires to hear direct news from God, perhaps as an antidote to the hearsay of the human world.

Gawaine plays a significant role in the dynamics of these scenes. He has reported the information about Lancelot at court in the same way that, earlier in Malory's text, knights have related their adventures. Gawaine is keeping that tradition, but now it serves to divide, another example of how the wholeness and unity of Arthur's court is disintegrating. Gawaine is not lying when he says what he says, so a further irony about this is that hearsay in this section is distinguished from falsehood. Gawaine has also revealed Lancelot's identity to Elaine; just after we are told that Elaine comes to Winchester, she asks her brother Lavayne how Lancelot is doing, and when Lavayne responds by asking her how she knew the knight was Lancelot, 'thenne she told hym how Sire Gawayne by his Sheld knewe hym' (XVIII, 15.524). A few lines later, Bors tells Lancelot that Guenevere is angry with him and that she knows Lancelot wore Elaine's sleeve, and 'there Sir Bors told hym alle, how Sir Gawayne disouered hit by youre shelde that ye left with the Fayre Mayden of Astolat' (XVIII, 16.525). Of course a further irony of this is that Bors is here engaging in the same activity as Gawaine has: he is revealing to Lancelot what Gawaine has revealed to others, although throughout Malory's text Bors seems to exercize a greater degree of discretion than Gawaine does. Lest we be too hard on Gawaine, it is also true that the last mention of Camelot occurs in XVIII, 13: 'Ryght soo Syre Gawayne took a squyer with hym vpon hakneis and rode al aboute Camelot within vi or Seuen myle, but soo he came ageyne and coude here no word of hym'(XVIII, 13.521). Gawaine's search for Lancelot is an attempt to keep the fellowship connected with its greatest knight; it is a noble attempt to save a fellow knight, and it is an attempt to hold Arthur's centre together. His riding 'about' Camelot looking for Lancelot reminds us of Camelot as Arthur's centre, but, in the tradition of Yeats' famous image, Arthur's centre cannot hold. Just as Gawaine fails to find Lancelot, so does Arthur's centre fail to withstand the forces acting upon it. After these lines, the signifier 'Camelot' does not appear again in Malory's text. The final image we have of the iconic signifier is of a knight unable to find what he is searching for.

The final references to the location formerly referred to as Camelot in Book XVIII and now referred to as Winchester occur in sections that also exhibit hearsay and division. Just after informing Lancelot about Gawaine's revealing of his identity, Bors also tells Lancelot about another tournament, '"that sholde be vpon Al Halowmasse Day beside

Wynchester'" (XVIII, 17.526). Later, Lancelot leaves a distraught Elaine, and he and Lavayne 'departed and came vnto Wynchester' (XVIII, 19.529). Here, the divisive tension generated by the Lancelot–Guenevere–Elaine triangle is again not associated with Camelot but rather Winchester. Arthur and Guenevere see Elaine's barge, and at that point Kay speaks of '"some newe tydynges"' to which Arthur replies '"goo thyder ... and take with yow Sire Brandyles and Agrauayne, and brynge me ready word what is there"' (XVIII, 20.530). The 'tydyings' Kay refers to and the 'word' Arthur requests, while not precisely hearsay, again focus attention on communication passed and shared among individuals. Later Lancelot tells Arthur that he was not responsible for Elaine's death: '"God knoweth I was neuer causer of her dethe by my wyllynge, and that wille I reporte me to her own broder ... here he is"' (XVIII, 20.531). Here the term 'report' is used, again not necessarily hearsay, but another allusion to person-to-person communication nevertheless. Thus this section concludes with Arthur asking for information, for 'word', and Lancelot naming Elaine's brother as a witness to his actions. In a section that has so prominently featured hearsay, the attempt to encourage truthful, eyewitness reporting would seem a way of addressing the damage that hearsay can cause, but, as we have seen, hearsay does not by definition imply falsehood. Gawaine and Bors have reported factual events; the effects of their words, the division caused by what Gawain in particular has said, is not a result of mere lies. Truthful reportage is not a remedy for the damaging effects of hearsay.[30]

Other than in Book XVIII, Malory refers to Winchester without mentioning Camelot in just two scenes, and both involve treachery. One instance occurs earlier in the text, when Lancelot attempts to prevent Sir Pedivere from killing his wife. Lancelot initially stops Pedivere from hurting her, but, at a moment when Lancelot is distracted, Pedivere beheads her. An angry Lancelot orders Pedivere to go to Guenevere, bearing the body and head with him: 'so Pedyuer departed with the ded lady and the hede and fond the queen and Kynge Arthur at Wynchester' (VI, 17.156). Despite this appearing earlier in the text, here again we see that when the situation involves treacherous and improper chivalric behaviour, and in this case division between a man and wife, there is no mention of Camelot. The other instance when only Winchester

---

[30] Malory does in fact present examples when statements of hearsay are outright falsehoods. For example, in the Tristram section a Saracen knight named Sir Corsabrin is in love with a damsel and tries to prevent her marriage to another by spreading falsehoods: 'for euer this Corsabryn noysed her and named her that she was oute of her mynde, and thus he lette her that she myght not be maryed' (X, 46.342). However, in the case of Bors and Gawaine in Book XVIII, they do not lie.

is mentioned appears in the opening scene of the ultimate betrayal of Arthur in Malory's final book: after forging letters that claim Arthur has been killed in battle, Mordred 'made a parlemente, and called the lords togyder, and there he made them to chese hym kyng ... and soo was he crowned at Caunterburye, and helde a feest there xv dayes, and afterward he drewe hym vnto Wynchester ... and there he took the Quene Gueneuer and sayd plainly that he wolde wedde hyr' (XXI, 1.584). 'Winchester', not Camelot, is the location, and it is now a place of betrayal and misinformation in the form of the forged letters. Furthermore, the association of Winchester with hearsay has now devolved into treachery that the usurping king is 'saying plainly' or openly. The dissolution of Camelot is complete; privy exchanges of hearsay have become openly known written communication. The lines are now blurred between truth and falsehood, hearsay and open communication. The disruption from within Camelot, now Winchester, is complete.

Thus Malory's Camelot is a signifier that encompasses Arthur's centre, but it is a shifting centre. At the beginning it is a point that fixes location and identity and that draws the best and contains the best. However, this signifier fades from view, and the location becomes exclusively Winchester. The glory of the old days of Arthur devolves into a contemporary locale that embodies all the social and political tensions of everyday life. For Malory, hearsay, division, treachery and betrayal, the forces too strong for Arthur's reign to withstand, are very much in the present and cause the Camelot of Arthur to implode. It is this implosion of Camelot in Malory that T. H. White recognized. We have no evidence that he specifically noticed the text's latter emphasis on Winchester as I have argued above, but he did nevertheless recognize the nuances in Malory's text involving the effects of gossip and hearsay on Arthur's iconic home. He also recognized the importance of Camelot *as* a home for Arthur. He knew that his own audience, like Malory's, would at least have heard of Camelot before they read his book, and thus most likely already had a stereotypical view of its significance, but White wanted to make sure his readers recognized the failures of Camelot as a pure and noble environment. Yes, it is Arthur's home, but it is a home that gradually fills with a poisonous atmosphere of betrayal and deceit. One change that White did make in order to emphasize the smudging of Camelot's reputation was to remove the Grail scene, as the Grail never appears at his Camelot. Indeed, his text states outright 'the Grail could not be brought to Camelot' (p. 482). As a place not worthy to hold one of the other best-known signifiers in all of Arthuriana, White's text eases the reader into the significant destructive forces at work.

White consistently uses the signifier 'Camelot' throughout his text, rather than 'Winchester', but there is no mention of Camelot in 'The

Sword in the Stone' section, which portrays Arthur's childhood. I will again focus on lines in the text where the linguistic signifier 'Camelot' appears except for the following consideration of this early section. By not mentioning Camelot until well into the story, White is able to achieve a unique effect, in that Arthur's youth is spent at Sir Ector's Castle of the Forest Sauvage, repeatedly emphasizing how this locale is a secure home for the boy. In the fourth chapter, after the young Arthur, nicknamed Wart, has returned with Merlin and retrieved the escaped hawk, he is welcomed back by Sir Ector and other members of the household: 'it was such a pleasure to be back home again with all his friends, and everything achieved' (p. 32). There is a similar 'immense reception' when the boys return home from their adventure with Robin Hood (pp. 114–17). Sir Ector's castle is a place of safety for many, for 'whenever there was a raid or an invasion by some neighboring tyrant, everybody on the estate hurried into the castle, driving the beasts before them into the courts, and there they remained until the danger was over' (p. 36). The castle 'was a paradise for a boy to be in' (p. 38), and, at one point after a description of the castle activities in the autumn, we are told 'everybody was happy' (p. 130). This statement occurs just after Wart has returned from his time with the ants, the result of which drastically contrasted with his security at home: 'the Wart was past hoping ... the dreary blank which replaced feeling ... the death of all but two values ... the total monotony more than the wickedness ... these had begun to kill the joy of life which belonged to his boyhood' (p. 129). At Christmas there is a huge feast, and the image is one of comfort and security: 'the boys lay curled up under the benches near the fire, Wart with Cavall [a dog] in his arms' (p. 139). To reinforce the concept of home and security, the first thing the badger says to Wart is '"I can only teach you two things – to dig, and love your home ... these are the true end of philosophy"' (p. 191). All of these passages reinforce the same theme of security, so when White does introduce Camelot in his text it is only after the reader has seen this depiction of castle life. When Camelot appears, therefore, there is already a standard and a degree of expectation against which it can be assessed. In White's text the question becomes whether or not the glorious Camelot can offer the same sense of security, the same sense of home, as the Castle of the Forest Sauvage.

White's first mention of Camelot is over 220 pages into the story, in the second chapter of 'The Queen of Air and Darkness' section, and *after* all these references to Sir Ector's castle as home. This placement of the introductory reference to Camelot offers a stark contrast in that sense. It is not the warm home of Arthur's innocent younger self. Arthur and Merlin are 'on the battlements of their castle at Camelot ... looking across the purple wastes of evening ... a soft light flooded the land below them, and the slow river wound between venerable abbey and stately castle, while the flaming water of sunset reflected spires and turrets and pennoncells hanging motionless in the calm air' (p. 224). We are also told that 'the world was laid out before the two watchers like a toy, for they were on a high keep which dominated the town' (p. 224). A few paragraphs later, Arthur is described as wearing a robe of velvet which had belonged to his father Uther, 'trimmed with the beards of fourteen kings who had been vanquished in the olden days' (p. 225). Two points about this passage are significant for this essay. First, the language White uses balances power with serenity. That is, we are reminded that Camelot is a castle with battlements, and it has a high keep which dominates the town. Yet these features are offset by the 'soft light', the slow, winding river and unmoving pennoncells in the 'calm air'. Arthur is wearing a velvet robe, but one that is literally made of those whom Uther had bloodily conquered. Here, I would argue, we see a facet of White's tendency to destabilize signs. Camelot is a place of strength and designed with war in mind, but at this point in the story it also represents peace, calm and its own kind of stability. By describing the scene in this way, White simultaneously establishes the iconic locale as a place of Arthur's glory, as a symbol of calm and unity, while at the same time reminding readers of the violence inherent in Arthur's world. The type of military security the castle offers is a very different type of security than that which Arthur knew in his youth. White destabilizes 'Camelot' as a linguistic signifier and upsets more conventional stereotypical connotations of the word. He does this elsewhere: referring to the great Arthur as 'Wart', creating a Merlin who is humorous and absent-minded rather than frightening and intimidating and presenting a Lancelot who is ugly rather than handsome all destabilize these names and characters as linguistic signs by offering variations on the more traditional interpretations of these figures. He does the same with Camelot as simultaneously signifying both the peaceful and the violent. While the technique differs from Malory's approach when he mentions Camelot, it is nevertheless consistent with Malory's overall presentation of his Camelot: seemingly stable as viewed from the exterior, but with significant inner tensions tugging at the seams.

The second point I want to raise regarding White's first passage naming Camelot concerns *where* in the text it occurs. Not only is it after the long opening section depicting Ector's Castle of the Forest Sauvage as home, but it also occurs just after the scene in which the young Gawaine and his brothers are retelling the story of Uther and Igraine. In that scene, the boys are in a cold, draughty tower where the chimney works in reverse and actually makes the room smokier, the walls sweat in damp weather, and the boys themselves have no beds and are forced to sleep on the floor (p. 217). This unhappy childhood provides another contrast to the introduction of Camelot in that it begins White's theme of the loss of innocence, as well as Arthur's ultimately failed attempt to 'find an antidote to war'.[31]

While on the battlements of Camelot, Arthur is nostalgically ruminating about the battle that has just occurred: "'I must say it is nice to be king ... it was a splendid battle'" (p. 225). Merlin reminds him, however, that 700 kerns were killed, something Arthur admits had not occurred to him.[32] The scene concludes with Arthur contemplating killing a kitchen worker by dropping a rock on his head from the top of the battlement, to which Merlin says "'you are the king ... nobody can say anything to you if you try'" (p. 230). Arthur does not do it, but the theme of arbitrary abuse of power has, if not emphasized, at the very least been suggested. White's first mention of Camelot, then, also shows us the great King Arthur contemplating the arbitrary use of brute force on the defenceless by the powerful. This specific scene does not occur in Malory, of course, but by this first view of Camelot presenting to the reader, White starts with a glimpse deeper behind the façade, showing us Camelot from the inside. While Malory anchors Camelot by using the term to refer to those travelling 'to' it or 'away from' it, or by presenting those who are 'of' it, White uses the signifier to emphasize the culture 'in' it.

He maintains the stark contrast between Camelot and Arthur's home of his youth throughout the entire story. In 'The Ill-Made Knight' section, in the chapters that deal with the Lancelot–Elaine story,[33] a longer passage contrasts Arthur's interpretation of his present circumstances with the experience of his youth:

> Arthur's feelings completed the misery of the court. He, unfortunately for himself, had been beautifully brought up. His teacher had educated him as the child is educated in the womb, where it lives the history of man from fish to mammal – and, like the child in the womb, he had been protected with love meanwhile. The effect of such an education was that he had grown up without any of the useful accomplishments for living – without malice, vanity, suspicion, cruelty, and the commoner forms of selfishness. Jealousy seemed to him the most ignoble of vices. He was sadly unfitted for hating his best friend or for torturing his wife. He had been given too much love and trust to be good at these things. (p. 406)

---

[31] White's phrase in a letter he wrote to Potts; Gallix, *Letters to a Friend*, p. 120.
[32] The term 'kern' refers to 'something living so it could be killed' (OD), so this may be anachronistic. There are numerous anachronisms in White's book, and White himself acknowledges in his letters that he knew he was including anachronisms. However, he may have intentionally used this term to draw attention to Arthur's insensitivity.
[33] White's story conflates the multiple Elaines in Malory's text into one character. He briefly mentions this change in a letter to Potts; see Gallix, *Letters to a Friend*, p. 117.

It is now Camelot where this catalogue of negative qualities is so prevalent, and so toxic.

At other points in his text White uses the signifier 'Camelot' to intensify the focus onto the tension and discord in Arthur's kingdom. Whereas Malory adds little other descriptive commentary to characters travelling to Camelot, White directs attention to the inner conflicts of his characters. For example, in the fourth chapter of 'The Ill-Made Knight' section, when Lancelot goes to Camelot for the first time, 'the hero-worshipper rode toward Camelot with a bitter heart' (p. 342). After Lancelot's madness, he is standing on the battlements of Bliant Castle 'looking towards Camelot with desperate eyes' (p. 433). Lancelot's association with Camelot is legendary, but White's colouring of that association with bitterness and desperation changes the tone significantly. This is not contrary to certain scenes in Malory, as it can be inferred that Lancelot at different times experiences these emotions, but it is White who lifts up these aspects to the forefront of his text and emphasizes them for his twentieth-century audience.

Another example occurs in White's depiction of a common medieval pastime. Falconry was a personal interest of White's, as the publication of his book *The Goshawk* makes clear, and there are references to the sport in his novel.[34] However, when White describes the sport at Camelot, it is tinged with conflict: 'so all the falconers at Camelot were trying to show that they were clever ones – by getting their hawks entered [into training] as quickly as possible – and, in all directions, if you went for a walk in the fields, there were atrabilious hawk-masters stretching out their creances and quarrelling with their assistants' (p. 346). A few lines later, Lancelot, 'and all the other angry men, went circling round Camelot in a bitter atmosphere of knots and competition and bating hawks' (p. 347). Camelot is a place of angry men and 'knots' and, by extension, a place of tension. The knot is an apt image of the negative forces at work in Camelot. Here again White presents the inner or everyday Camelot. This seemingly pleasurable pastime of hawking is, however, undercut by tension, in this case anger. Again, we see a Camelot that, beneath the surface, is far from harmonious.

White recognized the harmful effects of gossip and hearsay that permeate Malory's Camelot. Just before the scene in which Guenevere is accused of poisoning Sir Patrick, the atmosphere is drastically different

---

[34] White refers to his interest in falconry throughout his letters. See especially Garnett, *Letters*, pp. 24–5 and 30–1; Gallix, *Letters to a Friend*, pp. 80–2, 92–3 and 277 n. 1. S. T. Warner's biography of White also discusses his interest in falconry and gives some background regarding the publication history of *The Goshawk*: S. T. Warner, *T. H. White: A Biography* (New York, 1967), pp. 89–91 and 243–4.

from the environment of Sir Ector's Castle of the Forest Sauvage: 'there were eyes on Guenevere now – not the eyes of strong suspicion or of warm connivance, but the bored looks of calculation and the cold ones of society ... at the mouse-hole the sleek cats were still' (p. 505). Pelles' Castle of Corbin, which in Malory's text is a place miraculous and mysterious, is here reduced to a topic of hearsay: 'there had been a good deal of talk in Camelot about a certain King Pelles, who was lame and lived in the haunted castle of Corbin' (p. 384). White does reduce the religious allusions in his story, but the devaluing of this locale by reducing it to the level of commonplace gossip goes beyond a mere effort to minimize religious overtones. Rather, it suggests that hearsay can be blind to the wondrous, perhaps one of the greatest aspects of the entire story of Arthur. White's portrayal of hearsay's failure to recognize the wondrous privileges the provincial view over the broader, worldly view. This parallels the kind of selfishness that so often stifles the advancement of great ideals like the Round Table: a refusal or inability to acknowledge the wondrous hinders the individual from cultivating the broader view of things, which is precisely what is needed for Arthur's fellowship to succeed. As we know, it does not succeed, and Camelot, as Arthur's centre, will not withstand the internal pressures acting upon it. In another scene, towards the end of 'The Ill-Made Knight' section, White pithily encapsulates the pervasiveness of hearsay in Camelot. Lancelot remarks to Arthur that Morgause is pursuing Lamorak, even though she is a grandmother. When Arthur asks Lancelot how he knows this, his only reply is '"it's all over the court"' (p. 449). This short sentence is complete in its implication: hearsay is truly everywhere inside Arthur's Camelot.

VI

ΙΠΠΌΤΗΣ ῾Ο ΠΡΕΣΒΎΤΗΣ: THE OLD KNIGHT
AN EDITION OF THE GREEK ARTHURIAN POEM OF VAT. GR. 1822

Thomas H. Crofts
with a translation by Thomas H. Crofts and Dimitra Fimi

The medieval Greek poem called ῾Ιππότης ὁ Πρεσβύτης / *Hippotēs ho Presbutēs* (hereafter *The Old Knight*) is uniquely recorded in fols. 200r–205v of Biblioteca Apostolica Vaticana, Vat. gr. 1822, where it is last in a series of paper quires copied at different times between the thirteenth and fifteenth centuries. The manuscript's contents are all Greek and mostly grammatical treatises. *The Old Knight* itself is made up of 307 fifteen-syllable verses in the Byzantine 'political metre' and is a free translation into Greek of the first part of the first episode of Rustichello da Pisa's thirteenth-century French prose *Compilazione*, an extended narrative – or collection of narratives – which, in the form of a back-history, is a continuation of the Prose *Tristan*. The Greek poem gives a self-consciously, and humorously, pseudo-Homeric colouring to Rustichello's chivalric narrative, in which the elderly Sir Branor le Brun defeats the youthful Round Table knights in a series of jousts before coming to the rescue of a girl whose castle is subject to attacks by a 'King with a Hundred Knights'. Though the Greek text is fragmentary, it represents most of the first two distinct adventures of Rustichello's book. Since the manuscript is lacking only a single bifolium, it is likely that the Greek poet confined himself to these two first episodes. Though several adaptations of western romances exist in medieval Greek, *The Old Knight* is the only one to address the Matter of Britain and its heroes.[1]

---

[1] This project has benefitted from the generous help of Marina Brownlee, Keith Busby, Fabrizio Cigni, Eric Wirda, Luke Baugher, Patrick Harvey and Kathrin Lüddecke; a National Endowment for the Humanities stipend and seminar (2012) allowed me to undertake research at the Vatican Library and at the American Academy in Rome.

The present edition, based upon a new *in situ* examination and transcription of the manuscript, is aimed at readers who are interested in Arthurian literature (especially the matter of Tristan); late medieval romance continuation, compilation and translation; the commingling of Greek and Latin court culture in the medieval Mediterranean; or, in general, Greek literature of the late Palaeologan period. Because *The Old Knight* was written in the learned 'Atticizing' register – in which Byzantine writers composed expertly in the Greek of fifth-century Athens – and is thus accessible to readers of Classical and koinê Greek, it may also serve as a modest introduction to the world of medieval Greek romance. At all events – and without attempting to replace Francesca Rizzo Nervo's masterly edition[2] – the present one provides the first anglophone edition, with critical apparatus, of the Greek text of *The Old Knight*.

This translation is intended to introduce western medievalists and readers of Arthurian literature to a text largely unknown outside Byzantine studies. It strives to transmit, as closely as possible, the letter and spirit of the original, but also the knowing comedy of its rhetorical modulations. Two relatively recent, and excellent, articles on *The Old Knight*, by Marina Brownlee (2011) and Adam J. Goldwyn (2012), have appeared, each with an accompanying translation; prior to these, the only translation into English had been that of R. H. Martin (1977). While these renderings leave very little to improve upon, it is hoped that, by means of this edition and *en face* translation, *The Old Knight* may attract more admirers still.

Manuscript and poem

The manuscript containing the poem is a composite collection of texts copied between the thirteenth and fifteenth centuries, all on paper, and put into its present binding during the papacy of Pius IX (1846–78).[3] The quires were not uniformly trimmed, but none is very much larger or smaller than the one – the seventh and last – containing *The Old Knight* (fols. 200r–205v): it measures 225×150 mm, with twenty-two lines of text per page, continuing to the right hand margin regardless of where verses start, and an average of twenty-five political verses per page. The poem is the product of a single scribe whose hand dates from the middle of the fifteenth century, well within Pierre Breillat's watermark-derived range of 1424–62.[4] Moreover, since

---

[2] F. Rizzo Nervo (ed.), *Il Vecchio Cavaliere* (Catania, 2000).
[3] P. Canart, *Codices Vaticani Graeci: Codices 1745–1962*, 2 vols. (Vatican City, 1970), I, 217.
[4] C. M. Briquet, *Les Filigranes: Dictionnaire historique des marques du papier de s leur apparition vers 1282 jusqu'en 1600* (Paris, 1907), p. 174, nos. 3659, 3660 and especially 3668.

that watermark (in the shape of *forfices*, or scissors) matches that found in fols. 134r–139v in the third quire of the manuscript and since, in fact, the particular *hand* of our scribe is also found in that section (at fol. 139v),[5] we may suppose that *The Old Knight* was among the compiler's intended contents, and not an afterthought. The shared scribal production of these quires (III and VII) is an important detail, to which I shall return below.

Other than the Arthurian poem, Vat. gr. 1822 contains two historical extracts and a collection of Byzantine grammatical treatises. Most items appear in their own quires, the two exceptions being the group of short texts copied into the second quire and the lengthy *Schedographia* of Manuel Moschopoulos which takes up quires III and IV. The contents, listed by quire, occur in the following order:

- I. fols. 1r–16v. Excerpt from a Greek grammar showing verb conjugation
- II. fols. 17r–47v. Further Greek pedagogical treatises and excerpts:
  a. collection of anonymous *epimerismoi* (fols. 17r–36v)[6]
  b. on breathings (fols. 37r–41r)
  c. on accents (fols. 41r–43v)
  d. excerpt from a spelling book (fol. 43v)
  e. excerpts from Dionysios of Halicarnassos' *Roman Antiquities* and Plutarch's *Parallel Lives* (fols. 44r–47v)
- III. fols. 48r–109v, 111r–141v. *Schedographia* by Manuel Moschopoulos
- IV. fol. 110, fols. 142r–145v. *Schedographia* by Manuel Moschopoulos, cont'd.
- V. fols. 146r–194v. *First Introduction* [to Greek grammar] by Andronicos Contoblacas
- VI. fols. 195r–199v. *On Transitive and Intransitive Verbs* by Maximus Planudes
- VII. fols. 200r–205v. Ἱππότης ὁ πρεσβύτης (*The Old Knight*), untitled in the manuscript.

A table of contents in a hand of the seventeenth century appears on the first folio of the collection.[7] The six extant folios of *The Old Knight* were bound in incorrect order – and numbered in that order – so that the poem itself begins at fol. 203r (see p. 218) and continues to 205v, where the reader must turn back to fol. 200r to follow the poem to its last surviving line at fol. 202v. As mentioned, this quire represents the last in the codex, which,

---

[5] Rizzo Nervo, *Il Vecchio Cavaliere*, pp. 29–30.
[6] Attributed to Aelius Herodian by J. F. Boissonade, *Herodiani Partitiones* (London, 1819), p. 24; see also P. Botley, *Learning Greek in Western Europe, 1396–1529: Grammars, Lexica and Classroom Texts* (Philadelphia, 2010), pp. 4–5.
[7] See Canart, *Codices Vaticani*, p. 224, for a reconstruction of the manuscript's seventeenth-century life, which traces it to the possession of Nicola Maria Madaffari, Bishop of Bova in Calabria (1622–7).

with its disordered gathering, may suggest that the missing bifolium was lost at the time of the book's binding, or re-binding, in the nineteenth century.

The Greek Old Knight: date and provenance

An early but definite *terminus a quo* can be put at c. 1270–4, when Rustichello da Pisa, by the testimony of his prologue, presented his French *Compilazione* to 'Odoard, li roi d'Engleterre', that is, Edward I (though he had not acceded by the time of the book's first presentation). A *terminus ad quem* can be put at between 1424 (the date for our manuscript proposed by Pierre Breillat on the basis of its watermark and corroborated, on the basis of its handwriting, by Paul Canart) and 1477, the last date anything is known of Andronicos Contoblacas, author of the treatise at fols. 146r–194v.[8] Since Rustichello's book circulated widely (eleven manuscripts are extant and in three discrete redactions),[9] and because the Greek rendering is so free, it has been impossible to tell from what manuscript the Greek adaptor was working. However, two northern, and late, manuscripts of the *Compilazione* in Turin and in Geneva contain just the selection translated by the Greek poet, and a comparison of the Greek text with these may reveal further correspondences. In his 1932 francophone edition of the poem, Pierre Breillat noticed that its language bore distinct traces of the Cypriot dialect.[10] Such a provenance would place our text, or at least our scribe, in (or recently out of) the court of the Lusignan kingdom of Cyprus (1192–1571), which is for several reasons a highly plausible situation, as will be discussed below. In any case, the particular Frankish-Greek hybridity of the text presupposes an origin where the Latin and Greek literary culture were in close, even if not friendly, contact.

As to the script, Rizzo Nervo finds in our scribe's hand traces of two Cypriot styles, the Epsilon (from the twelfth and thirteenth centuries) and the so-called *chypriote bouclée* (from the fourteenth century; 'Cypriot curled [or buckled]').[11] The *Old Knight* scribe's is a fairly neat minuscule with majuscule forms employed here and there. He mostly observes

---

[8] P. Breillat, 'La *Table Ronde* en Orient: Le poème grec du Vieux Chevalier', *Mélanges d'Archéologie et d'Histoire* 55 (1938), 308–40 (pp. 323–4); Canart, *Codices Vaticani*, pp. 223–4.
[9] F. Cigni (ed.), *Il romanzo arturiano di Rustichello da Pisa: edizione critica, traduzione e commento* (Pisa, 1994), pp. 365–8.
[10] Breillat, 'Poème grec', pp. 322–6.
[11] Rizzo Nervo, *Il Vecchio Cavaliere*, p. 29. See also R. Browning and C. N. Constantinides, *Dated Greek Manuscripts from Cyprus to the Year 1570* (Nicosia, 1993), p. 13.

word divisions and includes diacritical marks systematically. The lines are written continuously to the right-hand margin, individual verses separated by points rather than line breaks and with a comma at each half-line. Heads of verses are marked clearly by a red, slightly oversized initial; distinct sections of the narrative are often set off with a rather larger initial (indicated in the present edition by indentation); when the head of a verse coincides with a new line of text, the initial is regularly placed in the margin and not in the body of the text. There are invariably twenty-two lines to the page, and no illustrations. The *Old Knight* quire is missing an outer bifolium whose eighty-odd lines must have contained the poem's beginning and end. Based on internal evidence, Roderick Beaton's account of the loss also suggests the near-completeness of the Greek poem's unique witness:

> There is indeed no need to suppose that any more than the isolated episode of 'The Old Knight' was ever translated into Greek: the six leaves of the extant manuscript cover all the episode except the beginning and end, which would have contained sufficient material for one lost folio at either end, to make up a normal quire of eight.[12]

The Greek poet's adventure of *The Old Knight*, then, is a loose translation – and compression – of the first episodes of Rustichello's *livre* (chapters 2–39). Rustichello's rather self-contained narrative within these chapters allows us to fill out the lost edges of the fragmentary Greek narrative.

Historical and cultural context 1: the poem

The Greek poem as preserved in Vat. gr. 1822 gives us no positive information about its provenance, but is rich in suggestion. The cultural hybridity of the text, for example, would seem to require a specific kind of reception, namely, that by a thirteenth- to fifteenth-century court audience reasonably comfortable with a mixture of Frankish and Greek language and literature. Cyprus would therefore suggest itself even without Breillat's observation of Cypriot dialect forms, and even if the scribe's hand did not (as Rizzo Nervo finds that it does) bear traces of Cypriot scribal practice. Since there are such clues, it seems worthwhile to follow them as far in the direction of Cyprus as they will take us.

Cyprus was dominated by crusader-aristocrats from 1191, when Richard the Lionheart conquered it, driving out Isaac Comnenos. The next year, Richard sold the island to the Templars for 100,000 bezants.

---

[12] Beaton, *Medieval Greek Romance*, p. 145.

Richard had only received the Templars' 40,000-bezant down payment before the Order, exhausted from supressing violent native revolts, prevailed on Richard to take it back. That same year, Richard sold it to Guy de Lusignan (d. 1194), who had been king of Jerusalem (through his wife Sybilla, d. 1190) and whose line maintained Cyprus until the *Tourkokratia* was extended there in 1571. Browning and Constantinides observe that in the thirteenth century

> the Lusignan court was quickly Hellenised, especially after the losses the Crusaders suffered in the Holy Land with the final loss of Jerusalem in 1244, and Acre in 1291. For apart from the refugees from Palestine and brides and bridegrooms from the West, very few reinforcements were added to the Catholic population of the island, mainly merchants. Thus the Catholic population declined in favour of the Orthodox. In 1285 the patriarch of Constantinople thought it was his duty to congratulate the new king of Cyprus Henry II and advise him to respect, as his father did, the rights of Orthodox subjects.[13]

Despite Cyprus' longstanding independence from the Patriarchate of Constantinople, then, the Lusignans continued to found and rebuild Orthodox churches and monasteries. Furthermore, 'a language essentially Greek was widely spoken and understood even in the Frankish court. It was into this language that the code of laws introduced by the Lusignan dynasty was translated.'[14] While it is very difficult to gauge the bilingualism of thirteenth-century crusader-kings, the insular situation of Lusignan Cyprus may have intensified the need for linguistic and cultural interchange.

Late medieval Cyprus also produced a number of important writer-scribes: Romanos Anagnostes, Demetrios Romanites, Georgios Lapithes and especially Constantinos Euteles Anagnostes,[15] compiler of the celebrated Vatican Library manuscript Vat. Pal gr. 367 (*c.* 1317–20) and who is recognized for his own minuscule, the *chypriote bouclée*, which is itself reflected in the hand of the *Old Knight* scribe. It is in fact Constantinos' book (Vat. Pal. gr. 367) that provides – alongside the Greek *Old Knight* – one of the few positive signs of an exchange between Latin and Greek literature in the period, and certainly one of the very few in Cyprus – one which merits a short digression. The work is a western-style cycle of mystery plays, preserved in a mixture of literary dialects which in general reflect the disparate origins of the text: passages taken from the canonical gospels are in koinê; material from the

---

[13] Browning and Constantinides, *Dated Greek Manuscripts*, p. 10.
[14] This was the 'Assizes of Jerusalem'. See Browning and Constantinides, *Dated Greek Manuscripts*, p. 17.
[15] Browning and Constantinides, *Dated Greek Manuscripts*, pp. 12–16.

Gospel of Nicodemus preserves its early Byzantine dialect; stage directions are in the Atticizing dialect used by Byzantine intellectuals.[16] From its first publication by Spyridon Lampros in 1916, the *Cyprus Passion Cycle* has inspired debate as to whether there was a native Cypriot Greek tradition of religious drama or whether the *Cycle*, unique to this manuscript, was a western work, translated by a Cypriot connected to the Frankish court. Adduced in support of the former are positions such as that of Mahr emphasizing 'the highly important dramatic tendencies (to say the least) in Byzantine homiletic literature' and presuming the text in Vat. Pal. gr. 367 to be 'the skeleton of a veritable drama which, moreover, was performed'.[17] Adduced in support of the position that the play is a Frankish transplant have been the canons of the Orthodox council *Quinisextinum*, or *In Trullo*, held at Constantinople in 692, which summarily forbade dramatic performance of any kind, with a specific provision against cross-dressing for dramatic roles.[18] Whatever the origins of the *Cyprus Passion Cycle*, we may conclude from its existence that Cyprus' literature was free to be more Cypriot-Frankish than Orthodox and, correspondingly, that its audience was receptive both to the Greek language and to Western literary forms, including liturgical drama and at least the possibility of its performance. Gilles Grivaud summarizes the situation as follows:

> Regardless of whether it was ever performed, the *Cyprus Passion Cycle* bears witness to the relatively early appropriation by the Greeks of a genre proper to Latin culture and of their desire to present it to a larger public. The *Cycle* represents a phenomenon of acculturation characteristic of a society that favoured discussions concerning forms of stylistic expression.[19]

---

[16] *The Cyprus Passion Cycle*, ed. August C. Mahr (Notre Dame, IN, 1947), p. 39.
[17] Ibid. p. 3.
[18] *A Select Library of Nicene and Post-Nicene Fathers of the Christian Church, Second Series. Vol. XIV: The Seven Ecumenical Councils*, ed. and trans. P. Schaff and H. Wace (New York, 1900), p. 393, quoting from 'In Trullo': 'The so-called Calends, and what are called Bota and Brumalia, and the full assembly which takes place on the first of March, we wish to be abolished from the life of the faithful. And also the public dances of women, which may do much harm and mischief. Moreover we drive away from the lives of Christians the dances given in the names of those falsely called gods by the Greeks whether of men or women, and which are performed after an ancient and un-Christian fashion; agreeing that no man from his time forth shall be dressed as a woman, nor any woman in garb suitable to men. Nor shall he assume comic satiric, or tragic masks; nor may men invoke the name of the execrable Bacchus when they squeeze out the wine in the presses; nor when pouring out wine in jars to cause to laugh, practising in ignorance and vanity the things which proceed from the deceit of insanity. Therefore those who in the future attempt any of these things which are written, having obtained a knowledge of them, if they be clerics we order them to be deposed, and if laymen to be cut off.'
[19] G. Grivaud, 'Literature', in *Cyprus: Society and Culture 1191–1374*, ed. A. Nicolau-Konnari and C. Schabel (Leiden, 2005), pp. 218–84 (p. 277).

These remarks might pertain equally to *The Old Knight*. Moreover, it is important to note that performance was itself a vital mode of reception in medieval Greek literary culture, even – or perhaps especially – in its hybridized form in Cyprus, and that *performance*, as we shall now see, is very much to the purpose of our inquiry.

Two thirteenth-century chroniclers of the Lusignan court record feasts at which Arthurian narratives were recited or enacted. One records a royal feast in 1225 in which 'hanno recitato le venture di brettagna et la Tavola Ronda et molti altri solazi' (they recited the adventures of Britain and the Round Table and many other pleasing tales) and another in 1286 in which 'hanno contrafatto la Tavola rittonda, la regina Femenia, cioè cavaglieri vestiti de donne che giostravano insieme; contrafaceno Lancilot, Tristan, Palamides et molti altri famosi valenthomini' (they performed the Round Table, the queen of the Femenye – that is, knights dressed up as women and jousted together; they enacted Lancelot, Tristan, Palamedes and many other famous valiant men).[20] David Jacoby, writing of western-chivalric social practices in the eastern Mediterranean, affirms that 'public readings or recitation provided manifestations of distinctive class values and mentality, and so did gestures, rituals and games people played. The appeal of tournaments, jousts, Round Tables and especially Arthurian performances was therefore obvious.'[21] In this light we may even see Rustichello's own positioning of the joust-spectacle of the Old Knight as the first in his book – a fictional spectacle with its own attentive audience – and likewise the Greek poet's decision to adapt a tale with such theatrical potential as deliberate.

The style of recital or enactment found in Lusignan Cyprus – not the same as the unscripted joust-pageants held in England, France and elsewhere – must be further considered in relation to its time and place.[22] While court recitals of romance texts are attested in twelfth-century Constantinople, the survival of this practice there, or in Cyprus, into the thirteenth and fourteenth centuries is a matter still under debate. We can say with Roderick Beaton, however, that 'it is at least likely that romances of this later period, like their predecessors of the twelfth century, would have been read aloud for the admiration of the writer's peers as well as to impress a more dignified personage, by whom he might hope to be

---

[20] *Chroniques D'Amadi et de Strambaldi*, ed. R. de Mas Latrie (Paris, 1891), pp. 119 and 217.
[21] D. Jacoby, 'Knightly Values and Class Consciousness', in his *Studies of the Crusader States and on Venetian Expansion* (Northampton, 1989), pp. 159–85 (p. 176).
[22] R. S. Loomis, 'Chivalric and Dramatic Imitations of Arthurian Romance', in *Medieval Studies in Memory of A. Kingsley Porter*, ed. W. R. W. Koehler, 2 vols. (Cambridge, 1939), I, 79–97.

rewarded.'[23] Beaton's remarks harmonize, in fact, with the metrical form of *The Old Knight*, the Byzantine *stichos politikos*. 'Political verse' is an accentual-syllabic metre (see Figure 1), whose unrhymed verses are of uniform measure: fifteen syllables with a caesura between the eighth and ninth. In all cases the fourteenth syllable is stressed and the fifteenth unstressed; otherwise the distribution of stresses is variable.

Figure 1: Stress Pattern of Political Verse[24]

Syllable	1	2	3	4	5	6	7	8	‖	9	10	11	12	13	14	15
Stress						(/	ˉ	ˉ)	‖							
	×	×	(ˉ)	(/)	(ˉ)	(ˉ	ˉ	/)	‖	×	×	(ˉ)	(/)	ˉ	/	ˉ
						(/	ˉ	/)	‖							
Key: / invariable stress; (/) frequent stress; × free in accentuation; (ˉ) rare stress; ˉ unstressed

An English analogy may be observed in the following line by Chaucer: 'For prykyng on the softe gras ‖ so fiers was his corage',[25] and in fact the Greek political verse is not alien in spirit from the demotic cosmopolitanism of Chaucer's tale.[26] Michael Jeffreys observes that 'the political line was chosen by some of the most learned men in Byzantium, but only for those works in which they were seeking to put aside their learning and to make communication with the half-educated, often members of the imperial family.'[27] Since almost all of the western-style romances translated into Greek were put into political verse, suggesting that they were intended for aristocratic patrons, it is unsurprising that *The Old Knight* should have been composed this way. Both in content and form, then, our

---

[23] Beaton, *Medieval Greek Romance*, p. 225. See also C. Cupane, 'Δεῦτε, προσκαταρή σατε μικρόν, ὦ νέοι πάντες. Note sulla ricenzione primaria e sul pubblico della letteraratura greca medievale', Δίπτυχα Ἑταιρείας Βυζαντινῶν καὶ Μεταβυζαντινῶν Μελετῶν 6 (1994–5), 147–68.
[24] Taken from M. Jeffreys, 'Political Verse', in *The Oxford Dictionary of Byzantium* (London, 1991).
[25] 'Sir Thopas', Fragment VII, 779–80, in *The Riverside Chaucer*, ed. L. D. Benson (Boston, 1987).
[26] D. B. Hull, *Digenis Akritas: The Two-Blood Border Lord* (Athens, OH, 1972). Introducing his translation, Hull provides an example from W. S. Gilbert's 'Periwinkle Girl' (p. xxix): 'I've often thought that headstrong youths ‖ of decent education, / Determine all-important truths ‖ with strange precipitation'.
[27] E. M. and M. J. Jeffreys, 'Nature and Origins of the Political Verse', *Dumbarton Oaks Papers* 28 (1983), 142–95 (p. 143).

poem would at first appear perfectly suited to an aristocratic audience; its literary dialect, however, very much complicates this matter.

Much of the apparent oddity of *The Old Knight* lies in its linguistic and rhetorical register, as Roderick Beaton points out:

> In language and style this fragment seems entirely independent of the other Greek romances, original or translated. Although it uses the unrhymed fifteen-syllable verseform, its language is marked by studied and often awkward archaism, with only a few concessions to the vernacular. Strangely, however, for a text in this relatively 'high' rhetorical register, its syntax is elementary, with a point of punctuation at the end of most lines.
> ... There is no sign either that The Old Knight was influenced by the Greek romance or that it exercised any direct influence upon it.[28]

All other western-style, political-verse romances, that is, are in 'vulgar' Greek (also called 'impure Greek' by the *grammatikoi*), reflecting the language as spoken in everyday life. But *The Old Knight* is composed in the high-literary 'Atticizing' register of the intellectual, professor or grammarian. Within this rarefied idiom, furthermore, the poem contains a rhetorical performance only the trained ear could have appreciated: that is, a chivalric romance – with a good deal of comedy – narrated with an epic fullness of expression, complete with Homeric syntax and diction. For a translation of a western romance, the Greek poem is notably devoid of Franco-Latin loan words, the single exception being *rex* (ῥήξ, and its adjectival form ῥηγικός) instead of *basileús* (βασιλεύς) to designate Arthur and kings subject to him. Though western chivalry had entered the Greek lexicon sufficiently to produce, by the thirteenth century, *kavallários* (καβαλλάριος), or *kavalláres* (καβαλλάρης), for western knights (and mercenaries),[29] the *Old Knight* poet invariably uses the Attic form *hippótēs* (ἱππότης). 'Neither demotic nor learned', as Rizzo Nervo observes, 'it is an artificial language not otherwise attested.'[30] Even in its Atticizing, then, the language of *The Old Knight* is peculiar.

Thus, while both the subject matter and the metrical form are appropriate to the 'middle' or 'low' registers of medieval Greek composition (and thus to an aristocratic readership), its highly-wrought Atticizing register is appropriate to a more bookish audience, one in a position not only to understand the dialect, but also to appreciate the rhetorical jokes in its presentation – *or* an audience being trained to recognize them. Remembering our crusader-kings, it seems then that the audience who

---

[28] Beaton, *Medieval Greek Romance*, p. 144.
[29] M. C. Bartsulos, 'The Kavallarioi of Byzantium,' *Speculum* 63 (1988), 343–50 (p. 343).
[30] Rizzo Nervo, *Il Vecchio Cavaliere*, p. 31.

would most enjoy a recital of this text's chivalric narrative is exactly the audience in want of the grammatical training to appreciate, or even to comprehend, what was being said. Whatever Greek was understood in the Hellenized Lusignan court, that is, was not *this* Greek. It must be remembered, too, that for a native Greek audience – who, for their part, would certainly have enjoyed the poet's take-down of Frankish hubris – this literary dialect might have presented the same difficulty.[31]

But the text's apparent exclusion of an aristocratic audience may in fact sharpen our picture of its original production, first by affirming the poem's satirical potential and secondly by placing it within the formal customs of the Byzantine literary circle, or *theatron*. *Theatron*, writes Margaret Mullet, 'was used during the Byzantine centuries for the meetings of groups of friends to read aloud and comment on literary texts written, perhaps from a distance, by absent members of the circle. ... The emphasis in these gatherings was on the *performance* to a learned literary audience of new works of art, a preview rather than a seminar.'[32] Evidence from letters suggests that this practice was current throughout the middle Byzantine period (tenth to twelfth centuries) – when, by the way, Constantinopolitan influence in Cyprus was at its peak[33] – and well into that of the western domination.[34] The *Old Knight* poet was writing, as Adam J. Goldwyn has observed, for an audience which knew the value of these forms. For example, Goldwyn points out that the maiden's speech to her retainers, in which she scolds them for deriding the Old Knight, turns on several key terms which imply a generic self-awareness on the part of the poet: she calls the situation 'τὸ δρᾶμα' (our drama) and promises that God will change their 'κωμῳδία' (comedy, mockery) into 'αἶνος' (encomium, praise). According to Goldwyn, 'These are technical words describing generic distinctions among types of Greek literature ... familiar to the poem's literate Greek audience.'[35] We may also observe this technical wordplay in the poet's use at line 146 of 'παίγνιος' (play,

---

[31] On Niketas Choniates' thirteenth-century Atticist *History*, for example, see Beaton, *Medieval Greek Romance*, p. 225.

[32] M. Mullett, 'Aristocracy and Patronage in the Literary Circles of Comnenian Constantinople', in *The Byzantine Aristocracy. Ninth to Thirteenth Centuries. Papers of the Sixteenth Spring Symposium of Byzantine Studies* (Edinburgh, 1982), ed. M. Angold, British Archaeological Report 221 (Oxford, 1984), 173–201 (pp. 174–5).

[33] Browning and Constantinides, *Dated Greek Manuscripts*, p. 8.

[34] P. Marciniak, 'Byzantine Theatron – A Place of Performance?', in *Theatron: Rhetorische Kultur in Spätantike und Mittelalter / Rhetorical Culture in Late Antiquity and the Middle Ages*, ed. Michael Grünbart (Berlin, 2007), pp. 277–85 (pp. 278–9).

[35] A. J. Goldwyn, 'Arthur in the East: Cross-Cultural Translations of Arthurian Romance in Greek and Hebrew, Including a New Translation of Ὁ Πρέσβυς Ἱππότης (The Old Knight)', *LATCH* (2012), 75–105 (p. 96).

sport) to describe how the women's laments sound to King Arthur's ears as he prepares for combat, since various forms of παίγνιος, or its verb form παίζω, were regularly used to describe political verse. As Theodore 'the Poor' Prodromos wrote quasi-apologetically to John Comnenos,

> I have had nothing, in my wretchedness, to bring before you, equivalent to your power and goodness, your majesty and graciousness, except again some unmetrical political verses, modest, playful (παίζοντας), but not shameless. For old men too play games (παίζουσι), but with more self-control.[36]

It is in such verses that the *Old Knight* poet sings his Matter of Britain: playful, but not undignified. In short, our poet's language, metre and diction all suggest the performative literature, as well as the knowing audience, proper to the *theatron*. While the performance of a text within the *theatron* is not to be equated with such costumed performances as took place at the Lusignan court, the likeliest original audience for such a strange mixture of romance, demotic metre and Atticized Greek as is found in *The Old Knight* was most likely the learned, high-literary atmosphere of the *theatron*, and it would seem natural to suppose that such conditions were met in thirteenth- through to fifteenth-century Cyprus. It is even possible that the future King Edward, patron and recipient of the Greek poet's source-text, could have met the well-travelled Rustichello da Pisa in Cyprus itself, when Edward stopped there around 1271 on his way to Acre, a tantalizing but entirely circumstantial proposition.[37]

Nevertheless, the Kingdom of Cyprus is not the only place where a text of this kind could have been produced. Interest in the Matter of Britain is attested throughout the Mediterranean from the twelfth century on, and especially in Rustichello da Pisa's Italy, as Rizzo Nervo notes:

> One can see in the tradition of Rustichello in particular – but more generally this is also true of the whole Arthurian tradition – that the Matter of Britain was widespread in Italy, where it was restructured and translated. In Italian courts, not only did manuscripts from France circulate, but manuscripts were also produced in French. Also the presence of Greek refugees, who often worked as scribes, in Italian courts is well documented by the fifteenth century (the date of the Vatican manuscript, which is, as mentioned, a scribal copy). Is it impossible that the Vatican manuscript was copied by a Cypriot scribe in Italy, as suggested by elements of writing and

---

[36] M. J. Jeffreys, 'Nature and Origins', p. 159.
[37] Cigni, *Il Romanzo Arturiano*, pp. 23–4.

language, or even that the work was 'translated' and then copied in Italy by a nostalgic Cypriot who was in contact with French Arthurian manuscripts? Of course, it is only a hypothesis.[38]

Given the evidence, though, and the circumstances of the poem's emergence in fifteenth-century Italy, to which we turn now, it is an extremely good hypothesis.

Historical and cultural context 2: the poem's place in Vat. gr. 1822

The Vatican Library catalogue identifies Vat. gr. 1822 as a 'miscellaneus [liber]', which, with its generically diverse contents and its gatherings varying so widely as to material, date, layout and script, would seem a safe bet indeed.[39] But in fact the manuscript shows a quite rational and discoverable principle of inclusion. The manuscript taken as a whole – both in its contents and its physical make-up – points clearly to its use, and possibly its compilation, by a Greek tutor, or his student, in northern Italy in the mid-to-late fifteenth century.

By this time, Greek learning had become indispensable to the humanist curriculum in the academies of Florence, Venice, Padua, Rome and elsewhere in the north, as well as across the Alps. This moment of Latin–Greek linguistic interchange, very different from any found in Lusignan Cyprus, yet has an equal claim on our attention since it is in Italy, somewhere in the triangle of Rome, Venice and Florence, that the Greek *Old Knight* emerged, in the pages of what is certainly an intermediate Greek school-text.

The first Greek Chair in the Florentine Studio, and in Italy, was that held from 1361 by Leonzio Pilato (Boccaccio's teacher); but it was after 1397, when that chair was taken up by Manuel Chrysoloras, that Greek language and literature became regularly and systematically taught in Florence, where Chrysoloras' students included Guarini Veronese and Leonardo Bruni. Chrysoloras also introduced the 'humanist' method of translating Greek texts to Italy. That is, instead of the – to Greek ears horrendous – *ad verbum*, 'word-for-word', method used by William of Moerbeke (for example), Chrysoloras' students were taught *transferre ad sententiam*, to translate the spirit, not the letter, of the text. This period saw the first creation and circulation (and quite soon the first printing) of

---

[38] Rizzo Nervo, *Il Vecchio Cavaliere*, p. 33.
[39] Canart, *Codices Vaticani*, p. 217.

Greek textbooks written for 'Latins'. These were invariably written by the Byzantine émigrés, including Chrysoloras, who came to occupy teaching posts in northern Italian centres in increasing numbers after 1397 – and especially after 1453. The most widely used grammars of the period were, more or less successively, those of Chrysoloras (*Erotemata, c.* 1400), Theodore Gaza (*Introductiva grammatica, c.* 1440s or 50s) and Constantine Lascaris (*Epitome,* 1463).[40] At the same time, and especially before these textbooks were printed, students and teachers would compile *ad hoc* school texts containing grammatical paradigms excerpted from the available grammars; they would also include short rhetorical treatises, word lists, glossaries and instructor-approved excerpts from Greek authors. The 1493 testimony of one of Guarino's students is telling:

> I have followed this method. First, I made notes on Constantine Lascaris's whole grammar, so that I might see what order he uses in teaching beginners. And hardly had Guarino explained to me the Greek declensions and conjugations than I had made a very well-organized little book of certain important extracts from Lascaris. I hope that this little book will be useful to you in learning the endings of the nouns and verbs: if you are diligent you will commit to memory what took me fifteen days in no more than eight. You will be pleased when you see this: in six short leaves I have sampled not only the endings but briefly, as much as a beginner needs, the words of the parts of speech, and I have written out the varied and complex conjugation of the verbs.[41]

Vat. gr. 1822 has all the marks of belonging to such a milieu. Besides containing grammatical treatises on breathings and orthography, its literary excerpts are from two of the most widely assigned authors in Italian schools: Dionysios of Halicarnassos and Plutarch. The rhetorical treatises, by Manuel Moschopoulos and Maximus Planudes, were likewise among those most frequently transmitted by Byzantine grammarians.[42] While these elements place the manuscript firmly in the world of northern Italian Hellenism, our manuscript contains yet another grammatical text which places it in an even more specific milieu: the unique Εἰσαγωγὴ ἀκρηβής / *Eisagōgē akrēbēs* [43] or *First Introduction* to Greek grammar

---

[40] Botley, *Learning Greek*, p. 16; D. J. Geanakoplos, *Constantinople and the West* (Madison, 1989), p. 74.
[41] Quoted from Botley, *Learning Greek*, p. 3.
[42] Gaza's grammar, for example. See Geanakoplos, *Constantinople and the West*, p. 75.
[43] The full title is Εἰσαγογὴ ἀκρηβὴς καὶ πάνυ ὠφέλιμος, περὶ στοιχείων καὶ προσῳδιῶν καὶ περὶ τῶν ὄκτω μερῶν τοῦ λόγου ἐκτεθεῖσα παρὰ Ἀνδρονίκου τοῦ Κοντόβλακα, or *A First and Very Helpful Introduction, Concerning the Letters and their Sounds, and Concerning the Eight Parts of Speech, Explained by Andronicus Contoblacas.*

(fols. 146r–194v) by the colourful, all too briefly glimpsed émigré scholar Andronicos Contoblacas. Contoblacas is of interest here not only by virtue of his grammar, but also his association with the Byzantine émigré and Roman Cardinal Basilios Bessarion (1403–72), who founded an academy in Rome for the study and translation of Greek and who had collected a massive library of Greek books, 'for the benefit', as he wrote, 'of my Greek countrymen who are left now, who, without these few vestiges of these excellent and divine authors which have been preserved, would differ in no way from barbarians and slaves.'[44]

Contoblacas is the author of three known works: besides the *First Introduction* in Vat. gr. 1822 (which remains unedited), they are a Latin oration on the study of Greek literature, *In laudem litterarum Graecarum*,[45] and, also in Latin, the *Dialogus invectivus*,[46] levelled at Guarino Veronese, the student of Chrysoloras mentioned above. It appears that on first arriving from Constantinople Contoblacas stayed with Cardinal Bessarion, whether in Rome or during Bessarion's stay in Bologna 1453–5. During this time he apparently made use of Bessarion's prodigious library of Greek manuscripts and at the same time earned the enmity of his host, though we do not know why the Cardinal called him 'a monster of nature' and 'a most ignorant man'.[47] Next, we know that, following a *contretemps* with Niccolò Botano, one of Guarino's students, he was imprisoned in Brescia, whence his invective levelled against that city in general and Guarino in particular, whom Contoblacas accuses of 'eating roasted frogs, cats, and dogs and drinking the urine of the crowd'.[48] Thereafter he travelled to Paris and later took up a Greek professorship at Basle. Aside from the invective, of course, Contoblacas' works seem calculated to advance a teaching career in Italy. While he was no master grammarian,[49] he did attract good students, notably among them the Swiss humanist Johann Reuchlin, who himself became a teacher of Greek.

The presence in Vat. gr. 1822 of Contoblacas' *First Introduction* helps us to historicize *The Old Knight* in at least two ways. First, it allows us

---

[44] Quoted in D. J. Geanakoplos, *Interaction of the 'Sibling' Byzantine and Western Cultures in the Middle Ages and Italian Renaissance (330–1600)* (New Haven, 1976), p. 172.
[45] W. O. Schmitt, ed., 'Eine unbekannte Rede zum Lob der griechischen Sprache und Literatur: Zur literarischen Biographie des Humanisten Andronikos Kontoblakes', *Philologus* 115 (1971), 264–77.
[46] J. Monfasani, 'In Praise of Ognibene and Blame of Guarino: Andronicus Contoblacas' Invective against Niccolò Botano and the Citizens of Brescia', *Bibliothèque d'Humanisme et Renaissance* 52 (1990), 309–21.
[47] Ibid. p. 315.
[48] Ibid. p. 313.
[49] Monfasani, 'In Praise', p. 311; Botley, *Learning Greek*, p. 32.

to suggest a rather narrow set of dates for the manuscript, as now constituted: that is, between 1453 – the earliest date for Contoblacas' arrival in Italy – and 1477 – the date of his last known activity. In 1472 we know he left Italy, perhaps via Milan, for Paris, where he was preceded by the letter from Bessarion with that warning to a friend that Contoblacas was a 'monster of nature'. By 1474 he was in Basle; the last we hear of him is a letter sent from that city (to his old student Johannes Reuchlin) in 1477. We cannot know whether the *First Introduction* was written somewhere in Italy, in Paris or Basle. The paper on which its unique witness survives in Vat. gr. 1822 bears watermarks associated with Rome and Brescia (as do other sections of the manuscript);[50] but there is no reason it could not have been composed at Basle (1474–7), brought back to Italy by his student Reuchlin in 1482, when Reuchlin visited Florence and Rome, and recopied at that time.

Secondly, the obscurity of Contoblacas' grammar, combined with the brevity and acrimony of his Italian career, make the survival of the *First Introduction* a matter of interest in itself, for it may be inferred that it stayed within his personal orbit. Certainly, given his habit of burning bridges, it was unlikely to have been adopted by any tutors or students who recognized the authority of Bessarion or Guarino. In short, to the extent that the itinerary of Contoblacas can be traced – Rome (or Bologna), Brescia, Milan (?), Paris, Basle – so perhaps may that of Vat. gr. 1822, or sections thereof. The manuscript's inclusion of *The Old Knight* – also unique, also not part of the standard curriculum – is no accident, then, and as integral to the book's contents as the *Schedographia* of Moschopoulos – in whose pages the *Old Knight* scribe was also at work and which shares the *forfices* watermark (to which Briquet assigns the number 3668) with *The Old Knight*.

Finally, on the subject of Contoblacas, the following irony, whether helpful or not to our inquiries, must be noted. At the end of his grammar (Vat. gr. 1822, fols. 193v–194r), in a later hand, is copied a set of glowing eulogies to Guarino Veronese, the main object of Contoblacas' calumnies in the Brescian *Invectivus*. These must have been added, at the earliest, at Guarino's death in 1460, and possibly with some satisfaction if their writer knew of their animosity.

In all, an Italian student of Greek in possession of Vat. gr. 1822, whether it was purchased, inherited or compiled by himself, would have been well supplied for his studies. The manuscript in fact bears many signs of such study: the margins are full of scholarly notes in many hands, including notes on conjugations, geography and spelling

---

[50] Vat. gr. 1822, fols. 118r, 134r–135r (Moschopoulos), 147r and 154r (Contoblacas).

(e.g. fols. 8v–9r and 24v); pronunciation of Greek double consonants (fol. 146r); marginal and interlinear glosses (e.g. quire II [fol. 17r–v] *passim*); and at fol. 193v (within the Contoblacas section) a short Greek–Latin glossary which begins 'ὁ αἰνεας ... aeneas'. Not only did he have the standard materials used and recommended by Byzantine scholars and teachers, but there is also the tantalizing possibility that he had some contact, perhaps direct, with Contoblacas, that scholar of such energy and more than a touch of that 'agitated and disturbed spirit' which, according to Geanakoplos, was 'so common a characteristic among almost all the exiled Greek refugees',[51] and whose bibliophilia somehow overstayed its welcome in Bessarion's library. Whether the Greek *Old Knight* was acquired in Bessarion's house or elsewhere in the north of Italy – where it would have been quite possible to lay hands on a contemporary redaction of Rustichello's text – it is possible that Contoblacas, or one of his students, may have had a hand in circulating the poem. We can at least say with reasonable certainty that the paper on which it is written was produced in Rome in 1454, which would correspond with Contoblacas' time in Bessarion's household, the year after the fall of Constantinople.

Even if they are just contingently connected with Contoblacas, the poem and its companion texts in Vat. gr. 1822 are without a doubt part of the scene which the 'monster of nature' shared with the more illustrious Bessarion and Guarino. And certainly the Greek poem could have been an exercise in *transferre ad sententiam*, that specifically humanist principle of translation, taking as its object Rustichello's popular text which in its fifteenth-century iteration (more on which below) circulated in northern Italy and of which one copy is even found north of the Alps. Beaton writes of *The Old Knight* that 'it is tempting to suppose that the date of the manuscript is also, in this case, the date of the translation'.[52] In fact, since the Greek poet only adapted the matter corresponding to Rustichello's chapters 2–39, two northern manuscripts of the *Compilazione* are of particular interest: Bibliotheca Bodmeriana, cod. 96 (Geneva), which contains only chapters 1–39, and Biblioteca Nazionale, R 1622 (Turin), which contains chapters 2–39. In my opinion it was one of these, or a close relation, which *c.* 1450–72 fell into the hands of our translator, himself perhaps Rizzo Nervo's nostalgic Cypriot scribe.

---

[51] Geanakoplos, *Constantinople and the West*, p. 111.
[52] Beaton, *Medieval Greek Romance*, p. 114. Beaton dates the poem to 1425–50.

The Greek poet's source: Rustichello da Pisa's Compilazione

Written about 1272, the *Compilazione* of Rustichello da Pisa (who would later write down Marco Polo's *Devisement dou monde* [1298]) represents an instalment in the thirteenth-century French prose romance tradition which began with the *Lancelot-Grail* cycle and reaches its greatest complexity in the massive Prose *Tristan*. The popularity of the Prose *Tristan* is attested not only by the number of manuscripts which survive (more than fifty complete, plus a great many fragments), but also by its translation or adaptation into Italian, Spanish, German, Old Norse, Galician, Dutch, Danish, Belarusian, Czech and, by Sir Thomas Malory, into English. Rustichello's book is not a continuation in the usual sense, but a development of the tradition by means of a back-history which deals mainly with the older generation, the fathers and uncles of the Round Table knights. Pickford called it 'a confused patchwork of adventures narrated without regard to chronology'.[53] But as subsequent scholarship, especially that of Fabrizio Cigni, has shown, Rustichello's book is a fascinating exploration of the possibilities of narrative compilation. 'Its contours', Cigni observes, 'are sometimes elusive, and its novelty vis-à-vis its sources lies precisely in its particular technique of montage, which was probably not subject to a predetermined narrative conclusion.'[54] Marina Brownlee observes of this 'Arthurian prequel' that Rustichello's concern is not with 'unity of time, space and character portrayal. His interest lies instead in the creative rewriting of carefully chosen narrative fragments that recontextualize well-known characters in exciting and unpredictable new ways.'[55] Like Malory, then, Rustichello was a conscious and skilled artist of *compilatio* who found a creative freedom in assembling narratives from many sources. These assessments are very much to the point, since Rustichello's book went on to insinuate itself into the tradition in ways Rustichello himself could not have predicted. While the textual permutations are very difficult to summarize, we can point out that the *Compilazione* exists in three redactions, called *a*, *b* and *c*, which may be distinguished as follows:

---

[53] C. Pickford, 'Miscellaneous French Prose Romances', in *Arthurian Literature in the Middle Ages: A Collaborative History*, ed. R. S. Loomis (Oxford, 1959), pp. 348–57 (p. 350).
[54] F. Cigni, 'French Redactions in Italy', in *The Arthur of the Italians*, ed. G. Allaire and F. R. Psaki (Cardiff, 2014), pp. 21–40 (p. 22).
[55] M. Brownlee, 'The Politics of an Arthurian Prequel: Rustichello, Palamedes, and Byzantium', in *La Pluma es a lengua del alma: Ensayos en honor de E. Michael Gerli*, ed. José Manuel Hidalgo (Newark, 2011), pp. 53–8 (p. 54).

a: the first iteration, dating from the 1270s, whose narrative is most strictly conceived as chronologically prior to, and dependent upon, the Prose *Tristan* and of which Bibliothèque nationale de France, fonds français 1463 is the earliest representative;

b: a subsequent development of the material (late fourteenth- to early fifteenth-century) which in its fullest expressions interpolates some or all of *Guiron le Courtois* before briefly returning to the Prose *Tristan*, to which is then added Rustichello's epilogue (absent from redaction *a*) and, *following* the epilogue, a set of new adventures attributed in the manuscripts to Rustichello himself;[56]

c: this family represents a still later refinement (late fifteenth-century) of the Prose *Tristan* in which Rustichello's texts are occasionally interpolated, whose primary witness – Bibliothèque nationale de France, fonds français 99 – dates from 1463 and is attributed to Michel Gonnot.

Rustichello's collection, depending upon the redaction in question, has been called variously *Palamedes*, *Guiron le Courtois* or *Meliadus* after Tristan's father. Neither Rustichello's preface, nor the epilogue ascribed to him in the *b*-redaction, names his book, referring to it only as 'cestui romainz'.

Rustichello's own preface is highly informative, memorializing the occasion of the book's production and its presentation to its patron. According to this preface – which is unlikely to have found expression in the missing first folios of the Greek version – Rustichello's book came about in the following way:

> And know full well that this romance was translated from a book of my Lord Edward, the king of England, at the time that he passed beyond the sea in the service of Our Lord God for the conquest of the holy sepulchre. And master Rusticanus of Pisa, he who is pictured above,[57] has compiled this romance, since he translated all the exceedingly marvellous tales which he found in this book, and all the greatest adventures; and will tell summarily all the great adventures of the world. But know that he will relate more of my lord Lancelot du Lac, and of my lord Tristan, son of king Meliadus of Leonoise, than any others, since without a doubt they were the best knights

---

[56] Paris, Bibliothèque nationale de France, fonds français 340 and 355, and Berlin, Hamilton 581.

[57] BNF f. fr. 1463, the basis of Cigni's edition used here (*Il Romanzo Arturiano*, p. 233 [Plate 21]), has an illustration of an author at the head of fol. 1, col. 1. Some witnesses, such as BNF f. fr. 340, reproduce the phrase 'pictured above' even though not so illustrated. J. F. Levy speculates that the figure in BNF f. fr. 1463, since it is crowned, is not Rustichello but King Edward: see his 'Livre de Meliadus: an Edition of the Arthurian Compilation of B.N.F. f. fr. 340 attributed to Rusticien de Pise' (unpublished Ph.D. dissertation, University of California, Berkeley, 2000), p. 421. See also P. M. Gathercole, 'Illuminations on the Manuscripts of Rusticien de Pise (Rustichello da Pisa)', *Italica*, 44.4 (1967), 400–8.

of their time and place. And the master will relate, concerning these two, more matters and more battles which they had between them than you can find in any and all the other books, because the master found them written in the king of England's book.[58]

Edward, son and heir of Henry III, was prince rather than king when he went on crusade in 1270; he succeeded to the throne while abroad in 1272 and left Acre for home that same year. Edward's itinerary is certainly a matter of interest, since it took him through Sicily, Sardinia and Cyprus on his way to the Holy Land. At any of these places, according to Cigni, Edward 'could easily have come into contact with a Pisan writer. For that matter Acre, where Edward landed in May 1271, was an intensely active commercial centre for Pisans, Genoese and Venetians.'[59] That Edward landed in Cyprus and that Rustichello *could* have been in Cyprus, is, as mentioned above, certainly enough to set our imagination working: could our Cypriot-Greek poet have been have been involved with this text's transmission from the time of Rustichello's presentation of the *Compilazione* to Edward? If the Greek poet could be shown to have been working from the *a*-redaction of Rustichello's book, there would be grounds for supposing this. Unfortunately, the Greek translation is too loose and its dialect too undatable to be identified, on linguistic grounds, exclusively with either the *a*- or the *b*-redaction.

The reference to 'the *king* of England's book' might indicate that the presentation was made between 1272 and 1274, but nothing would have prevented a later scribe bringing Edward's royal title up to date if the book had been first presented between 1270 and 1272. Pickford suggests that Edward's book must have been either a manuscript of *Palamedes* or of the thirteenth-century Prose *Tristan*, or a book containing portions of each.[60] Tantalizingly, such a book, a '*liber Palamedes*', appears to have been commissioned by Frederick II from one 'Johannes Romanzor' as of 1240.[61] As Frederick's is the first text we know of bearing the title

---

[58] The version of the preface translated here is that of redaction *a*; the version found in redaction *b* – the one most likely consulted by the Greek poet-translator – differs in minor particulars. Translation is my own (as elsewhere unless otherwise attributed), based on Cigni, *Il Romanzo Arturiano*. See also Levy, 'Livre de Meliadus,' pp. 1–2. The action of Rustichello's entire book is summarized in E. Löseth's *Le Roman en prose de Tristan* (Paris, 1890), pp. 423–74, as well as in Levy, 'Livre de Meliadus', pp. iii–vii and lxxxv–xc.

[59] Cigni, *Il Romanzo Arturiano*, pp. 23–4.

[60] Pickford, 'Miscellaneous French Prose Romances', pp. 350–2.

[61] A letter written by Frederick (February 5, 1240) acknowledges receipt of 'LIIII quaternis scriptis de libro Palamedes qui fuerunt quondam magistri Johannis Romanzor' (fifty-four quaternions of a Palamedes book which was once written by master Johannes Romanzor). See A. Huillard-Bréholle, *Historia diplomatica Friderici secondi*, 6 vols.

Palamedes, it is not impossible that, as Jacoby suggests, it was a recension of Romanzor's *Palamede* which Prince Edward obtained in Acre in May 1271[62] and which he provided to Rustichello. But no such book, nor anything by 'Romanzor', survives.[63] Rustichello's book does contain narrative material unattested elsewhere – including the 'Old Knight' episode itself – which is probably his own. In the epilogue, Rustichello tells us there were other sources ('pluseurs hystories' and 'pluseurs croniques'[64]) from which Edward requested extracts to be included, but does not name them.

Rustichello's first episode, the challenge of the Old Knight, can be summarized as follows: an unnamed, unknown elderly knight, accompanied by a young girl of exceeding beauty, challenges King Arthur's knights to single combat, offering as a prize the hand in marriage of the girl, who is his niece. Always declining to give his name – and forbidden by the maiden from using a lance – the Old Knight defeats, one by one, Palamedes, Gawain, Lamorak, Gaheris, Bors, Yvain, Sagremor, Bleoberis, Segwardes, Saphar, Hector and Guivret de Lamballe. When Lancelot and Tristan rise to the challenge, he departs from the script and does them the honour of using a lance; they are also defeated. When the knights have all been vanquished, Arthur himself takes up the challenge and is knocked out cold. From out of nowhere, then, King Karados arrives with thirty other kings to form a second wave of combatants; all are just as quickly defeated.

At this moment a second plot opens up: a strange damsel has come to seek a champion against the wicked Count Guiot who with his Hundred Knights is attacking her widowed mother's estate. Arthur has promised his help but kept her waiting, and now the girl, having seen the Old Knight's performance, begs his help instead; when he agrees she reveals herself to be the niece of Lamorat de Listenois. The Old Knight accompanies the girl home, withstands the ridicule hurled by her mother's retainers and the next day vanquishes Guiot. At last, he seals the peace by a marriage between Guiot and Lamorat's niece. Thereafter, the Old Knight remains at the castle for a month. On taking his leave the Old Knight asks that a letter be sent to King Arthur revealing his name, Branor le Brun; he

---

in 12 (Paris, 1852-61), II, 722; see also R. Lathuillère, *Guiron le courtois:* Étude *de la tradition manuscrite et analyse critique* (Paris, 1966), p. 30 n. 47.

[62] Jacoby, 'Knightly Values', p. 168.

[63] It is also impossible to say whether 'Romanzor' was a proper name or the occupational title 'romancer'.

[64] Rustichello's epilogue is found only in Bibliothèque nationale de France, fonds français 350 (redaction *b*). See Löseth, *Roman en Prose du Tristan*, p. 472; Levy, 'Le Livre du Meliadus', p. 419.

then rides through the forest for many days, encountering and defeating recreant knights and rescuing their victims, until he reaches home and dies peacefully at the age of about 120.

The Greek poet includes, and compresses, only the first two adventures, the joust and the defence of the widow's town, and into these he introduces a number of variations, many of them comic, both in the behaviour of the characters and the use of a self-consciously pseudo-Homeric style. The rendering of Arthur's leave-taking from Guenevere as he goes to fight the Old Knight, for example, presents a feverishly emotional parody of Hector's final farewell to Andromache in *Iliad* VI.482–502. Again, as if to complement the old age of their challenger, the Greek poet consistently infantilizes the Round Table knights, making them out to be vain, hot-tempered and sexually immature. So Rex Artoúzos, Palamédes, Gaoulbános, Galaiótos, Tristános and Lanselótos ek Límnēs take their place in Greek literature as tyros who get beaten up by an old man.

Other variations are more substantial. When Arthur himself rides out to face him, the Old Knight, rather than summarily knocking him to the ground as in the source text, lectures him on the impropriety of his attempt to win the hand of the beautiful maiden. The Old Knight reminds him that should the king be victorious, he would be bound by the letter of the challenge to marry the Old Knight's niece, thus committing himself to bigamy:

> Seeing him standing there, the Old Knight
> knew truly it was the king who had come.
> He willingly descended from his saddle to the ground,
> approached and greeted him, kneeling like a vassal,
> and said: 'Depart, my lord, lest something happen contrary to law.
> My niece is offered as a reward for your knights,
> and your consort by law is Guenevere – may she live long!
> So, regally and suitably, glorify your crown;
> do not approach this beautiful maiden's bed.' (150–8)

Whereas this possibility never crosses the mind of Rustichello's Old Knight, the Greek one is mindful of domestic imperatives and uses the occasion to teach correct behaviour to the king: for even the staged combat of jousting may have consequences that go beyond physical trial. Just by entering the lists, he says, Arthur has wronged Guenevere (as she herself seemed to feel in the leave-taking scene), whether through short-sightedness or out of lust. Similarly – and again in a departure from Rustichello – the Greek poet's Old Knight does not, at the second adventure's conclusion, enforce a marriage between the maiden and her now-pacified tormentor. In the Greek poem a feast to honour the Old Knight, who gets the nickname 'White-Winged Swan', is held, but there is no wedding.

It is easy to see how for a Greek poet of the Paleologan period, with little enough investment in Frankish aristocratic self-aggrandizement, Rustichello's tale might have provided the occasion for an Arthurian spoof. This would have been very much in the vein of medieval Greek humour and literary parody.[65] Where better for our anonymous poet to use his command of Homeric simile to comic effect, as he does in this joust passage:

> But is it necessary for me to speak at length, adding up all the men
> who drove their spears at the old man's chest?
> All were thrown from their saddles and laid out on the ground.
> All except the steadfast Tristan and glorious Lancelot,
> for these did not drive their spears at his chest.
> And the sturdy old knight did them an honour,
> since all who drove their spears at his chest
> were always flung from the saddle to the ground.
> Even as a boat being hit by violent waves
> and crashing on the rocks under the force of the gale,
> is smashed into pieces by the force of the blow,
> in the same way they all fell, and all seemed powerless.
> For the strong and steadfast old knight
> stood sturdy as a pillar, laughing down the young men. (71–84)

Another trenchant joke runs through the Old Knight's reception by the retainers of the besieged castle he has come to liberate. At first they are thrilled to have a knight of the Round Table as their champion. Soon, however, the Old Knight removes his helmet to reveal his age:

> But, when they saw that the knight was old and white-haired,
> they mocked him, faulting the maiden's sagacity,
> for it must have escaped her notice that she had brought an old man,
> useless, wasted, in the extremity of age.
> They would have preferred Lancelot to come to their aid,
> or Tristan the glorious, or indeed Palamedes,
> or, as a second-best option, one of the banqueters
> from the Round Table of the king of Britain,
> or at least not an old man leaning on his stick.
> 'This one will rather be asking us for help!
> Therefore, let a bed be brought for this poor old man,
> and let him go back home in peace.

---

[65] Beaton, *Medieval Greek Romance*, pp. 192–5. For a discussion of Byzantine humour at the expense of Latins, see J. Haldon, 'Humour and the Everyday in Byzantium', in *Humour, History and Politics in Late Antiquity and the Early Middle Ages*, ed. G. Halsall (Cambridge, 2002), pp. 48–71.

> But you, run once more to the king of Britain
> and fetch one of his knights as soon as possible,
> so that he is with us by early morning,
> before the tyrants, with their depredations, are upon us.'
> But the maiden, standing bright-eyed before them,
> answers: 'Do not scorn what I have done.
> It was not possible to bring a knight of the Round Table,
> not Lancelot whom you mention, nor yet Tristan,
> nor strong Palamedes, nor Gawain for that matter.
> This man alone has undertaken to help us.' (218–39)

The frustrated retainers wish for the very heroes the Old Knight has so recently, and so effortlessly, defeated. Their rude complaint expresses verbally the immaturity and lack of chivalry which Arthur and all his knights have just demonstrated in the lists.

The poet of *The Old Knight* is a trenchant satirist. His knowing comedy strikes a note not unlike that of the Latin *Draco Normannicus*, *De ortu Waluuanii* and *De Arturo et Gorlagon lycanthropo*,[66] the Auchinleck *Sir Tristrem*, *Sir Gawain and the Green Knight* and Chaucer's *Sir Thopas* itself. Like the authors of these narratives, the Greek *Old Knight* poet shows his firm grasp of the tradition and also a master's awareness of style. When the maiden scolds her mother's retainers, who have been mercilessly teasing the Old Knight, she speaks one of his finest lines:

> Θεὸς δὲ τρέψει τὰς ἡμῶν πρὸς αἶνον κωμῳδίας
> (but God will turn their mockery of us to praise) [243]

This line, which has no equivalent in Rustichello's text, allows the reader a new degree of play in his or her understanding of 'us' ($ἡμῶν$). Does she mean herself and her champion, who are being openly mocked? Does she mean herself and her mother's retainers? Perhaps she means herself and her mother, and thus perhaps women in general, poor creatures dependent on the strength and goodwill of immature, unreliable men. The line demonstrates the damsel's surpassing wisdom: as she now sees, her plight has gone from bad to ridiculous. But unlike her audience of jeering

---

[66] The three Latin texts – *Draco Normannicus* by Etienne de Rouen, *De ortu Waluuani nepotis Arturi (The Rise of Gawain, Nephew of Arthur)* and *Narratio de Arthuro rege et rege Gorlagon lycanthropo (The Tale of King Arthur and King Gorlagon the Werewolf)* – are edited and translated in M. L. Day, *Latin Arthurian Literature*, Arthurian Archives 11 (Cambridge, 2005). See also E. Archibald, 'Questioning Arthurian Ideals', in *The Cambridge Companion to the Arthurian Legend*, ed. E. Archibald and A. Putter (Cambridge, 2009), pp. 139-53, and *The Arthur of Medieval Latin Literature: The Development of the Arthurian Legend in Medieval Latin*, ed. Sîan Echard (Cardiff, 2011).

retainers, and certainly unlike the knights of Arthur's court, she knows that the ridiculous can be redeemed, can in fact be turned into something triumphant. This notion, in turn, is not the worst justification for tales of imaginary knights.

Note on the text

Since this edition aims to be accessible to readers of the most diverse training in Greek – not Byzantine specialists only, but also students of Attic, Hellenistic and koinê – and since the forms employed by the poet of *The Old Knight* are generally Attic in form, I have, following all previous editors, brought the poem's orthography the short distance required into the Attic forms; I have however retained the manuscript's Cypriot genitive singular in –ω. Manuscript readings, where they differ from those in this edition (except where I have added iota subscript in dative singular forms, see note 1 below), appear in the notes to the edition. Conventional abbreviations are silently expanded. The following should also be noted.

1. Whether nouns or verbs, the scribe does not typically include iota subscript.
2. Double consonants are typically reduced by the scribe to a single consonant, except where an ambiguity would be introduced.
3. The following regularised spellings are substituted for scribal forms: ἅμιλλαν for ἅμιλαν, γεννάδας for γενάδας, στερρόν for στερόν, ἄπιθι for ἄπειθι, κλεινός for κλινός, ἀρωγήν for ἀρογήν.
4. Breillat reads in the manuscript ῥύγες instead of ῥῆγες: 'Toujours υ dans ce mot, comme dans Παλαμύδης (v. 6)'. The scribe's η, often merely two minims, is sometimes hard to distinguish from his υ. In practice, however, my readings in these cases are the same as Breillat's. Similarly, the digraph by which the scribe indicates αι often looks like ε (as in αἰσχύνης [15], and δαιτυμόνες [97]).
5. Readings not in the manuscript are bracketed, e.g., [Ἡ] κόρη (234).
6. Footnotes refer to the manuscript and previous editions as follows:
    Edd. = according to all previous editors
    MS = Biblioteca Apostolica Vaticana, Vat. gr. 1822
    RN = Francesca Rizzo Nervo (ed.), *Il Vecchio Cavaliere* (Catania, 2000)
    B = Pierre Breillat, 'La *Table Ronde* en Orient: Le poème grec du Vieux Chevalier', *Mélanges d'Archéologie et d'Histoire* 55 (1938), 323–5
    E = Adolf Ellissen, *Versuch einer Polyglotte der europäischen Poesie, Erster Band: Poesie der Kantabrer, Kelten, Kymren und Griechen* (Leipzig, 1846)

H = F. H. von der Hagen (ed.), 'Poema graecum de rebus gestis regis Arturi, Tristani, Lanceloti, Galbani, Palamedis aliorumque equitum tabulae rotundae, e codice Vaticano editio prima', *Monumenta Medii Aevii Plerumque Inedita* (Bratislava, 1821).

Note on the translation

The line-by-line verse translation does not attempt to approximate the Greek political verse, nor to find an equivalent line in English, since there is none, despite some superficial similarity to the English fourteener. The Greek political line is exact in its syllable-count – invariably fifteen – and much less so in the distribution of accentual stress. Dr Fimi and I have given our five-beat lines a similar freedom in the placement of accents, including the freedom to exceed five beats, if unavoidable, rather than to enjamb. We have also decided to retain the poet's frequent changes in tense, which, while sometimes jarring, preserve the character of the poem's oral delivery.

Ἱππότης ὁ Πρεσβύτης

1   ... ἔχοντες τὰς ἀξίας.   f. 203r
Νέοι, παιδίσκαι σὺν αὐτοῖς, μητέρες εὐτεκνοῦσαι
καὶ ῥῆγες ὑποκείμενοι ῥηγὶ τῷ Βρετανίας
ὁρῶντες ἐκπληττόμενοι τὸ θάρσος τοῦ πρεσβύτου,
5   τὸ κάλλος δ᾽ ἐπεθαύμαζον τῆς ἐπελθούσης κόρης.
ὁ Παλαμήδης σὺν βοῇ βαρβαρικῇ[1] καὶ σθένει
ὠθεῖ[2] τὸν ἵππον κατ᾽ αὐτοῦ, βάλλει τῷ δορατίῳ.
Ἀτρέμας δ᾽ ὁ πρεσβύτατος ἵστατο ῥωμαλέος,
ὥσπέρ τις λίθος ἀκλινής, σκοπὸς τοῖς βουλομένοις.
10 Ἐν τῇ χειρὶ συνέτριψε τὸ δόρυ Παλαμήδης
κἀξ ἐφεστρίδος κατὰ γῆς ἐκπετασθεὶς ἐρρίφθη,[3]
ὥσπέρ τις[4] λίθος ἀφεθεὶς ἐκ πετροβόλου σκεύους
πρὸς πέτρον δὲ παραβαλών[5] αὖθις παλινδρομεῖται,
τὸ πλῆττον ἀσθενέστερον φανὲν τοῦ πληττομένου.
15 Καὶ μετ᾽ αἰσχύνης ἀπελθὼν ῥίπτει[6] τὴν πανοπλίαν
πρηνής[7] τῇ κλίνῃ κείμενος, μὴ φέρων τὸ πρακτέον.
Διττῶς καὶ γὰρ ἐτάραττον οἱ λογισμοὶ τὸν ἄνδρα,
χάριν τῆς πτώσεως αὐτοῦ καὶ πόθου τοῦ τῆς κόρης,
μὴ που καί τις ἐκ τῶν αὐτῶν ταύτην λαβεῖν ἰσχύσει.
20 Καὶ θροῦς ἐγγίνεται πολὺς καὶ θόρυβος[8] τοῖς πᾶσιν.

---

[1] MS: *βαρβαρικήν*
[2] MS: *ὀθεῖ*
[3] MS: *ἐρύφθη*
[4] MS: *τϊ*
[5] MS: *παραβαλλών*
[6] MS: *ῥυπτει*
[7] MS: *πρϊνής*
[8] MS: *πολλϋς καὶ θώρυβος*

The Old Knight

1   ... the ones holding rank.

      The young men, maidens and mothers blessed in offspring,

      and the kings subject to the King of Britain,

      seeing, in utter amazement, the old man's courage,

5   marvelled also at the beauty of the girl at his side.

      Palamedes, with barbaric shout and main force,

      now spurs his horse against him and smites with his spear.

      But the ancient one, unmoving, stood strong,

      like a stone set up as a target, for anyone to try.

10   Palamedes' spear shattered in his hand

      and he was flung from his saddle to the ground.

      Just as a stone, launched from some siege engine,

      striking rock, returns again to the thrower,

      so the one striking fared worse than the one being struck.

15   Departing in shame, he throws down his armour

      and lies face-down on his bed, unable to bear the outcome.

      In two ways the man's thoughts disturbed him:

      both because of his defeat and his yearning for the maiden,

      lest somehow one of the others win through and claim her.

20   There was much murmuring and comment in the throng,

Καὶ γὰρ οἱ πάντες ἴσασι τὸ σθένος Παλαμήδους
καὶ τὸ στερρὸν ἐθαύμαζον ἱππότου τοῦ πρεσβύτου.
Ἐπεὶ δὲ σχύνης ἔμπλεος ἀπῆλθε Παλαμήδης,
ἀδελφιδοῦς ὁ τοῦ ῥηγός, ἀνδρεῖος Γαουλβάνος,
25 γονυπετῶν ἐφθέγξατο ῥηγὶ τῷ θείῳ τάδε·
'Προσήκει μέν, ὦ δέσποτα, μὴ προπετῶν ἐκτρέχειν
πρὸς ἅμιλλαν ἢ συμπλοκὴν δίχα τῇ σῇ προστάξει.
Ἀλλ' ἀναχάζει⁹ μ᾽ οὐκ ἐᾷ τὸ Παλαμήδους φίλτρον.   f. 203v
Οἶδας καὶ γὰρ ὡς φιλικῶς διάκρινε¹⁰ πρὸ χρόνων,
30 τὴν δ᾽ ἧτταν ἀνασώσασθαι πειρῶμαι τοῦ φιλοῦντος.᾽
Ὁ ῥὴξ δ᾽ αὐτὸν ἐνδίδωσι τοῖς ὅπλοις ἁμιλλᾶσθαι.
Μετ᾽ εὐθυμίας δ᾽ ἐξελθὼν φθάνει τῷ δωματίῳ.¹¹
Ἐκτείνας δὲ τὴν δεξιάν· 'Χαῖρε,' φησίν, 'ἱππότα,
ὁ τὴν αἰσχύνην ἀληθῶς ἐμπλήσας Παλαμήδην.
35 Ἐγὼ τὴν ἧτταν ἔρχομαι ζητῆσαι τοῦ φιλοῦντος.
Ἐκ γὰρ μακροῦ τυγχάνει μοι¹² φίλος ὁ Παλαμήδης.᾽
Ὁ δὲ πρεσβύτης εἴρηκεν· 'Χαῖρέ μοι, Γαουλβᾶνε,
ὁ τοῦ ῥηγὸς ἀδελφιδοῦς᾽ Ἀρτούζου Βρετανίας.
Ἀλλ᾽ ἄπιθι, μακρύνθητι, μή μου προσψαύσεις ὅλως.
40 Ὁμολογῶ τὰς χάριτας μητέρι σου Μοργαίνῃ
καὶ πάππῳ σου τῷ θαυμαστῷ ῥηγὶ τῷ Βρετανίας,
τὴν κλῆσιν ἐπιφέροντι Οὐτέρω Παντρεγόρω.¹³

---

⁹ MS: *ἀναγάζει.* I follow RN, who partially accepts H and edd. αναχάζειν, but who preserves 'the infinitive without final *ν* which also occurs in verse 151' (RN, p. 35).
¹⁰ *διάκρινε·* RN finds previous emendations *διέκειτο* (H), *διέκρινε* (EB) unnecessary: 'Verbs are found without augment in vv. 76, 101, 202, 254' (p. 35). This judgment is followed here.
¹¹ MS: *τῷ δωματίῳ,* Cypriot genitive singular.
¹² MS: *μϊ*
¹³ MS: *Οὐτέρω Παντρεγόρω,* Cypriot genitive singular. B adds iota subscript, for *Οὐτέρῳ Παντρεγόρῳ,* dative singular agreeing with *Μοργαίνῃ.*

since all were aware of Palamedes' might,
and they marvelled at the old knight's strength.
    When, covered in shame, Palamedes had departed,
the nephew of the king, the manly Gawain,
25 kneeling, addressed the divine king thus:
'It is fitting, lord, not to rush out, put oneself forward
in contest or fight without your sanction.
But, for the love I bear Palamedes, I cannot recoil.
And, you know, having been his friend for so long,
30 I must try to avenge my friend's defeat.'
He is granted by the king to contend in arms
and in high spirits he hastens from the lodging
and, stretching forth his right hand, says: 'Greetings, knight,
you who have quite covered Palamedes in shame.
35 I have come to avenge my friend's defeat,
since Palamedes happens to be an old friend of mine.'
    The old man answered: 'Greetings, Gawain,
nephew of King Arthur of Britain.
But go, keep your distance, touch me not at all.
40 I declare my loyalty to your mother, Morgan,
and your illustrious grandfather, the King of Britain
who bore the name Uther Pendragon.

Εἰ δ' ἴσως πλήττει σου ψυχὴν ἡ πτῶσις τοῦ φιλοῦντος,
γνῶθι σαφῶς ὡς σὺν αὐτῷ τὸ πάθος κοινωνήσεις.'
45 Καὶ ταῦτ' εἰπόντες, ἵσταται μακρόθεν Γαουλβᾶνος,
καὶ βάλλει τὸ δοράτιον τοῖς στέρνοις τοῦ πρεσβύτου
καὶ Παλαμήδει κοινωνεῖ τῇ πτώσει καὶ τῷ πάθει.
  Ὁ Γαλαιῶτος ὁ κλεινὸς Τιτάνων ὁ δεσπότης,
ἰδὼν τὸν ἀδελφόπαιδα ῥηγὸς, ὡς Παλαμήδην,
50 ἐξ ἐφεστρίδος κατὰ γῆς σφοδρῶς ἐκπετασθέντα,
αἰτεῖ ῥηγὶ πρὸς ἄμιλλαν γενέσθαι τοῦ πρεσβύτου.
  Ὁ δὲ κ'αὐτὸν ἐνδίδωσιν τοῖς ὅπλοις ἀμιλλᾶσθαι.
Καὶ προσκαλέσας τοὺς αὐτοῦ παῖδας καὶ ταγματάρχας   *f. 204r*
πλουσίως ἐφοπλίζεται κατὰ τοῦ πρεσβυτέρου.
55 Βλέπει δ' αὐτὸν ὁ γηραιὸς ἐκεῖνος ὁ γεννάδας,
ὑπογελᾷ τὸ προσῶπον, μέμφεται τὸ χρυσίον,[14]
καταμωκᾶται μάλιστα τούτου τὴν ἀφροσύνην.
  Ὁ δὲ γεννάδας καρτερὸς ἱππότης Γαλαιῶτος
ἐζήτει τοῦ καταμαθεῖν τὴν κλῆσιν τοῦ πρεσβύτου.
60 Ὁ δὲ φησίν· 'Οὐκ ἀρεστὸν τοῦτο ἐμοὶ τυγχάνει
Οὐδὲ γὰρ εἷς ἐπάξιος τὴν κλῆσιν μου γνωρίσαι.
Ὅτι μὲν εἷς[15] ἀφ' ὑψηλοῦ καὶ ῥηγικοῦ τοῦ γένους,
τοῖς πᾶσιν δῆλον γίνεται τοῖς οὖσι Βρετανίας,
ἀλλὰ πρὸς γνώμην τὴν ἐμὴν παιδάριον ἀχρεῖον.
65 Οὐκοῦν μακρύνθητι καὶ σὺ κατὰ τὸν ἴσον τρόπον
καὶ δεῦρο βάλλε κατ' ἐμοῦ τὸ δόρυ[16] ῥωμαλέως,
ὡς ἀδελφόπαις τοῦ ῥηγὸς στερρὸς ὁ Γαουλβᾶνος,
καὶ πρότερος ὑπὲρ αὐτὸν γεννάδας Παλαμήδης.'

[14] MS: *χρίσίον*
[15] MS: *ῆς*
[16] MS: *δώρυ*

But, if your friend's downfall so wounds your spirit,
know truly you will share the same misfortune.'
45 These things having been said, Gawain places himself at a distance
and drives his spear at the old man's chest
and shares Palamedes' downfall and misfortune.
   Galehaut the famous, the lord of the Titans,
seeing the nephew of the king, like Palamedes,
50 cast roughly from the saddle to the ground,
petitions the king to let him contend with the Old Knight;
and the king grants him to contend in arms.
And, calling forth his squires and retainers,
he is sumptuously armed for combat with the old one.
55 When the old man, that noble warrior, sees all this
he smiles openly; he scorns his gilded stuff
and above all mocks the young man's lack of wits.
   Then the noble knight, the mighty Galehaut,
asks if he might know the old man's name.
60 But he says: 'That does not happen to please me,
for you are not worthy of knowing my name.
That you are of high and kingly parentage,
is obvious to everyone in Britain,
but in my judgment you are a useless child.
65 Therefore, place yourself at the same distance
and thrust your spear at me, right here, as hard as you can,
just as the king's nephew did, the steadfast Gawain,
and before him the noble Palamedes.'

Ὁ δὲ πεισθεὶς δοράτιον βάλλει κατὰ τῶν στέρνων.
70 κἀξ ἐφεστρίδος κατὰ γῆς ἐρρίφθη[17] σὺν τοῖς πρῴην.
Καὶ δεῖ με λέγειν τὰ πολλὰ καὶ 'παριθμεῖν τοὺς ἄνδρας
τοὺς βάλλοντας τὰ δόρατα τοῖς στέρνοις τοῦ πρεσβύτου;
Οἱ πάντες ἐξερρίφησαν[18] πρὸς γῆν ἐξ ἐφεστρίδων,
πλὴν τοῦ Τριστάνου τοῦ στερροῦ, κλεινοῦ τοῦ Λανσελώτου.
75 Αὐτοὶ καὶ γὰρ οὐκ ἔβαλον[19] τὰ δόρατα τοῖς στέρνοις.
Τίμησε τούτους ὁ στερρὸς ἱππότης ὁ πρεσβύτης,
ἐπεὶ δὲ πάντες ἔβαλον[20] τὰ δόρατα τοῖς στέρνοις
κἀξ ἐφεστρίδων[21] κατὰ γῆς ἐρρίπτοντο[22] καθάπαξ.
Ὥσπέρ τις ναῦς τοῖς κύμασιν σφοδρῶς χειμαζομένη   f. 204v
80 καὶ τῇ φορᾷ[23] τοῦ πνεύματος προσκρούσασα τοῖς λίθοις
καὶ συντριβεῖσα[24] καθ' αὑτὴν τῆς πλήξεως τῇ βίᾳ,
οὕτως καὶ πάντες ἔπιπτον ὡς ἀδρανεῖς[25] φανέντες.
Ὁ γὰρ στερρὸς καὶ καρτερὸς ἱππότης ὁ πρεσβύτης
ὡς κίων[26] ἵστατο στερρός, καταγελῶν τοὺς νέους.
85 Αὐτὸ δ' οὐκ ἦν καθ' ἡδονὴν ῥηγὶ[27] τῷ Βρετανίας
οὔτ' αὖ τοὺς ὄντας σὺν αὐτῷ καὶ προὔχοντας τοῦ κράτους.
Ἐλπίδας δ' ἐπεσάλευον ἐν μόνῳ τῷ Τριστάνῳ
καὶ Λανσελώτῳ τῷ στερρῷ τοῖς ὅπλοις καὶ τῇ ῥώμῃ,

---

[17] MS: ἐρύφθη
[18] MS: ἐξερίφησαν
[19] MS: ἔλαβον
[20] MS: ἔλαβον βαλλείν. Either ἔβαλον or βαλλεῖν would fit grammatically, and one was probably meant for deletion. I follow B and RN in choosing the more metrical reading. As elsewhere I have reversed the scribe's metathesis (ἔλαβον for ἔβαλον).
[21] MS: καὶ ἐξεφεστρίδων. Emended for metre following B and RN.
[22] MS: ἐμίπτοντο
[23] MS: φρουρα
[24] MS: συντριβῆσα
[25] MS: αὐδρανεῖς
[26] MS: κύων
[27] MS: ῥίγι

Thus persuaded, he drives his spear at his chest
70 and is flung from his saddle to the ground like the others.
But is it necessary for me to speak at length, adding up all the men
who drove their spears at the old man's chest?
All were thrown from their saddles and laid out on the ground.
All except the steadfast Tristan and glorious Lancelot,
75 for these did not drive their spears at his chest.
And the sturdy old knight did them an honour,
since all who drove their spears at his chest
were always flung from the saddle to the ground.
Even as a boat being hit by violent waves
80 and crashing on the rocks under the force of the gale,
is smashed into pieces by the force of the blow,
in the same way they all fell, and all seemed powerless.
For the strong and steadfast old knight
stood sturdy as a pillar, laughing down the young men.
85 This was not pleasing to the King of Britain
nor to those with him, the chief men of rank.
Hopes were now riding alone on Tristan
and powerful Lancelot, on their arms and might.

καὶ ποτνιῶνται τοῦ λαβεῖν τὴν ἄμιλλαν πρεσβύτου.
90 Ἡ ξυνωρὶς δὲ παρευθὺς τὸ κελευσθὲν τελοῦσα,
τὰς πανοπλίας αἴρουσα παρίστανται σταδίῳ.
Καὶ Λανσελῶτος ὁ κλεινὸς ᾔτησεν τῷ Τριστάνῳ
ἀναλαβέσθαι πρότερον τὴν ἄμιλλαν πρεσβύτου.
Δέδοικε γὰρ ὡς ἀληθῶς τὴν ῥώμην τοῦ Τριστάνου,
95 μή πως αὐτὸς ἀναδειχθῇ βελτίων[28] τοῦ πρεσβύτου.
καὶ τὴν νικῶσαν ἀληθῶς λήψεται τῆς τραπέζης.
Οἱ δαιτυμόνες[29] καὶ στερροὶ τοῖς ὅπλοις κηρυχθέντες,
ὁ δὲ Τριστάνος ἐν αὐτοῖς ἀρτιφαὴς ὑπῆρχεν.
Δωρεῖ τ' αὐτῷ τὴν αἴτησιν Τριστάνος Λανσελώτῳ,
100 ἀλλὰ καθάπαξ τὴν ψυχὴν ἠνίασε τὸ δρᾶμα,
[ἐ]πεὶ κ'αὐτὸς ὡς ἀληθῶς δεδοίκει[30] Λανσελῶτον,
μή που νικήσας τὸν στερρὸν ἐκεῖνον τὸν ἱππότην
ἕξει καὶ γέρας παρ' αὐτοῦ, τὴν ἐπελθοῦσαν κόρην,
αὐτὸς δ' ἀγέραστος λειφθεὶς λειφθήσεται ἀμίλλης.[31]
105 Ἐπεὶ δ' οὐκ ἦν ἀποφυγεῖν[32] τὴν αἴτησιν Τριστάνῳ,
ὁ Λανσελῶτος ἔρχεται· 'Χαῖρε,' φησὶν, 'ἱππότα.' f. 205r
Ὁ πρέσβυς ὁ πανθαύμαστος, ὁ βρυχητίας[33] λέων,
ἀντίχαριν δὲ δεδωκὼς πυνθάνεται τὴν κλῆσιν.
·'Εγω,' φησίν, 'ὡς ἀληθῶς, ἐκ Λίμνης Λανσελῶτος.'
110 Ὁ δὲ πρεσβύτης εἴρηκεν· 'Χαῖρε, τῶν νέων κλέος,
ἀλλ' οὔπω δὲ γεγένησαι τῶν πρεσβυτέρων ἴσος.[34]

---

[28] MS: *ἀναδιχθῇ βελτιόν*
[29] MS: *δαιτιμῶνες*
[30] MS: *δεδοίκη*
[31] MS: *λειφθήσεις τῆς ἀμίλης*
[32] MS: *ἀποφυγὴν*. See similarly structured line and manuscript reading at line 143.
[33] MS: *βρυχίτιαις*
[34] MS: *ἴσως*

Everyone cried for them to join the old man in fight,
90　and the pair now did what was needful.
Armed and ready, they are side by side on the field.
And now glorious Lancelot appealed to Tristan
to let him challenge the old knight first.
For he plainly feared the strength of Tristan,
95　lest he somehow prove better than the old one
and truly become the Round Table's champion.
The banqueters having lately been summoned, stalwart in arms,
Tristan had risen to distinction among them.
And Tristan does grant Lancelot his boon
100　but instantly it torments him in his soul,
since he also plainly fears Lancelot,
lest he somehow beat that powerful knight,
and win his companion, the girl, for his prize
and leave him empty-handed and without the honour of fighting.
105　　But since it was not for Tristan to deny him,
Lancelot went ahead. 'Greetings, knight', he says.
The marvellous old man, the bellowing lion,
having returned the greeting, asks for his name.
'Truly', he says, 'I am Lancelot of the Lake.'
110　And the old knight says: 'Greetings, glory of the young!
But even so you remain unequal to your elders.

Ὅμως κἀγὼ παρέξω³⁵ σοι γέρας ὑπὲρ τοὺς ἄλλους,
καὶ λάβω τὸ δοράτιον, βάλλων³⁶ κατὰ τῶν στέρνων.'
Καὶ μακρυνθέντες βάλλονται τοῖς δόρασιν ἀλλήλοις.
115 Συντρίβεται δοράτιον χειρὶ τοῦ Λανσελώτου.
Ὁ δὲ πρεσβύτης κατὰ γῆς πετάσας Λανσελῶτον,
παλινδρομήσας ἵσταται τῷ χώρῳ τῷ προτέρῳ.
Ὕστατος³⁷ πάντων ἔρχεται Τριστᾶνος ὁ γενναῖος
καὶ χαῖρε προσφθεγξάμενος ἀντίχαιρε λαμβάνει.
120 Καὶ χαίρει μὲν ἐπαληθῶς κρυφίως τῇ καρδίᾳ,
ὡς ὕστατος³⁸ γενόμενος ἕξει τὸ γέρας μόνος
ὅτι καὶ κρείττων κηρυχθῇ στερροῦ τοῦ Λανσελώτου.
Τοῦτον³⁹ δ' ἰδὼν ὁ γηραιὸς ἱππότης ὁ γεννάδας,
τὴν κλῆσιν ἐπυνθάνετο καὶ γένος καὶ πατρίδα,
125 οὐ γὰρ ἐδόκει κατ' αὐτοὺς εἶναι τῆς Βρετανίας.
'Υἱός,' φησίν, 'ὁ τοῦ ῥηγὸς ὑπάρχω Λιονόης,
ἀδελφιδοῦς δὲ τοῦ ῥηγός τοῦ Μάρκου Κορναλίας.
Τριστᾶνος δὲ καλούμενος⁴⁰ ὑπάρχω παρὰ πᾶσιν.'
Ταῦτα δ' ἀκούσας ἔχαιρεν ἱππότης ὁ πρεσβύτης,
130 ὡς ὁ Τριστᾶνος κατὰ γῆς ῥιφθῇ⁴¹ σὺν Λανσελώτῳ.
Καὶ τῷδε γέρας δίδωσι τοῦ βάλλειν δορατίῳ,
καὶ μακρυνθέντες βάλλονται τοῖς δόρασι κατάμφω.
Καὶ πάντα γέγονεν αυτῷ τοῦ Λανσελώτου τρόπῳ.   f. 205v
Ὁ ῥὴξ ὠχροῦται⁴² πρόσωπον καὶ βρύχει τοὺς ὀδόντας,

---

35 MS: *παρέξο*
36 MS: *βάλλον*
37 MS: *ίστατος*
38 MS: *ίστατος*
39 MS: *τούτων*
40 MS: *καλλούμενος*
41 MS: *ρυφθῆ*
42 MS: *όχροῦται*

Still, I shall grant you a greater privilege than the others,
for I shall take my spear and drive it at your chest.'
So, standing apart, they rushed against each other with their spears.
115 Lancelot's spear is shattered in his hand,
while the old knight, with Lancelot laid out on the ground,
turns again, taking up his old position.
    Last of all, then, comes the valiant Tristan,
and calling out 'Greetings!' he is greeted in return.
120 And truly, in his heart he secretly rejoices
since, being last, he alone will have the prize
and be proved stronger than mighty Lancelot.
Seeing him, the venerable old knight
asked to know his name, his birth and homeland,
125 because he seemed unlike the other Britons.
'I am the son', he said, 'of the king of Lyonesse,
nephew of King Mark of Cornwall,
and I am known to all as Tristan.'
Hearing these things, the old knight rejoiced
130 since Tristan would be flung to the ground like Lancelot.
To him, too, he grants the privilege of a joust.
Taking their places, they rush at each other with their spears,
and everything happens just as with Lancelot.
    Now the king's face goes white, he grinds his teeth,

135 ἀνακαχλάζει τῷ θυμῷ, σφοδρῶς ἐξαγριοῦται.
Καλέσας δὲ τοὺς παρ' αὐτῷ τὴν πανοπλίαν αἴρει.
Ἡ δὲ Ντζενέβρα δέδοικεν μή τι καὶ χεῖρον ἔλθῃ.[43]
Γονυπετοῦσα φθέγγεται[44] μὴ τοῦτο τελεσθῆναι.
Ὁ δὲ κλεινὸς καὶ θαυμαστὸς ὁ ῥὴξ τῆς Βρετανίας,
140 '"Απιθι,' φάσκει πρὸς αὐτήν, 'μηκέτι φθεγγομένην,
γυναικωνῖτιν[45] εὐπρεπῶς κοσμοῦσα καὶ παιδίσκας.[46]
Ἐγὼ δὲ καθοπλίσομαι[47] τῶν συνδειπνούντων χάριν.'
Ἐπεὶ δ' οὐκ ἦν ἐπιτυχεῖν[48] τὴν αἴτησιν [Ν]τζενέβρᾳ,
παίει χερσὶ τὰς παρειάς, τὰς τρίχας ἔξω τίλλει.[49]
145 Καὶ πάντες οἱ θεράποντες ἐβόουν, ἐθορύβουν.[50]
Ἀλλ' ἦν ῥηγὶ πρὸς παίγνιον τῶν θεραπόντων θρῆνος.
Καὶ κατελθὼν τοῦ δώματος[51] παρίσταται σταδίῳ,
οὔτ' αὖ τὸ χαῖρε προσειπών, οὐ δεξιὰν ἐκτείνας,
ἀλλ' ἔστη βλοσυρόματος[52] ὥσπερ λεόντων[53] σκύμνος.
150 Τοῦτον[54] δ' ἰδὼν ἱστάμενον ἱππότης ὁ πρεσβύτης,
ἔγνω τὸν ῥῆγαν ἀληθῶς τυγχάνει τὸν ἐλθόντα.
Κἀξ ἐφεστρίδος κατὰ γῆν καθῆλθεν ἑκουσίως,
καὶ προσελθὼν ἠσπάσατο γονυπετῶν ὡς δοῦλος.
'"Απιθι,' λέγων, 'δέσποτα, μὴ παρὰ θέμιν δρᾶται.
155 Τὸ γέρας γὰρ τῶν ἱπποτῶν, ἀδελφιδοῦς μοι 'πάρχει

[43] MS: *ἔλθη*
[44] MS: *φθύγγεται*
[45] MS: *γυναικονίτην*
[46] MS: *καὶ παρθένος παιδίσκας*
[47] MS: *καθοπλήομαι*
[48] MS: *ἐπιτυχεῖν*. See similarly structured line and manuscript reading at line 105.
[49] MS: *τείλει*
[50] MS: *ἐθωρύβουν*
[51] MS: *δόματος*
[52] RN: *βροσυρόμματος*
[53] MS: *λεώντων*
[54] MS: *τούτων*

135 he seethes in his heart, exasperated beyond measure.
Calling to his men, he takes up his armour.
But Guenevere, fearing worse things to come,
falls to her knees and loudly voices her dissent.
But the renowned and marvellous King of Britain,
140 'Go!' he says to her. 'No more wailing!
Look after the maidens in their apartments, as is fitting.
But I shall arm myself for the sake of these dinner-guests.'
Since it was not for Guenevere's plea to hit the mark,
she strikes her cheeks with her hands and tears out her hair,
145 and all the servants were wailing and making a noise.
But their lament was, to the king's mind, childish.
And, going out, he takes his place in the field.
Not giving him greeting, nor extending his right hand,
he stood angry-eyed, like a lion's whelp.
150 Seeing him standing there, the Old Knight
knew truly it was the king who had come.
He willingly descended from his saddle to the ground,
approached and greeted him, kneeling like a vassal,
and said: 'Depart, my lord, lest something happen contrary to law.
155 My niece is offered as a reward for your knights,

ἡ σὴ δὲ ζήτω σύνευνος Ντζενέβρα κατὰ θέμιν,
ὡς εὐκλεῶς, ὡς εὐπρεπῶς κοσμοῦσά σου τὸ στέφος,
καὶ μὴ πρὸς κοίτην ἔλθης σὺ κόρης εὐπρεπεστάτης.
Εἰ δὲ καὶ πλήττει σου σφοδρῶς τῶν ἱπποτῶν ἡ πτῶσις *f. 200r*
160 κἀγώ γε φίλος ἀληθῶς καὶ λάτρις σου τυγχάνω.
Κ'οὐκ ἀπὸ ξένοις πρὸς ὑμᾶς ἦλθον ἐκ γῆς μακρόθεν.
Εἰ δὲ[55] καὶ κρείττων φαίνομαι τῶν ἱπποτῶν τραπέζης,
καὶ τοῦτό σοι πρὸς κλεϊσμὸν τυγχάνει τὸ πρακτέον.
Ἔχεις καὶ γὰρ ἰσόρροπον[56] θεράποντα τοῖς πᾶσιν.'
165 Ταῦτα δ'ἀκούσας ὁ κλεινὸς Ἀρτοῦζος ὁ γενναῖος
ἐξ ἐφεστρίδος πρὸς τὴν γῆν κατῆλθεν ἑκουσίως.
Περιπλακεὶς[57] δ' ἠσπάζετο γενναίῳ τῷ πρεσβύτῃ
καὶ πρὸς τοὺς δόμους ἀγαγεῖν ἠνάγκαζεν ἐξόχως
τοῦ συνδειπνῆσαι τῷ ῥηγὶ καὶ πᾶσι τοῖς ἱππόταις.
170 Ὁ δ' ἔφη· Μου καθ' ἡδονὴν ὑπάρχει σοῦ τὸ ῥῆμα.
Ἀλλ' οὔτε κλῆσιν τὴν ἐμήν, οὔτε τὴν ὄψιν ὅλως
ἔχω τοῦ δοῦναι παρ' ὑμῖν ἐν τοῖς πρακτέοις.'
Καὶ ταῦτ' εἰπὼν ἠσπάσατο, τὴν δεξιὰν ἐκτείνας,
καὶ λύσιν ἔλαβεν ἐλθεῖν αὖθις πρὸς κατοικίαν.
175 Ἐν τούτοις δὲ τοῖς δράμασιν ἧκει παιδίσκη κόρη,
θυγάτηρ οὖσα γυναικὸς ἀφ' ὑψηλοῦ τοῦ γένους
καὶ χηρευούσης ἐν μακρῷ τῷ χρόνῳ ταλαιπώρως,
προσαπολέσασα[58] κακῶς καὶ πᾶσαν τὴν οὐσίαν,
τὰς πόλεις, τὰ πολίχνια,[59] τὰ θρέμματα, τοὺς παῖδας,

---

[55] MS: *οὐ δὲ*
[56] MS: *ἰσόροπον*
[57] MS: *περιπλακίς*
[58] MS: *προσαπωλέσασα*
[59] MS: *πολύχνϊα*

and your consort by law is Guenevere – may she live long!
So, regally and suitably, glorify your crown;
do not approach this beautiful maiden's bed.
If the defeat of your knights pains you terribly,
160 I happen, truly, to be your friend and supporter.
Nor have I come to you from abroad, a foreigner.
And if I appear stronger than the Round Table knights,
even this fact increases your glory:
for you have one servant equal to all the rest.'
165   Hearing these things the glorious and valiant Arthur
gladly descended from his saddle to the ground.
Embracing the valiant old man, he welcomed him
and keenly urged him to enter into his house,
to be a dinner-guest of the king and all his knights.
170 But he replied: 'Your words give me pleasure.
But neither my name, nor indeed my appearance,
can I reveal to you in the present circumstance.'
Saying these things he paid his respects, extending his right hand,
and took his leave, about to return to his home.
175   But in the midst of all this action, a young girl has arrived,
being the daughter of a nobly-born woman
who, widowed for a long time and long having suffered,
had been evilly deprived of all her possessions:
towns, villages, livestock, servants;

180 ἐπείπερ ἀπηφάνισται[60] πατρὸς καὶ κασιγνήτων.
Γείτων καὶ γὰρ ἐτύγχανεν αὐταῖς ὁ δυναστεύων,
τῶν ἱπποτῶν τῶν ἑκατὸν[61] ὁ ῥὴξ ὁ κεκλημένος
καὶ παρανόμους ἁρπαγὰς ἠργάσατο πλειστάκις.
Ἐπεὶ δ' οὐκ ἦν ἀντέχεσθαι τὴν ῥώμην τοῦ δυνάστου,   *f. 200v*
185 βουλὴν βουλεύεται σοφὴν πάνυ συνετωτάτην·
Κ' ἡ κόρη παραγίνεται ῥηγὸς ἐν τοῖς μελάθροις,
ἡ μήτηρ δὲ προσέμενεν τῇ φυλακῇ φρουρίου
....[62]
ἐκ δαιτυμόνων τῶν λαμπρῶν τραπέζης τῆς στρογγύλης.
Ἐπείπερ κατεμανθάνον τὴν ἔλευσιν δυνάστου,
190 ὁ ῥὴξ δ' αὐτὴν ἀμείβεται βιαίως καὶ δυσήχως·
'Ὁρᾷς, παιδίσκη, τὴν αἰδῶ τὴν ἐπελθοῦσαν ὧδε,
ὡς πάντες κατῃσχύνθησαν τῇ ῥώμῃ τοῦ πρεσβύτου.
Ἄπιθι τοίνυν πρὸς τὴν σὴν μητέρα καὶ τοὺς δόμους.
Ἐν ἄλλοις δέ σοι πρύτανις[63] ἐξ ἱπποτῶν γενέσθαι.'
195 Ἡ δ' ἐκ δόμων[64] ἔρχεται δακρυρροοῦσα[65] πάνυ.

[60] RN (p. 36) sums up the situation of ἀπηφάνισται· 'In his apparatus Breillat offers the correction ἀπηρφάνισται on the grounds that the word ἀπαφανίζω is not attested, and that in the Cypriot dialect the attestation of ἀρφανός for ὀρφανός ... may suggest a verb *ἀπαρφανίζω. One doubts whether to accept Breillat's proposal, given the presence of Cypriot forms in the text. In the Cypriot dialect is also attested the word ἀρφανεύκω > ἀρφανεύω... In the end, a conservative position on the manuscript reading has prevailed.'
[61] MS: ἱκατῶν
[62] The difficulty of construing lines 187-190 leads me to suspect that text is missing between lines 187 and 188; the missing line or lines would have supplied the substantive direct object, or objects, of προσέμενεν ('awaited') + ἐκ + partitive genitive, on the model of lines 222-225 (following the verb ἤθελον, 'they would have preferred'):
Ἤθελον ἂν πρὸς ἀρωγὴν γενέσθαι Λανσελῶτον,
ἢ τὸν Τριστᾶνον τὸν κλεινόν, ἤγε καὶ Παλαμήδην,
ἢ κατὰ πλοῦν τὸν δεύτερον ἕνα τῶν δαιτυμόνων
ἐκ τῆς τραπέζης τοῦ ῥηγὸς στρογγύλης Βρετανίας.
[63] MS: πρίτανις
[64] MS: ἐκ τῶν δόμων. / follow RN who omits τῶν on metrical grounds.
[65] MS: δακρυροοῦσα

180   and the girl had lost her father and brothers.
      It happened that a local tyrant was terrorising the women:
      he was called the King of the Hundred Knights,
      and had made many unlawful raids against them.
      Since it was impossible to withstand the tyrant's strength,
185   a wise and altogether judicious decision was taken:
      the girl would travel to the court of the king
      while the mother safe in her citadel, awaited
      ....
      from the bright banqueters of the Round Table.
      But when they learned of the tyrant's incursion,
190   the king answers her abruptly and harshly:
      'Do you see, girl, the shame that completely covers us?
      All of us humiliated by the strength of that old man?
      But go now, to your mother and your house,
      and seek a champion from among other men.'
195   She departs from the chamber then, all in tears.

Ἰδόντες⁶⁶ κατοικτείροντο πάντες οἱ προστυχόντες
καὶ γνώμην δίδωσιν αὐτὴν πρεσβύτην προσαιτῆσαι
πρὸς ἀρωγὴν σύναρσιν καὶ 'μύνην τοῦ δυνάστου.
Ἡ κόρη πείθεται σοφῶν μαθοῦσα βουλευμάτων
200 καὶ ποτνιᾶται κάμπτουσα τὸ γόνυ τοῦ πρεσβύτου.
    Ὁ δὲ φησί· 'Μου κέκμηκεν, θύγατερ, τὸ σαρκίον.
Ἀλλ' ἐπειδὴ πρὸς ἀρωγὴν αἰτήσω τὸν ἱππότην
καὶ τῆς αἰσχύνης αἴτιον εὑρέθη σοι καθάπαξ,
ἐγὼ λοιπὸν πορεύομαι πρὸς ἀρωγήν σου, κόρη,
205 ὁ τὴν αἰσχύνην ἀληθῶς ἐμπλήσας τοῖς ἀνδράσιν.
Γενοῦ μοι τοίνυν ποδηγὸς ἄχρι τοῦ πολιχνίου.'
Καὶ ταῦτ' εἰπὼν ἐξέρχεται ῥηγὸς τῶν δωματίων.⁶⁷
Καὶ πρὸς ἑσπέραν ἔρχονται κάτενδον τοῦ φρουρίου.
Καὶ πάντες κατησπάζοντο τὴν ἔλευσιν τῆς κόρης.   f. 201r
210 Τῇ δὲ 'στεραίᾳ⁶⁸ παρ' αὐτοῖς⁶⁹ ἐκδέχοντο δυνάστας.
Ἐπεὶ δὲ γέγονεν ἐντὸς ἱππότης δωματίων,⁷⁰
αὐτοῦ τὴν ἀδελφόπαιδα ταῖς γυναίξιν ἐνώσας,
αὐτὸς ταμίω⁷¹ γίνεται, παρακαθίσας κλίνην.⁷²
Τὴν κεφαλὴν ἐγύμνωσε τῆς κόρυθος⁷³ ὁ πρέσβυς,
215 ἀπέθετο τὸν θώρακα, πᾶσαν τὴν πανοπλίαν,
καὶ πρὸς ἀνάπαυλαν, ἰδού, τρέπεται τοῦ σαρκίου.
Καὶ γίνεται φιλότιμον τὸ⁷⁴ δεῖπνον τῷ πρεσβύτῃ.

---

⁶⁶ MS: *οἰδόντες*
⁶⁷ MS: *δοματίων*
⁶⁸ i.e., ὑστεραίᾳ, 'on the following day'.
⁶⁹ MS: ἀτῆς. Emended for sense following RN and B.
⁷⁰ MS: *δοματίων*
⁷¹ MS: *ταμίω*. Cypriot genitive singular.
⁷² MS: *παρακαθήσας κλήνην*
⁷³ MS: *κόρινθος*
⁷⁴ MS: *τῶ*

Seeing this, the dinner-guests all pitied her,
and they advise her to petition the old knight
for his help and protection from the tyrant.
The girl, hearing this sage advice, is persuaded
200 and falling to her knees she loudly implores the old one.
    And he answers, 'Maiden, my body is exhausted,
but since you have asked a knight for assistance
and made the cause of your shame known to all,
I will come, child, alone as I am, and help you,
205 I who truly filled these men with shame.
Now be my guide until we get to your village.'
Having said these things, he quits the king's chambers,
and towards evening they arrive at the castle.
And everyone celebrated the girl's arrival,
210 for they expected the tyrants at their gates the next morning.
Once the knight was within the house,
his niece having joined the other ladies,
he is lord of the feast, reclining on the couch.
Then the old man doffed his crested helmet
215 and laid his breast-plate down and all his armour,
and now, know well, he turns his body toward rest.
And a feast was laid to honour the old man.

Εἰπόντες δὲ τὸν γηραιὸν λευκότριχον ἱππότην
κατεμωκῶντ᾽,[75] ἐμέμφοντο τὴν σύνεσιν τῆς κόρης
220 ὅπως λαθοῦσα παρ᾽ αὐτοῖς παρήγαγεν τὸν πρέσβυν
ἀχρεῖον καὶ ταλαίπωρον[76] ἐκ μακροτάτου χρόνου.
Ἤθελον ἂν πρὸς ἀρωγὴν γενέσθαι Λανσελῶτον,
ἢ τὸν Τριστᾶνον τὸν κλεινόν,[77] ἦγε καὶ Παλαμήδην,
ἢ κατὰ πλοῦν τὸν δεύτερον[78] ἕνα τῶν δαιτυμόνων[79]
225 ἐκ τῆς τραπέζης τοῦ ῥηγὸς στρογγύλης Βρετανίας,
οὐ μήν γε δ᾽ ἐρειδόμενον τῷ νάρθηκι[80] πρεσβύτην.
Αὐτὸς δὲ μᾶλλον παρ᾽ ἡμῶν τὸν ἀρωγὸν[81] αἰτήσει.
Δοθήτω[82] κλίνη τοιγαροῦν τῷ ταλαιπώρῳ πρέσβει,[83]
καὶ μετ᾽ εἰρήνης πρὸς αὐτοῦ τοὺς δόμους πορευέσθω.
230 Σύ[84] δ᾽ αὖ γε τρέχε πρὸς αὐτὸν τὸν ῥῆγαν Βρετανίας
καὶ ἕναν ἱππότην παρ᾽ αὐτοῦ λάμβανε κατὰ τάχος,
ἵν᾽ ὅπως γένη μεθ᾽ ἡμῶν πρωίας ἐπελθούσης,
πρὸ τοῦ δυνάστας πρὸς ἡμᾶς πρὸς ἁρπαγὴν ἐλθόντας.᾽

[Ἡ] κόρη δ᾽ αὖ ἐν χαροπῷ σταθεῖσα τῷ προσώπῳ *f. 201v*
235 ἀμείβεται· ʽΜὴ μέμφεσθαι τόδε μου τὸ πρακτέον.[85]

---

[75] MS: *κατεμωκόντ*
[76] MS: *ταλαίπορον*
[77] MS: *κληνόν*
[78] ἢ *κατὰ πλοῦν τὸν δεύτερον*. Thus RN for MS: *ἢ καταπλοῦν τὸν δεύτερον*. B: *ἢ καταπλοῦν τὸν δεύτερος*. H: *ἢ᾽᾽ Γαυλβᾶνον τὸν δεύτερον*. E: *ἢ Γαυλβᾶνον τὸν στερρόν*. RN summarises the situation of this much-emended half-line as follows (p. 37): 'All the editors have considered this passage to be seriously corrupt because they did not know the expression, attested already in Plato and Aristotle, and which later became proverbial.'
[79] MS: *δαιτυμώνων*
[80] For MS: τὴν ἄρτι καί, following B.
[81] MS: *ἀρογόν*
[82] MS: δωθήτω
[83] MS: *πρέσβυ*
[84] For MS: *οὐ*, following B.
[85] MS: *τωδε μου τὸ πρακταίον*

But, when they saw that the knight was old and white-haired,
they mocked him, faulting the maiden's sagacity,
220 for it must have escaped her notice that she had brought an old man,
useless, wasted, in the extremity of age.
They would have preferred Lancelot to come to their aid,
or Tristan the glorious, or indeed Palamedes,
or, as a second-best option, one of the banqueters
225 from the Round Table of the king of Britain,
or at least not an old man leaning on his stick.
'This one will rather be asking us for help!
Therefore, let a bed be brought for this poor old man,
and let him go back home in peace.
230 But you, run once more to the king of Britain
and fetch one of his knights as soon as possible,
so that he is with us by early morning,
before the tyrants, with their depredations, are upon us.'
But the maiden, standing bright-eyed before them,
235 answers: 'Do not scorn what I have done.

Οὐδὲ γὰρ ἴσχυσα λαβεῖν ἕνα τῶν[86] τῆς τραπέζης,
οὐ Λανσελῶτον ὅν φατέ, οὔτε γε τὸν Τριστᾶνον,
οὐ Παλαμήδην τὸν στερρόν, οὔτ' αὖ γε Γαουλβᾶνον.
Ἀυτὸς καὶ μόνος πρὸς ἡμᾶς ἤρετο τοῦ γενέσθαι.
240 Τὸ δ' αἴτιον τοῦ δράματος ἐν ἄλλοις ἐκδιδάξω.
Νῦν δὲ πορεύεσθαι λοιπὸν πρὸς παῦλαν τοῦ σαρκίου.
Τοιγὰρ[87] ἐν τάχει παρ' ἡμῖν ἔσται τῶν ὅπλων χρεία.
Θεὸς δὲ τρέψει τὰς ἡμῶν πρὸς αἶνον κωμῳδίας.'
Καὶ πάντες ἐπορεύοντο, τῆς ὥρας ἀπαιτούσης,
245 βαρυθυμοῦντες, στένοντες, μεμφόμενοι τὸν πρέσβυν.
Τῇ δ' ἐπιούσῃ, καθαρῶς μὴ λάμψαντος φωσφόρου,
σκοπὸς ἐγγίνεται βοῶν τὴν ἔλευσιν δυνάστου.
Καὶ πάντες εὐτρεπίζουσιν ἵππους καὶ πανοπλίας.
Ὀψέ ποτε πρὸς γηραιὸν πορεύονται κ' ἱππόται
250 ἐγρηγοροῦσι, φάσκουσι τὴν ἔλευσιν δυνάστου.
Ὁ δ' ἐκ τῆς κλίνης ἀναστὰς αἰτεῖ τὴν πανοπλίαν.
[Αἰ]τεῖ δ' ὁ γέρων παρ' αὐτῶν βρῶσιν καὶ πόσιν πρώην,[88]
καὶ τοῦτο μάλ' ἀπαίσιον ἔδοξε τοῖς ἀνδράσιν.
Ἀλλὰ παιδνὸν τοῦ γηραιοῦ νόμιζον καὶ τὸ σθένος,
255 εἰπόντες δὲ ταῖς γυναιξίν· 'Δότε τρόφην τῷ πρέσβει,'[89]
αὐτοὶ πρὸς ὅπλα γίνονται καὶ 'μύνην[90] τοῦ δυνάστου.
Ἐπεὶ δ' ὁ πρέσβυς βέβρωκεν, πέπωκεν[91] ἀνθοσμίαν,
λαμπρῶς κατεφωπλίσατο, πρὸς ἄμυναν[92] ἐξῆλθεν. *f. 202r*

---

[86] MS: *τόν*
[87] MS: *τηγάρ*
[88] MS: *πωσιν πρόην*
[89] MS: *πρέσβυ*
[90] MS: *μίνην*
[91] MS: *πέποκεν*
[92] MS: *καθἐφωπλήσατο πρὸς ἅμιναν*

It was not possible to bring a knight of the Round Table,
not Lancelot whom you mention, nor yet Tristan,
nor strong Palamedes, nor Gawain for that matter.
This man alone has undertaken to help us.
240 The reason for this action I shall tell you later.
But now it remains to give our bodies to rest,
for soon enough we shall have need of arms,
but God will turn their mockery of us to praise.'
And all went away as the hour demanded,
245 with heavy hearts, groaning, cursing the old man.

    The next day, before the morning star has clearly shone,
the watchman is shouting, announcing the tyrant's approach.
And all are readying their horses and armour.
Only later do the knights go find the old man.
250 They wake him up, inform him the tyrant is coming.
So, rising from his bed, he asks for his armour.
But first the old man asks for food and something to drink.
And this seemed most ill-omened to the men.
They valued the old man's strength as much as a boy's,
255 and, telling the women 'Give the old man some nourishment',
they take their arms and go to hold off the tyrant.
But when the old one had broken his fast and drunk fragrant wine,
he armed himself brightly and went out to the defence.

Καὶ μετ' αὐτῶν οὐ γίνεται τῶν ἔνδον[93] πολιχνίου,
260 ἀλλ' ἔτι μόνος καθορῶν τὸ τέλος τῆς ὑσμίνης.
Ἰδόντες δ' ἐμυκτήριζον, ἐγέλων τὸν πρεσβύτην,
ὡς ἀδρανῆ, ὡς ἀσθενῆ, ὡς κεκμηκότα πάνυ.
Ἐπεὶ δ' ἐντὸς ἐγένοντο βελῶν οἱ τοῦ δυνάστου,
τὰς δεξιὰς ἐκτείναντες, ἑλκύσαντες τὰ ξίφη,[94]
265 τροποῦνται πάντας ἔνδοθεν εἰσάγουσι[95] φρουρίου.
Ἁρπάζουσι βοσκήματα, τέμνουσι παραδείσους,
λεηλατοῦσι, φθείρουσι, γυμνοῦσιν ἀροτῆρας.[96]
Ὁ πρέσβυς δ' ἦλθεν παρ' αὐτοῖς· 'Χαίρετε,'[97] φάσκ' ἱππόται.'
Ἀντέχαιρε δεξάμενος ἠρώτα τὴν αἰτίαν,
270 τοῦ χάριν γέγονεν αὐτοῖς τοῦ πολιχνίου 'σμίνης.[98]
Οἱ δ' ἔνδοθεν[99] ἱστάμενοι πάντες κατεμωκῶντο,
ἐκ τῶν ἐπάλξεων αὐτῶν γελώντων[100] τὸν πρεσβύτην
καὶ τὴν αὐτοῦ καλέσασαν δεσποίνης θυγατέραν.
Ὡς δ' ἔγνω γέρων παρ'[101] αὐτῶν ἀδίκως πεπραγμένα,
275 δίδωσιν γνώμην πρὸς αὐτούς, βουλεύεται τὰ λῶστα,
τοῦ στρέψαι τὰ βοσκήματα, τοῦ λῦσαι τὴν ὑσμίνην.
Ἐπεὶ δ' οὐκ ἔπειθεν αὐτούς, πειρᾶται τοῦ κατέχειν.
Οἱ δ' ἐμωκῶντο[102] γέροντος τὴν σύνεσιν καὶ ῥώμην,
καὶ τὴν ὁδὸν προβαίνωσιν,[103] παλινδρομοῦσι δόμοις.

---

[93] MS: *ἔνδων*
[94] MS: *ξίφει*
[95] MS: *ἰσάγουσι*
[96] MS: *ἀρωτῆρας*
[97] MS: *χαίρεται*
[98] MS: *πολυχνίου μίνης*
[99] MS: *ἔνθοθεν*
[100] MS: *γελόντων*
[101] Emended from MS: *γαρ*, following RN.
[102] MS: *ἐμακῶντο*
[103] Cypriot form of *προβαίνουσιν*

He does not place himself alongside the townsmen,
260 but keeps apart, perceiving how the battle will end.
Seeing this, they scoffed and derided the old man
as powerless, feeble and entirely overcome with age.
But when the tyrant's men got there, firing arrows,
stretching out their right hands, drawing their swords,
265 they are routed all and retreat to the stronghold.
The raiders seize livestock, ravage the fields,
they plunder and destroy, they rob the peasants.
   The old man now approached them: 'Greetings, knights', he says.
Saluted in return, he inquires into the matter,
270 why the war was waged by them on the town.
All those inside the castle were mocking him,
from the battlements deriding the old man,
and also her who had brought him, their mistress's daughter.
But since the old one knew the raids were committed unjustly,
275 he gives his opinion, what is best for them to do:
to give back the livestock and to dissolve the battle.
Since he did not persuade them, he prepares to use force.
They mocked the old man's prudence and strength
and started down the road, heading to their homes.

280 Ἐπεὶ δ' οὐκ ἦν τοῦ κατασκεῖν εἰ μὴ τῇ ῥώμῃ μόνῃ,
ἕλκει τὴν σπάθην παρευθὺς, τὴν δεξιὰν ἔκτεινας.
Συλλήβδην[104] πάντας ἐξωθεῖ τοῦ μεταιχμίου χώρου,   f. 202v
καὶ ζωπυρεῖ τοὺς ἔσωθεν, θαρσύνει, παροτρύνει.
Καὶ βάλλουσι δοράτια, τοὺς ἔξωθεν τροποῦνται.
285 Ἐν δεξιοῖς, ἐν τοῖς λαιοῖς καὶ κατ' εὐθεῖαν τέμνει,
ἀσπίδας ῥίπτει κατὰ γῆς, τοὺς θώρακας συντρίβει.
Τέμνει καὶ στερροχάλκευτα τῶν ἱπποτῶν τὰ κράνη.
Πάντες λιπόντες ἔφευγον τοῦ χώρου τραυματίαι.[105]
Οἱ πλεῖστοι δ' ἔργον γίνονται μαχαίρας τοῦ πρεσβύτου.
290 Αὐτὸς δ' ὁ σκύμνος στρέφεται τῇ μάνδρᾳ πολιχνίου.[106]
Πάντες δ' ἐφήμουν[107] στέφοντες λευκόπτερον τὸν κύκνον,
ἄνδρες, γυναῖκες σὺν αὐτοῖς παισὶ καὶ τοῖς πρεσβύταις,
ἀρεϊκόν, καρτερικὸν τὸν ῥύστην τοῦ δυνάστου.
Καὶ τράπεζα πολυτελής, ἄνει[108] τὰς εὐφημίαν.
295 Ἡ κόρη καθηρμήνευσεν τὴν πτῶσιν τῶν ἀνδρείων
καὶ πάντα τὰ γινόμενα ῥηγὶ τῷ Βρετανίας.
Ἐδόκει θαῦμα παρ' αὐτοῖς καθάπερ ἦν τὸ δέον.
Τῇ δ' ἐπιούσῃ τάχιστα παλινδρομεῖ πρὸς δόμους
πρέσβυς ὁ νέους ἀφειδῶς συντρίψας ῥωμαλέους.[109]
300 Ἡ δὲ φρουρίου δέσποινα σὺν θυγατρὶ καὶ δούλοις,
γονυπετοῦσα φθέγγεται, πρεσβύτῃ ποτνιᾶται
γέρας λαβεῖν ἐκ τῶν αὐτῆς τῶν θησαυρῶν[110] ἀφθόνως.

---

[104] MS: *συλίβδην*
[105] MS: *λειπόντες ... τραυματίαν*
[106] MS: *πολιχνίω*
[107] Demotic form of *εὐφήμουν*
[108] MS: *ἄνοι*
[109] MS: *ῥωμαλαίους*
[110] MS: *θησαυρὸν*

280　Since there was no stopping them except by force,
　　　he draws his sword quickly, stretching out his right hand.
　　　Soon he thrusts back all those around him in the host
　　　and fires the blood of the townsmen, inciting and urging them on.
　　　They hurl their spears, they turn back the invaders.
285　He cleaves on the right, on the left and in the centre,
　　　shields he casts to the ground and smashes breast-plates.
　　　He cleaves even the strong copper helmets of the knights.
　　　Everyone was in retreat, wounded ones fled the place,
　　　but most become fodder for the old man's blade.
290　Like a lion's whelp, then, he returns to the enclosure of the town.
　　　Surrounding him, all praised 'The White-Winged Swan',
　　　men and women together, children and the old,
　　　their warlike, steadfast deliverer from the tyrant.
　　　And a lavish feast-table concludes the praises.
295　The girl now related the downfall of the mighty ones
　　　and all the events at the court of the King of Britain.
　　　And it seemed miraculous to them, as indeed was fitting.
　　　　The next morning, he is eager to return to his home,
　　　the old one who so vanquished the able-bodied young.
300　And the lady of the castle, with her daughter and servants,
　　　falling to her knees, loudly implores the old man
　　　to take some reward, freely, from her treasury.

Ὁμολογεῖ τὰς χάριτας δεσποίνῃ καὶ τοῖς οὖσι,
γέρας δ' αἰτεῖ τοῦ παρασχεῖν αὐτῷ τῶν πονημάτων,
305 ὅτι τὴν κόρην ἀπελθεῖν πρὸς ῥηγικοὺς τοὺς δόμους
καὶ δοῦναι τὸ γραμμάτιον ῥηγὶ τῷ Βρετανίας.
Καὶ ταῦτ' εἰπὼν ἀπαλλαγήν[111]...

---

[111] MS: *ἀπαλαγήν*

He declares his loyalty to the lady and her people,
but only requests as a reward for his labours
305　that the young girl depart to the royal lodgings
and convey a letter to the King of Britain.
And having said these things, his departure ...

Commentary

3. Neither the French source nor the Greek text is any more specific than 'other kings' or 'kings'; ὑποκείμενοι implies, but does not denote, vassalage.

6. *Palamedes, with a barbaric shout.* The poet's word βαρβαρική is appropriate to Palamedes as the pagan knight of the Tristan cycle. In medieval Greek the word not only signifies 'not Roman' (i.e., not Rhomaios, as the Byzantines called themselves) but was also freely used, most pejoratively, of Latin crusaders. Eustathius of Thessalonika, for example, writes of the Norman invasion of Thessalonika: 'The barbarians, having entered every part of the city, beginning from the eastern gates, cut down our men and piled them on the ground, those thick manciples of human crops that Hades loves to feed on.' See *L'espugnazione di Tessalonica*, ed. S. Kyriakedes (Palermo, 1960), p. 112; translated in *Byzantium*, ed. D. J. Geanakoplos (Chicago, 1984), p. 367.

7. The Greek term for 'spear' in this text is either τό δοράτιον or, interchangeably, τό δόρυ. In the Byzantine army, the spear was the weapon of the infantry, but John Kinnamos (b. before 1143, d. after 1185) in his *Epitome* records that the Emperor Manuel I Comnenos taught his cavalry to fight with long, almost body-length shields and long spears (δόρατα ... μακρά) instead of with rounded shields and bows, and, in training, to charge one another on horseback 'with blunted wooden spears' (δόρασιν ... αὐτοξύλοις).[1]

9. The stone used as a mark or target is the Greek poet's development of Rustichello's '*quintaine*'. See also the Greek poet's 'pillar' at line 84 (and see note to lines 76–84).

12. *siege engine.* The Byzantines used torsion catapults and (more often) weight-driven trebuchets called the *cheiroballistron* and *cheiromanganon* similar to western models. But the *Old Knight* poet, perhaps wanting to seem unfamiliar with modern, un-Homeric weaponry, here uses 'πετρόβολος σκεῦος' – 'catapult-thing' or 'stone-throwing apparatus' – which we have rendered in equally unspecific terms.

---

[1] J. Kinnamos, *Epitome*, ed. A. Meineke (Bonn, 1836), pp. 124–5.

16. The bed – not mentioned in Rustichello's text – is probably to be understood as within Palamedes' own tent or pavilion; if the effect seems emasculating, the poet probably meant it.

18. In Rustichello's version the knights are motivated much less by the prize than the threat to their reputation.

48. There is no consensus as to what the Greek poet means by calling Galahaut 'Lord of the Titans', but it is likely a gesture of mockery, and the Old Knight's scorn of Galehaut's gold may reflect the frequent Byzantine characterization of Franks as gold-hungry barbarians, as in Choniates, *Historia*, ed. J.-L. van Dieten (Berlin, 1975), pp. 647–51; see also A. Komnena, *The Alexiad*, trans. E. R. A. Sewter (Harmondsworth, 1969), pp. 311–13.

56. *He smiles openly.* A very different smile from the inward and invidious rejoicing of Tristan at line 120.

71. *But is it necessary for me...?* Whereas previous editors Hagen and Ellissen had emended the Greek reading to 'καὶ δεῖ μή' (it ought not to be necessary), Breillat restored the manuscript reading, followed here, which as he points out 'agrees so well with the sentence, so frequent in Rustichello: *Que vos diroie-je?*'[2]

74. *All except the valiant Tristan and glorious Lancelot.* Prolepsis; the sense is not that these two were not, or would not be, thrown to the ground, but that they would be thrown to the ground with a difference.

76–84. Simile and trope of the shipwreck. To the shame which Rustichello's text already reserves for Palamedes, the Greek poet adds a highly kinetic account of his impact upon the immovable Old Knight, complete with an epic simile. Supplying the necessary weather, but without the maritime imagery, Rustichello's text runs as follows:

> All these knights, which were twelve, went all one after the other to charge at the knight, and to each the knight was a tilting-block, and all they broke their lances on it, but they could not remove him from the saddle. But before well nine of these twelve had fallen, there was a great noise throughout the court, and it was thought a great marvel,

---

[2] Breillat, 'Poème Grec', p. 329.

and they said that this one was not a knight at all, but a lightning-bolt and a tempest.[3]

As if not content with the tilting block or *quintaine* – here transformed to a pillar – the Greek poet is perhaps moved by Rustichello's 'foudre et tenpestez' to deploy a total *naufragium*. But McCabe has also pointed out that *naufragium*, or *naufragion*, was regularly used in hippodrome mosaics to indicate a chariot crash.[4]

98. *Tristan had just risen to distinction among them*. According to E. Kriaras' *Lexicon of Medieval Greek Demotic Literature 1100–1669*, 'ἀρτιφαής' – an unusual word – means something or someone that is shown or distinguished recently. Kriaras cites this line from *The Old Knight* in his entry.[5]

134–45. *Now the king's face goes white*. Breillat and Goldwyn and others have viewed this scene as a laughably over-heated version of Hector's leave-taking of Andromache at *Iliad* VI.490–502.[6] Breillat speaks of a '*rire grec*' unique to our poet's account. Goldwyn persuasively explores further comic parallels between *The Old Knight* and the *Iliad*.

149. *like a lion's whelp*. The epithet λεόντων σκύμνος is used of Judah in Septuagint, Genesis 49. 9: 'σκύμνος λέοντος Ἰουδα· ἐκ βλαστοῦ, υἱέ μου, ἀνέβης· ἀναπεσὼν ἐκοιμήθης ὡς λέων καὶ ὡς σκύμνος· τίς ἐγερεῖ αὐτόν;' (Judah is a lion's whelp; from the prey, my son, you have gone up. He stooped down, he couched as a lion, and as a lioness; who dares rouse him up?). Also, the *Physiologos* identifies the lion cub, said to be stillborn until his father breathes life into him on the third day after his birth, as a figure of Christ; used of King Arthur here, and of the Old Knight at line 290, the epithet may well have echoed the *Physiologos* to an educated ear.

264. *drawing their swords*. Whereas the invaders draw ξίφη (singular ξίφος; the most general Greek word for 'sword'), the Old Knight's

---

[3] Cigni, *Il Romanzo Arturiano*, p. 234. My translation.
[4] A. McCabe, 'Horses of the Hippodrome', in *Hippodrom Atmeydan: Stanbulun Tarih Sahnesi*, ed. B. Pitarakis and P. Müzesi (Istanbul, 2010), p. 75.
[5] E. Kriarias, Λεξικο της μεσαιωικής ελληνιής δημώδους γραμματείας *1100–1669 / Lexiko tēs mesaiōnikēs hellēnikēs dēmōdous grammateias 1100–1669*, 16 vols. (Thessaloniki, 1968–).
[6] Breillat, 'Poème Grec', p. 318; Goldwyn, 'Arthur in the East', p. 81.

sword (281) is the σπάθη—a long two-edged sword named after the Greek for 'weaving rod' or 'spattle.' Since ξίφη and σπάθη are metrically interchangeable, some distinction may be intended; either term describes weapons in use by Byzantine infantry and cavalry. At line 289 the Old Knight is said to wield a μαχαίρα, according to Liddell and Scott 'a large knife or dirk worn by the heroes of the *Iliad* next the sword-sheath'; also, generally, 'a knife for cutting up meat'.

Vatican gr. 1822, fol. 203r © 2016 Biblioteca Apostolica Vaticana. Reproduced by the permission of Biblioteca Apostolica Vaticana, with all rights reserved.

CONTENTS OF PREVIOUS VOLUMES

Details of earlier titles are available from the publishers

XXII (2005)

Benn Ramm	Locating Narrative Authority in Perlesvaus : *Le Haut Livre du Graal*
Fanni Bogdanow	Micheau Gonnot's Arthuriad Preserved in Paris, Bibliothèque Nationale, fr. 112 and its Place in the Evolution of Arthurian Romance
Annette Völfing	Albricht's *Jüngerer Titurel*: Translating the Grail
Helen Fulton	Arthurian Prophecy and the Deposition of Richard II
Julia Marvin	Arthur Authorized: The Prophecies of the Prose *Brut* Chronicle
Norris J. Lacy and Raymond H. Thompson	The Arthurian Legend in Literature, Popular Culture and the Performing Arts, 1999–2004

XXIII (2006)

Andrew Lynch	Beyond Shame: Chivalric Cowardice and Arthurian Narrative
P. J. C. Field	Malory's Forty Knights
Joyce Coleman	Fooling with Language: Sir Dinadan in Malory's *Morte Darthur*
D. Thomas Hanks Jr	William Caxton, Wynkyn de Worde and the Editing of Malory's *Morte Darthur*
Raluca L. Radulescu	Ballad and Popular Romance in the Percy Folio
Margaret Robson	Local Hero: Gawain and the Politics of Arthurianism
Martin Connolly	Promise-postponement Device in *The Awntyrs off Arthure*: a Possible Narrative Model
Norris J. Lacy	*L'Atre perilleux* and the Erasure of Identity
Fanni Bogdanow	The Theme of the Handsome Coward in the Post-Vulgate *Queste del Saint Graal*
Tony Grand	A Time of Gifts? Jean de Nesle, William A. Nitze and the *Perlesvaus*
Robert Gossedge	Thomas Love Peacock's *The Misfortunes of Elphin* and the Romantic Arthur

XXIV (2007)

Norris J. Lacy	Perceval on the Margins: a Pan-European Perspective
Lori J. Walters	More Bread from Stone: Gauvain as a Figure of Plenitude in the French, Dutch and English Traditions
Cora Dietl	Artus – ein Fremdkörper in der Tristantradition?
Stefano Mula	Dinadan Abroad: Tradition and Innovation for a Counter-Hero
Marjolein Hogenbirk	Gringalet as an Epic Character
Sarah Gordon	Consumption and the Construction of Identity in Medieval European Arthurian Romance
Linda Gowans	Lamenting or just Grumbling? Arthur's Nephew Expresses his Discontent
Joseph M. Sullivan	Youth and Older Age in the Dire Adventure of Chrétien's *Yvain*, the Old Swedish *Hærra Ivan*, Hartmann's *Iwein* and the Middle English *Ywain and Gawain*
Frank Brandsma	Degrees of Perceptibility: the Narrator in the French Prose *Lancelot*, and in its German and Dutch Translations
Susanne Kramarz-Bein	Die altnorwegische *Parcevals saga* im Spannungsfeld ihrer Quelle und der mittelhochdeutschen und mittelenglischen Parzival-Überlieferung

Martine Meuwese	Crossing Borders: Text and Image in Arthurian Manuscripts

XXV (2009)

Nikolai Tolstoy	Geoffrey of Monmouth and the Merlin Legend
Carolyne Larrington	The Enchantress, the Knight and the Cleric: Authorial Surrogate in Arthurian Romance
Michael Twomey	'Morgan le Fay, Empress of the Wilderness': A Newly Recovered Arthurian Text in London, BL Royal 12.C.ix
Ralica L. Radulescu	Malory's Lancelot and the Key to Salvation
Martine Meuwese	Chrétien in Ivory
Stewart Mottram	'An Empire of Itself': Arthur as Icon of an English Empire, 1509–1547

XXVI (2009)

Derek S. Brewer	Introduction to the *Morte Darthur*, Parts 7 and 8
Jonathan Passaro	Malory's Text of the *Suite du Merlin*
Amanda Hopkins	Why Arthur at all? The Dubious Arthuricity of *Arthur and Gorlagon*
Thomas Hinton	The Aesthetics of Communication: Sterility and Fertility in the *Conte del Graal* Cycle
Siân Echard	'Whyche thyng semeth not to agree with other histories …': Rome in Geoffrey of Monmouth and his early modern readers
Norris J. Lacy	Arthurian Texts in their Historical and Social Context
Ronald Hutton	The Post-Christian Arthur
Raymond Thompson and Norris J. Lacy	Supplement: The Arthurian Legend in Literature, Popular Culture, and the Performing Arts, 2004-2008

XXVII (2010)

Emma Campbell	Commemoration in *La Mort le roi Artu*
Andrew Lynch	'… "if indeed I go"': Arthur's Uncertain End in Malory and Tennyson
Aisling Byrne	The Intruder at the Feast: Negotiating Boundaries in Medieval Insular Romance
P. J. C. Field	What Women Really Want: The Genesis of Chaucer's *Wife of Bath's Tale*
Sue Niebrzydowski	Monstrous Appetite and Belly Laughs: A Reconsideration of the Humour in *The Weddyng of Syr Gawen and Dame Ragnell*
Megan G. Leitch	Speaking (of) Treason in Malory's *Morte Darthur*
Karen D. Robinson	*Lancelot of the Laik*: A Scottish Mirror for Princes
Kenneth Hodges	Prince Arthur's Archers: Innovative Nostalgia in Early Modern Popular Chivalry

XXVIII (2011)

Christine Francis	Reading Malory's Bloody Bedrooms
Megan G. Leitch	[Dis]Figuring Transgressive Desire: Blood, Sex, and Stained Sheets in Malory's *Morte Darthur*
Helen Phillips	Bewmaynes: The Threat from the Kitchen
Carolyne Larrington	Sibling Relations in Malory's *Morte Darthur*
Lydia A. Fletcher	'Traytoures' and 'Treson': the Language of Treason in the Works of Sir Thomas Malory

Kate McClune	'The Vengeaunce of My Brethirne': Blood Ties in Malory's *Morte Darthur*
Sally Mapstone	Malory and the Scots
Caitlyn Schwartz	Blood, Faith and Saracens in 'The Book of Sir Tristram'
Maria Sachiko Cecire	Barriers Unbroken: Sir Palomydes the Saracen in 'The Book of Sir Tristram'
Anna Caughey	Virginity, Sexuality, Repression and Return in the 'Tale of the Sankgreal'
Catherine LaFarge	Launcelot in Compromising Positions: Fabliau in Malory's 'Tale of Sir Launcelot du Lake'

XXIX (2012)

Christopher Berard	Edward III's Abandoned Order of the Round Table
Julian Luxford	King Arthur's Tomb at Glastonbury: The Relocation of 1368 in Context
Joshua Byron Smith	Benedict of Gloucester's *Vita Sancti Dubrucii*: An Edition and Translation
Sjoerd Levelt	New Evidence for an Interest in Arthurian Literature in the Dutch Low Counties in the Fifteenth and Early Sixteenth Centuries
P. J. C. Field	Malory's Source-Manuscript for the First Tale of *Le Morte Darthur*
L. M. Gowans	Malory's Sources – and Arthur's Sisters – Revisited
Ryan Naughton	Peace, Justice and Retinue-Building in Malory's 'The Tale of Sir Garethy of Orkney'
Dorsey Armstrong	Mapping Malory's *Morte*: The (Physical) Place and (Narrative) Space of Cornwall
Bart Besamusca and Jessica Quinlan	The Fringes of Arthurian Fiction

XXX (2013)

Helen Fulton	Magic and the Supernatural in Early Welsh Arthurian Narrative: *Culhwch ac Olwen* and *Breuddwyd Rhonabwy*
Michael W. Twomey	How Green was the Green Knight? Forest Ecology at Hautdesert
Richard Barber	Edward III's Arthurian Enthusiasms Revisited: *Perceforest* in the Context of Philippa of Hainault and the Round Table Feast of 1344
Nigel Bryant	Pagan Gods and the Coming of Christianity in *Perceforest*
Aisling Byrne	Malory's Sources for the *Tale of Sankgreal:* Some Overlooked Evidence from the Irish *Lorgaireacht an Tsoidigh Naomhtha*
Carol J. Chase	'Transmuer de rime en prose': The Transformation of Chrétien de Troyes's 'Joie de la Cour' episode in the Burgundian Prose *Erec* (1450–60)
Patricia Victorin	La Rétro-écriture ou l'écriture de la nostalgie dans le roman arthurien tardif: *Ysaïe le Triste, Le Conte du Papegau et Mélyador* de Froissart
Siân Echard	Remembering Brutus: Aaron Thompson's *British History* of 1718

XXXI (2014)

Irit Ruth Kleiman	Chrétien's *Conte Du Graal* between Myth and History
Karen Cherewatuk	Malory's Thighs and Launcelot's Buttock: Ignoble Wounds and Moral Transgression in the *Morte Darthur*
Keven S. Whetter	Weeping, Wounds, and Worshyp in Malory's *Morte Darthur*
Megan G. Leitch	Sleeping Knights and 'Such Maner of Sorow-Makynge': Affect, Ethics and Unconsciousness in Malory's *Morte Darthur*
Erin Kissick	Mirroring Masculinities: Transformative Female Corpses in Malory's *Morte Darthur*
Joan Tasker Grimbert	Tristan and Iseult at the Cathedral of Santiago de Compostela
Roger Simpson	Trevelyan Triptych: A Family and the Arthurian Legend
Tara Foster	*Kaamelott*: A new French Arthurian Tradition

XXXII (2015)

Larissa Tracy	Wounded Bodies: Kingship, National Identity and Illegitimate Torture in the English Arthurian Tradition
Marco Nievergelt	The Place of Emotion: Space, Silence and Interiority in the Stanzaic *Morte Arthur*
Ralph Norris	Another Source for Malory's 'Tale of Sir Gareth'
Lisa Robeson	'Warre and Worshyppe': Depictions of Battle in Malory's *Le Morte Darthur*
Richard Sévère	Malory's 'Chivalric Cliques': Public and Private *Felyshyp* in the Arthurian Community
David Eugene Clark	Scribal Modifications to Concluding Formulae in the Winchester Manuscript
Sarah Randles	Heraldic Imagery in the Embroidered Tristan Narratives
Jaakko Tahkokallio	Update to the List of Manuscripts of Geoffrey of Monmouth's *Historia regum Britanniae*

Printed in the United States
By Bookmasters